Perspectives from the Disciplines

PERSPECTIVES FROM THE DISCIPLINES
Stanford Online High School

edited by
Jeffrey Scarborough
Raymond Ravaglia

CSLI
PUBLICATIONS
Center for the Study of
Language and Information
Stanford, California

Copyright © 2016
CSLI Publications
Center for the Study of Language and Information
Leland Stanford Junior University
Printed in the United States
20 19 18 17 16   1 2 3 4 5

Library of Congress Cataloging-in-Publication Data

Names: Scarborough, Jeffrey, 1976- editor. | Ravaglia, Raymond, 1965- editor.

Title: Perspectives from the disciplines : Stanford Online High School /
  [edited by] Jeffrey Scarborough and Raymond Ravaglia.

Description: Stanford, California : Center for the Study of Language and
  Information, [2016] — Includes bibliographical references and index.

Identifiers: LCCN 2016043435 (print) | LCCN 2016054348 (ebook) | ISBN
  9781575867403 (pbk. : acid-free paper) | ISBN 1575867400 (pbk. :
  acid-free paper) | ISBN 9781575867427 (electronic)

Subjects: LCSH: Stanford Online High School (Stanford, Calif.) | Stanford
  Online High School (Stanford, Calif.)–Curricula. | Web-based
  instruction–Curricula–California–Stanford. | Gifted
  children–Education–California–Stanford–Computer-assisted instruction.

Classification: LCC LD7501.S9147 P37 2016 (print) | LCC LD7501.S9147 (ebook)
  | DDC 373.794/73–dc23

LC record available at https://lccn.loc.gov/2016043435

CIP

∞ The acid-free paper used in this book meets the minimum requirements of the
American National Standard for Information Sciences—Permanence of Paper for
Printed Library Materials, ANSI Z39.48-1984.

CSLI was founded in 1983 by researchers from Stanford University, SRI International, and
Xerox PARC to further the research and development of integrated theories of language,
information, and computation. CSLI headquarters and CSLI Publications are located on the
campus of Stanford University.

Visit our web site at
http://cslipublications.stanford.edu/
for comments on this and other titles, as well as for changes
and corrections by the author and publisher.

To the parents and families of the SOHS whose tireless efforts and devotion to the original vision of the school serve as the wellspring from which the SOHS is born anew each year. And to those dedicated instructors and staff who return each year to ensure that the students find the school they deserve.

And to those recognized in the first book of this set. The sentiments expressed therein only continue to increase over time.

Contents

Contributors

KATHRYN BALSLEY Division of Ancient and Modern Languages, SOHS, Stanford University, California
kathryn.aftosmis@gmail.com

KIM FAILOR Division of Sciences, SOHS, Stanford University, California
kfailor@stanford.edu

CLAIRE GOLDSMITH Malone School Online Network, Washington DC
claire.goldsmith@gmail.com

KAREN KENKEL Divisions of Philosophy Core and Humanities, SOHS, Stanford University, California
kkenkel@sonic.com

MARGARET LAMONT Division of English, SOHS, Stanford University, California
melamont@stanford.edu

GREG NUCKOLS Division of Mathematics, SOHS, Stanford University, California
gnuckols@stanford.edu

RAYMOND RAVAGLIA Ravaglia and Associates, California
ray@ravaglia.net

JEFFREY SCARBOROUGH SOHS, Stanford University, California
jeffrey.scarborough@gmail.com

MICHAEL SLETCHER Department of History, Division of Humanities, SOHS, Stanford University, California
sletcher@stanford.edu

TRACY STEELE Department of Counseling and Student Services, SOHS, Stanford University, California
sletcher@stanford.edu

Acknowledgments

We wish to thank the students and faculty of the Stanford Online High School (SOHS) for their tireless dedication to making the idea of this school a reality. And to their families for bringing them to the school and tolerating their periodic departures down the rabbit hole.

Secondly, we wish to thank all members of the faculty who were willing to take precious time outside the all-consuming job that is teaching at the SOHS to share their perspectives on the school and the perspectives of their disciplines. Further thanks goes to their colleagues, past and present, who have indirectly contributed to the writing of this volume through myriad conversations and through their instructional practice. May the result of our efforts be pleasing, and if not, may they inspire you to add your own perspectives to future volumes.

Finally, an infinite debt of gratitude is owed to our publisher, Dikran Karagueuzian, without whose combination of persistence and tolerance this volume would have remained merely an undelivered catalog entry.

Preface

1 From School to Class

When writing the first book, we wanted to focus on how the SOHS worked in general, and on the interplay of the *schoolness* and the *onlineness* in particular. At that point we were focused on making crystal clear what we were doing, both in the abstract and in the idealized cases that constitute the fodder for educational writing. We were explaining why we had done things differently than the mainstream for ten years, often swimming against the popular current, and doing what was hard, but right, rather than what seemed expedient.

Having now demonstrated the coherence and efficacy of the blended-flipped synchronous seminar approach, we can turn to what actually happens in our classrooms when our instructors use this approach to teach their students. In the earlier volume, we knew that by not going deep into the classroom we were stopping short of a full description of what makes the school work. We have always stressed when talking to parents that the 'secret sauce' of the school had nothing to do with the technology and everything to do with getting the right teachers together with the right students and getting out of their way.

With this book we have endeavored to get out of the way of the teachers and to let them tell their own stories about how they solved their own particular problems of teaching their disciplines within the environment of the SOHS and how often in doing so they found they made curricular or pedagogical innovations with implications beyond online instruction. In this way we see a myriad of distinct solutions develop to a common problem. One might be tempted to say that if the SOHS is the elephant, the first book described the elephant as an ideal while this book gives the perspective of each of the blind philosophers as to what elephants are in particular. But the better analogy is given in the companion volume: 'Such a reader would be in the position of the novice sports fan, who after seeing the players and all their actions, wonders where to find the famous *esprit de corps*: so much of the school is the students and the teachers and their interaction.[1]

So as not to disappoint such readers, we have devoted two chapters exactly to the *esprit de corps*, the first being an examination of how one safeguards the mental and emotional health of students that one may never meet face to face, and the second an in-depth examination of how one develops school spirit and emotional connectedness within an online school. We have stressed throughout its history that the SOHS is not an online day school but rather is more akin to an online boarding school. These chapters underscore the importance of taking a comprehensive view of one's students when developing a school online.

Beyond this discussion there is certainly plenty that could be said about online education, where it may be heading, and what the schools of the future may look like. The discussions of the courses and curricula in this book, taken with the broader discussions in the first book of this set shine a bright light on where we have been and tell the story of how we arrived at where the school is today. As to where things may be tomorrow, we touch briefly upon such topics at the end of the introduction, but a deeper discussion must be left for another day.

Raymond Ravaglia
Jeffrey Scarborough
October 2016

---

[1] J. Scarborough and R. Ravaglia, *Bricks and Mortar: The Making of a Real Education at the Stanford Online High School* (Stanford, CA: CSLI Publications, 2014) 52.

1

Introduction

RAYMOND RAVAGLIA

When this two volume series was originally conceived in May 2013, part of the purpose was to put a stake in the ground for what could be accomplished with the blended-flipped synchronous seminar approach to online learning that defines the Stanford Online High School (SOHS), in opposition to what was then a rising tide of enthusiasm for MOOCs and other versions of computer-based instruction that downplayed the importance of the human instructor-student interaction. Coursera and Udacity had just emerged from Stanford University and the Khan Academy was in the headlines every week. The hope of these efforts seemed to be, simplistically put, that if superstar instructors could just record the perfect lecture once, then everyone hearing it would have perfect knowledge arise within them, and little more would ever need to be done. Or failing that, whatever was left to be fixed would be the job of lower-paid, lower-skilled individuals. To put it another way, if only one could have filmed Socrates and the slave boy from the *Meno*, and put it up on YouTube, then no one would ever need to teach the proof of the Pythagorean Theorem again.

At some point in that conversation people became lost, moving from the understandable enthusiasm they had for the potential of large classes and of students working together from recorded media to bring education into arenas where it could not otherwise be had, to the belief that somehow this type of education would be superior. The dubious conclusion was that the promise of the idealized zero-to-one instructor to student ratio implicit in the idealized image of the 'electronic Aristotle' would win out over the dynamic interactive human quality

Perspectives from the Disciplines.
Jeffrey Scarborough and Raymond Ravaglia.
Copyright © 2016, CSLI Publications.

represented by the image of Socrates and his students in the Agora.[1]
In the period from 2009 to 2013 the world of online learning was drunk
on the possibility of what the electronic Aristotle, augmented with 'big
data' might accomplish, and we were one of a few contrarian voices
within that world insisting that the goal of education, at least the goal
of the best type of education represented by independent schools, was
not to move everything in the direction of the MOOCs and the Khan
Academy, but to stand fast on traditional values of good teaching that
stress the interaction between teacher and student and look for how the
technology might expand access without sacrificing quality. To us the
goal was not to see how cheap and wide we could go, but to see whether
we could use the technology to make possible a great education online.

As we complete this book, three years after its initial conception
and two years after the completion of the companion volume, we find
ourselves at times in the unenviable position of the man who has been
telling a long slow joke, with carefully orchestrated pacing, slowly building to a climax, only to have someone across the room say in a stage
whisper, 'I know this one—it turns out that . . .' giving the punchline
away. The man telling the joke still wants to finish the story, but also
realizes that the pacing does not really matter much anymore. That
said, we believe that the story should be told for the school has important things to say, not just about how one should teach these courses
online, but also about the curricula themselves; in working in a unique
medium we have gained insights that are more broadly applicable.

1   Aspirational to No Discernible Difference to Better

To understand the context in which SOHS came into being and the
degree to which its instructional model represented a departure from
the received wisdom of 2006, it is worthwhile to review briefly some
seminal moments in the development of the modern structure of online
efforts at the university and secondary school levels. This sketch is not
intended to be complete or in depth but rather to provide a first-hand
sense of where things were and where they seemed to be going.

In the spring of 1992, a number of representatives of different research efforts into the use of computers in education, gathered at the
invitation of A. Frank Mayadas and Ralph Gomory at the midtown
Manhattan offices of the Alfred P. Sloan Foundation for a first discussion of what everyone was doing at their respective institutions with
an eye towards systematically harnessing the power of such courses to
improve the availability of quality education to students everywhere.

---

[1]Scarborough and Ravaglia, *Bricks and Mortar*, 7.

This effort would initially become known by the phrase 'Asynchronous Learning Networks' and then as Sloan Consortium (or Sloan-C).[2] I was in attendance at this meeting because I was leading a team that had developed courses in secondary-school mathematics and we had received funding from the Sloan Foundation to use these courses in remediation efforts with university students in community colleges. At this point the effort was focused largely on the power of 'Anytime, Anywhere' learning with an emphasis on university-level instruction delivered asynchronously.[3] At this meeting, there was a variety of presentations from grant recipients on how they were using computers to support student learning. Most of the work presented had a fairly standard computer-based training approach, and all of the work was around asynchronous use of computers, with at least one group using the phrase 'virtual classroom' and trying to treat that phrase as something trademarked.[4] At this meeting there was also some nascent excitement about the emerging potential of multimedia. CD-ROMs had just become available on personal computers, and while CD-ROM production was still expensive—cutting your own required $7,000 in hardware and software, and blanks were $45 each—there was speculation that emerging internet technology would allow audio and video lectures to be captured and delivered to students. While not demonstrated at the meeting, the technology we had developed, which was a simple system for screen casting with graphics and audio combined, produced lectures that looked rather much like those that Salman Khan would produce to great effect a decade and a half later.

Following this meeting at the Sloan Foundation, the internet entered the mainstream, the age of websites was at hand, and cheap tools allowing anyone to produce bad courses had become commonplace. Companies like Blackboard and Web-CT developed their models of 'course as syllabus with containers' and it became progressively easier for people to assemble courses. Fully embracing the anytime-anywhere *zeitgeist*, the model that proliferated for 'online courses' was that of students essentially sitting down and working through a stack of precollected materials that were organized in syllabus fashion, with the reading embedded, with comprehension questions and quizzes scattered through-

---

[2]Ultimately this effort was incorporated into the organization called the 'Online Learning Consortium'.

[3]In fact 'Anytime, Anywhere' became the mantra for most of the second half of the 1990s with various Department of Education calls for funding under that name.

[4]For an example of the phrase 'Virtual Classroom' used with a trademark symbol, see Hiltz and Turoff: http://files.eric.ed.gov/fulltext/ED388215.pdf, accessed August 28, 2016.

out, with the ability to email the instructor integrated, and with an ability to post to discussions and to comment on the discussions and other posts. This model was easy to produce and easy to manage and deploy, and since it sat upon an intuitive structure, i.e. the syllabus, it was conceptually easy to adopt. It also forced a very homogeneous vision of what it meant to teach and learn online: online learning should be fundamentally an asynchronous affair, with students having the advantage of being able to move at their own pace through the curriculum and with instructors only being proactive when building courses and otherwise only reacting to student work.

In August 2002, the North American Council for Online Learning (NACOL), since renamed the International Council for Online Learning (iNACOL), came into being following a conference on online learning that took place in Santa Cruz, California.[5] The Bill and Melinda Gates Foundation and the William and Flora Hewlett Foundation provided the seed money to allow a group of industry leaders to come together for the purposes of developing their own standards and guidelines for what constituted good online learning and for promulgating those standards.

At this point any number of schools and groups were represented, with the most prominent being the Florida Virtual School, The Virtual High School, The Michigan Virtual High School, and the University of California College Preparation Initiative. Each of these groups was in the business of developing and offering online courses to high school students, sometimes for a fee, sometimes for free, and sometimes both depending on where the student lived. All used basically the same model for how courses worked, how teachers taught, and how students learned.

In this conference and in the ensuing years these types of efforts were increasingly ubiquitous. Activities that had seemed novel even for universities ten years earlier at the inception of Sloan-C were becoming commonplace even at the secondary school level. And it was not just states and universities that were developing courses. Companies like Apex, K-12.com, and Connections Learning came into being, developing virtual charter schools and other models of distribution. By 2005 anyone who wanted to receive an online course in a given subject would have no difficulty in finding one that they could take without charge, typically from their state association.

Noticeable about these efforts was the tendency to focus on keeping the instructional model individualized, self-paced, and asynchronous. One motivation for doing so was the convenience of the student: learn-

---

[5]I was at the conference in Santa Cruz, and was present through the inception of the NACOL, serving as founding member of the board of directors.

ing anytime, anywhere was, after all, deeply appealing. Another was the convenience of the institution: having students act asynchronously is very easy to handle from a scheduling and resource allocation point of view, and makes it possible to enlist the support of instructors from overseas.

That such an approach was intellectually justifiable was also being supported by the research that was coming out at the time. Beginning in 2003, and concluding with their publication in 2004, Robert Blomeyer and his team at Learning Point Associates had been conducting an exhaustive meta-analysis of the research into the efficacy of online instruction compared with face-to-face instruction. The results were promising and were supportive of the overwhelming optimism of the day. Quoting from the abstract:

> The community of K-12 education has seen explosive growth over the last decade in distance learning programs, defined as learning experiences in which students and instructors are separated by space and/or time. While elementary and secondary students have learned through the use of electronic distance learning systems since the 1930s, the development of online distance learning schools is a relatively new phenomenon. Online virtual schools may be ideally suited to meet the needs of stakeholders calling for school choice, high school reform, and workforce preparation in 21st century skills. The growth in the numbers of students learning online and the importance of online learning as a solution to educational challenges has increased the need to study more closely the factors that affect student learning in virtual schooling environments. This meta-analysis is a statistical review of 116 effect sizes from 14 web-delivered K-12 distance education programs studied between 1999 and 2004. The analysis shows that distance education can have the same effect on measures of student academic achievement when compared to traditional instruction. The study-weighted mean effect size across all outcomes was -0.028 with a 95 percent confidence interval from 0.060 to -0.116, indicating *no significant difference* [italics mine] in performance between students who participated in online programs and those who were taught in face-to-face classrooms. No factors were found to be related to significant positive or negative effects. The factors that were tested included academic content area, grade level of the students, role of the distance learning program, role of the instructor, length of the program, type of school, frequency of the distance learning experience, pacing of instruction, timing of instruction, instructor preparation and experience in distance education, and the setting of the students.[6]

---

[6]C. Cavanaugh et al.,"The Effects of Distance Education on K-12 Student Outcomes: A Meta-Analysis," Learning Point Associates/North Central Regional Edu-

At the time of its publication and in the years following, the phrase most often heard at conferences on online learning was that of 'no significant difference'. Since there was no significant difference we were free to run ahead as far and as fast as we wished, embracing the new technology, and the concomitant new models for instructional delivery, without fear that we were somehow shortchanging our students. For those who were excited about online learning, this was music to the ears, confirmation that what they were doing was reaching students and leading to outcomes as positive as those in traditional classrooms.

And yet at the same time, if one pauses for a moment to reflect on the claim of 'no significant difference', what exactly were we achieving? Were we happy with the achievement of our students in our schools? Were these not the same schools that other publications routinely pointed to as failing? Was it not the common refrain that the typical American school was woefully behind that of much of the rest of the industrialized world? Should we have not viewed 'no significant difference' as a ridiculously low standard, if not an outright indictment of failure?

Now if the goal is primarily expanding reach and access, then anything that gets the courses to the students who need them, and that can do it cheaply, is an endeavor worthy of pursuit. So it was no wonder that initiatives driven by this goal or by the goal of access embraced the technology that was available at the time and were happy achieving those results. But if the goal is to deliver the best education possible, *to become the best school in the world*, as was the case with SOHS, then one needs to look for other models, models that promise more than 'no significant difference'.

2 The Blended-Flipped Synchronous Seminar Model

As we discussed in the first chapter of the companion volume, our goal in creating SOHS was to capture what was best about quality education, namely dynamic student-teacher interaction, and to enshrine it in a model we would use to build a school online. We had experimented with synchronous methods of online instruction as early as 1993 in a course in multivariable calculus for gifted high school students, and then more aggressively with courses for teaching writing to middle and high school students. But it was only when we had begun to think about creating a school that we seriously began to think about synchronous instruction in all its potential as a component of online courses.

We wanted a synchronous model, because we saw it as essential for

cational Laboratory (NCREL), 2004, accessed June 18, 2016, http://files.eric.ed.gov/fulltext/ED489533.pdf.

good instruction, but we also saw the efficiency of the asynchronous approach and did not want to abandon it entirely. We knew that scheduling synchronous sessions more than twice a week for a class would be prohibitively difficult. We also knew that college courses could cover the same material as high school courses, in the same number of weeks, meeting just twice a week for seventy-five minute seminars, because of the expectations placed on students to do work outside of class. We reasoned that if the same type of expectations could be placed on talented high school students, augmented by additional lectures to help support students doing the work, we could attain this right mix of quality, economy, and efficiency.

Thus was born the blended-flipped synchronous seminar model employed by the SOHS. The model was blended because it mixed synchronous and asynchronous educational modalities: synchronous in having a real-time online classroom component used for seminars, and asynchronous in using recorded lectures and other preexisting materials. The model was flipped in that the lectures were consumed prior to coming to class and the classroom time was used for discussion. Lastly the model employed a college-style schedule in which classes meet for seminars two-to-three times per week rather than daily. This model was assembled as a way to capture what was essential about high quality education but difficult to do online (namely the regular seminar component) and embellish it with what was easy to do online (namely asynchronous lectures and review materials) in order to round out a course experience that would be able to cover all of the course content, but that could do it in a manner that was strategic in its employment of the live seminars.

While the companion volume discusses this model and its success in great length, what is noteworthy in the context of this discussion is that concurrent with our embrace of this model, the rest of the world was beginning to wake up to the possibility that blending face-to-face with online might actually produce superior results than exclusively online asynchronous material.

In 2010, year five in the SOHS calendar, the US Department of Education published the results of a comprehensive meta-study evaluating best practices in online learning. This study showed that students who learned in blended contexts showed superior results to those who were purely online or purely in person. While blended here was defined as a combination of face-to-face and online, we would argue that similar findings should hold if one treats the blending as a combining of synchronous and asynchronous, since the dominant feature of the 'at school' component is its synchronous nature and the dominant feature

of the 'online component' examined was its asynchronousness.
The findings of the study are summarized as follows:

> A systematic search of the research literature from 1996 through July
> 2008 identified more than a thousand empirical studies of online learn-
> ing. Analysts screened these studies to find those that (a) contrasted
> an online to a face-to-face condition, (b) measured student learning
> outcomes, (c) used a rigorous research design, and (d) provided ade-
> quate information to calculate an effect size. As a result of this screen-
> ing, 50 independent effects were identified that could be subjected to
> meta-analysis. The meta-analysis found that, on average, students in
> online learning conditions performed modestly better than those re-
> ceiving face-to-face instruction. The difference between student out-
> comes for online and face-to-face classes—measured as the difference
> between treatment and control means, divided by the pooled stan-
> dard deviation—was larger in those studies contrasting conditions that
> blended elements of online and face-to-face instruction with conditions
> taught entirely face-to-face.[7]

With such a ringing endorsement of the efficacy of blended learning,
it is not surprising that in the ensuing years the trend towards ever more
focus on blended education has certainly been a dominant driver. While
commercial considerations continue to lead providers to push purely
asynchronous modalities, few people implement them where there are
alternatives, especially if the objective of the effort is quality. Indeed,
the ubiquitous nature of blended learning as the dominant way in which
online learning is manifested in independent schools has had its impact
in the nomenclature. There is a consortium of schools in the San Francisco Bay Area choosing to call itself 'Blend-Ed' for its emphasis on
blended education. The organization formerly calling itself the 'Online
Education Symposium for Independent Schools' or OESIS, decided to
embrace its initialism as its name, since 'online' has been roundly sub-
sumed under blended in the context of independent schools. Perhaps
most strikingly, after failing to see online learning disrupt class in the
way that they had envisioned, the next book from the Christensen Institute was entitled *Blended–Using Disruptive Innovation to Improve
Schools*.[8]

This is not to say that all the benefits of blending were coming from

---

[7]B. Means, et al., *Evaluation of Evidence-Based Practices in Online Learning:
A Meta-Analysis and Review of Online Learning Studies* (Washington, DC: US Department of Education Office of Planning, Evaluation, and Policy Development), accessed June 18, 2016, http://www2.ed.gov/rschstat/eval/tech/evidence-based-
practices/finalreport.pdf.

[8]M. Horn and H. Staker, *Blended – Using Disruptive Innovation to Improve
Schools* (San Francisco: Jossey-Bass, 2014).

the blending per se. Part of the impact, and this is stated clearly in the report, may be due to the fact that:

> Studies using blended learning also tend to involve more learning time, additional instructional resources, and course elements that encourage interactions among learners. This confounding leaves open the possibility that one or all of these other practice variables, rather than the blending of online and offline media per se, accounts for the particularly positive outcomes for blended learning in the studies included in the meta-analysis.[9]

So it may just be that better schools tend to bring more resources to hand when teaching and that as a result these students both experience online only as blended and do so in the context of a generally richer environment. While interesting as a question for study, this type of finding is in line with the success we have had at SOHS where the goal has never been to find adequacy but has always been to bring whatever resources are required to ensure student success.

3 Now Everybody Wants to Blend

Despite their initial impulse, even the MOOCs have found that a blended approach, where students have an opportunity to come to a physical location and meet synchronously with each other and subject experts, can yield markedly better results than the pure model where students run through the course reading the material and completing the assignments with only asynchronous interaction. While a review of that literature would be out of place in this introduction, a web article from July 2015 nicely sums up the direction of thinking that institutions who had created MOOCs had begun exploring.

> When Massive, Open Online Courses (also known as MOOCs) made their debut in 2009, many believed that they would fundamentally change the face of education...Over the past six years, however, MOOCs have failed to disrupt education...Instead, educators are finding ways to repurpose MOOC content for their own brick-and-mortar classes. 'Recycling' MOOC content in this way provides two main benefits to institutions: cost recovery, and enabling support for blended learning scenarios.

> First, universities can maximize the investments they've made in creating MOOC content by repurposing the videos for other courses. MOOCs can cost tens of thousands of dollars to produce....

---

[9]B. Means et al., *Evaluation of Evidence-Based Practices in Online Learning.*

> Second, MOOC content can be used to support blended learning scenarios such as lecture capture and flipped learning in traditional classes... Class time is then allocated for specific questions and more in-depth discussions.

> By outsourcing some elements of the course to MOOC videos viewed outside of class, Professor McDermott has found that his students are producing better work and learning more during class time.[10]

The beauty of this piece is that it is neither a set of scholarly observations nor the detailed findings of a study, but it is essentially an advertisement from a service that is helping universities repurpose their MOOC investments into something more useful. The reality of dissatisfaction and sunk costs associated with MOOCs is so prevalent that businesses are cropping up to help universities recoup benefit from their failed investments. After investing large sums in producing lectures for MOOCs, universities are finding that it may be more effective to take these recorded lectures and use them to support a blended approach wherein the classroom time can be spent more like a seminar, in the SOHS model. In the companion volume we discussed how MOOCs are like text books, albeit text books that have multimedia components. This piece shows that some formerly MOOC-friendly institutions are reaching the same conclusion.

At the end of the day, most discussions of the advantages of blended learning sound rather like someone saying 'You know, there is something good about seminars, but there is also something good about books. I am thinking about maybe using books to support my seminar next semester.'

4   Stirred, Not Shaken

While the world at large has been stumbling into recognizing the value and efficacy of the SOHS instructional model, and the intrinsic superiority of the blended-flipped synchronous seminar model more generally, the world of college admissions and high school rankings has been increasingly recognizing the value of SOHS itself, and the fact that what students have been learning in the classrooms of SOHS is exactly what colleges want students to be learning.

In the previous book we discussed at length the success that the students from SOHS had achieved in gaining admission to colleges, and in their academic performance in those colleges once they had

---

[10]Panopto, "Trending in Blended Learning: Recycling MOOCs", July 28, 2015, accessed June 18, 2016, https://www.panopto.com/blog/trending-in-blended-learning-recycling-moocs/.

arrived. This trend has continued, and if anything, broadened, with students from the original classes now having success in graduate and professional schools as well as in their careers.

What has often been most surprising to people is that the graduates of SOHS seem indistinguishable from the graduates of other elite independent secondary schools. Even though the education they have received has been predominately delivered online, one can honestly say that there is 'no significant difference' between these *online* students, and the students in top secondary schools, not only in measures of academic performance, but in the formation of character, leadership, and the panoply of social-emotional skills that such schools pride themselves on developing within their students.

In the companion volume we discussed how our goal from the moment of creation of the SOHS was to become the best school in the world, and not just the best online school. While the science of school rankings is imprecise and any measure of 'best' would be across too many dimensions to produce a single answer, ratings can be used as an accurate measure of perception. And in this way there is much to suggest that SOHS is increasingly perceived as having realized this goal.

The first review of significance was in *Business Insider* in March 2015. In an article entitled "The 50 Smartest Private High Schools in the US" SOHS placed number six. In particular, the article noted that 'Though completely online, creating a community and fostering relationships are two of the main priorities at Stanford's Online High School' making it clear that SOHS is about providing a complete education and not just getting students through advanced courses.[11]

The K-12 rankings from the website Niche, which specializes in ranking neighborhoods, schools, and colleges, placed SOHS number three among private high schools, behind Philips Academy Andover and Philips Academy Exeter.[12]

We cite these rankings not to make the case that somehow SOHS actually is the best school in the world, but only to indicate that no one laughs or shakes their heads these days when a purely online school that has only been around for ten years is listed as comparable to institutions that have been around for several centuries.

---

[11] E. Martin, "The 50 Smartest high schools in the US," *Business Insider*, March 24, 2015, accessed June 18, 2016, http://www.businessinsider.com/smartest-private-high-schools-in-the-us-2015-3.

[12] "2016 Best Private High Schools in America," *Niche*, accessed June 18, 2016, http://k12.niche.com/rankings.

5   The Implications of All This

When the claim was that there was 'no significant difference' from students learning online and in the regular classroom, it was easy enough for the top independent schools to sit back and chuckle to themselves 'not significantly different from what happens in average schools, you mean.' But with the development of SOHS and its blended-flipped model of synchronous seminars, and with the success that such approaches have had, both as documented broadly in the research literature, and more importantly, as documented in the success of its students, and in this context, its perceived success in the popular press, we have a compelling case that it is indeed possible to deliver an education online that is on par with that of the best schools in the world. And that it is not just on par from the perspective of content knowledge, but from the perspective of a complete education.

How this pertains to the structure and operation of different classes at the SOHS, and what implications this has for how one teaches and should teach different subjects, will be the focus of much of this book. Most notably, substantiating the claim that SOHS is offering a complete independent school education requires not just pointing to the outcomes but showing course-by-course, service-by-service how this is done.

As regards the deeper implications: if the success of SOHS is not *sui generis* but rather emblematic of the kind of result that any effort constituted on foundational principles similar to SOHS could have, then it raises significant challenges to long cherished beliefs about how to build a high achieving school. Does in fact one need to spend upwards of seventy to one hundred million dollars, or more, to create such a school, as has been the case with schools such as Keystone Beijing, or schools created by Avenues or GEMS? Or would one be better off spending a fraction of this amount on physical plants and instead invest in one's teachers and deliver the education online using the blended-flipped synchronous seminar model? When we used to think that only by attending a college-like secondary school could one experiences the full range of independent school virtues, this may have made sense. Knowing as we now do that such success can be accomplished without any buildings, why should we continue to invest so heavily in new physical plants?

Even if we do decide to have buildings, the SOHS model has implications for how they might best be used. The blended-flipped synchronous seminar approach, coupled with a college-style schedule, changes how we think about physical space. Such an approach does not require students to live thousands of miles away from campus; any school that is willing to flip its classes and blend them with seminars could adopt this model. One of the upsides of such an approach would be a reduction in the amount of time each student in each course spends in class each week from over four hours to just over two. This shift, carried across a school, has the potential to reduce classroom utilization by thirty to fifty percent. Adopting this model would allow a school to grow its enrollment without having to construct a single building. Of course one would still need to put the students somewhere, so one cannot simply double the number of students on campus without having a concrete plan. That said, a twenty-percent increase in enrollment could be managed by most schools without appreciable impact. While schools that are struggling to fill the seats they have may ask 'what good is this increased capacity?', the answer is that what is good is not the increased capacity per se, but the increased efficiency of the system. Given that the typical independent school has seen increases in tuition outpace inflation for the last twenty-five years or more, any gain in efficiency is important. The same holds true for boarding schools. If SOHS really is more akin to a virtual boarding school, rather than a virtual day school, what might be possible to accomplish if dormitory facilities were available? At SOHS, students have an option of coming to the Stanford campus for up to two weeks each summer. What might happen if students at such a school could come into residence more often than that? What if they were on campus several times a year for extended stays? How might the academic program change? What might one do in person and what might one do online? What might be gained and what might be lost? And if these models proved successful, what then? If one takes seriously the implications of the example of SOHS, the future may be a very different place indeed.

References

"2016 Best Private High Schools in America." *Niche*. Accessed June 18, 2016. http://k12.niche.com/rankings.

Cavanaugh, C., K. J. Gillan, J. Kromrey, M. Hess, and R. Blomeyer. "The Effects of Distance Education on K-12 Student Outcomes: A Meta-Analysis." Learning Point Associates/North Central Regional Educational Laboratory (NCREL), 2004. Accessed June 18, 2016. http://files.eric.ed.gov/fulltext/ED489533.pdf.

Hiltz, S. R., and M. Turoff. "Virtual Classroom Plus Video: Technology for Educational Excellence." In *Educational Multimedia and Hypermedia*, 1994. 26-31. Accessed August 28, 2016. http://files.eric.ed.gov/fulltext/ED388215.pdf.

Horn, M. and H. Staker. *Blended – Using Disruptive Innovation to Improve Schools*. San Francisco: Jossey-Bass, 2014.

Martin, E. "The 50 Smartest high schools in the US." *Business Insider.* March 24, 2015, Accessed June 18, 2016.
http://www.businessinsider.com/smartest-private-high-schools-in-the-us-2015-3.

Means, B., Y. Toyama, R. Murphy, M. Bakia, and K. Jones. *Evaluation of Evidence-Based Practices in Online Learning: A Meta-Analysis and Review of Online Learning Studies.* Washington, DC: US Department of Education Office of Planning, Evaluation, and Policy Development. Accessed June 18, 2016.
http://www2.ed.gov/rschstat/eval/tech/evidence-based-practices/finalreport.pdf.

Scarborough, J., and R. Ravaglia. *Bricks and Mortar: The Making of a Real Education at the Stanford Online High School.* Stanford, CA: CSLI Publications, 2014.

Part I

The Academic Disciplines

2

Preface to The Academic Disciplines

1   Introduction

Writing about Stanford Online High School, particularly about its 'schoolness' rather than its 'onlineness', it's hard to escape the fact that this is a school situated at Stanford University, filled with academically talented and passionate students, and staffed by teachers and administrators with advanced academic backgrounds. The first volume in this collection showed how such a school could flourish; how the blended-flipped synchronous seminar model could make it possible to deliver a world-class education to a far-flung but ultimately closely-knit population of students. Two years later, with such a general demonstration already in place, our focus in writing about the school is different.

It is particularly true for the academic disciplines at SOHS that the online setting of instruction is not the sole or sometimes even the primary driver of innovation in their work. Rather, it is in the efforts of our talented instructors to address and meet the curricular and pedagogical needs of our talented and advanced students that the broader innovations happen. The six chapters in this first academic part of this book pay considerable attention to the findings and strategies that have been successful for our students, and that are directly applicable to schools serving a similar demographic of students.

To be sure, accomplishing these academic goals online requires a deep resourcefulness within the online setting. In this volume, we are able to characterize the nuances and application of broad strategies of teaching in a live online context to the particular instructional needs of individual disciplines. These practices pertain not simply to the technological tasks of executing an effective live class—using the tools available to perform the activities—but also to the pedagogical strategies and activities themselves that make the best use of the precious class time for the purposes of the respective disciplines. Some of these strategies, again, are not tied to online instruction; rather, they reveal some of the promise and advantage of approaches that had their origin in the necessities of teaching online, but that might be extended back into a brick-and-mortar setting. It is rare, in any case, that these practices are uniquely tied to the distinctness of SOHS courses—despite their origins, they are largely relevant to instruction in settings of varied academic intensity.

Perhaps the signal lesson from the first ten years at SOHS has been the importance of community to a school environment, and in turn, to our online school. At every turn, our students have thrived in response to measures and innovations that bring them into closer and more substantial contact with one another and their teachers. From clubs, online study groups, all manner of physical gatherings, on-campus summer programs, travel, and competitions, to the original premise of real-time group seminars, the points of connection students have to one another have immeasurably enriched not only their experience at the school, but also their learning. Teachers at SOHS have seen the place of community in their classrooms from the first day. So it is small wonder that their strategies, and even the curriculum, reflect support for students learning together.

2 Findings about Teaching

Each of the disciplines has grappled in its own ways with the mandate of meeting the mission of the school in practice—to stimulate, support, and challenge talented and dedicated students. Still, several common threads of innovation run through their collective experiences.

A convenient, though relatively superficial, way to approach the school's unique calibration to the needs and abilities of talented students would be simply to open the course catalog. While the traditional subjects make their appearances, course offerings stand out. Math listings continue past Calculus with various flavors, before heading into the terrain of undergraduate majors; similarly for physics. Each discipline has developed courses that explore material at a college level and with similar methodologies. Courses like these are not tacked on to entirely conventional early high school sequences. History courses focus on themes like empire or rebellion, allowing deeper exploration and authentic practice of historical tools. And English courses wear their characteristic attention to argumentation, evidence, and writing in their titles. To be sure, the real work of these features of the curriculum in the various disciplines is accomplished by details that can't be read off the catalog; laying out these curricular innovations and how they harness and refine the talents of our students is part of the work of the respective chapters.

What does stand out even at the mundane level of academic disciplines is the Philosophy Core. This sequence of philosophically informed courses required in each year of high school is a centerpiece of the SOHS student experience. At the inception of the school there was a desire for a unique curricular experience that would pull students together across their varied interests and academic achievements, and help define the culture of the school. So the original mandate for Core envisioned a collection of interesting concepts and material drawn from across the disciplines, equipping students with a distinctive intellectual framework while falling conveniently outside of their previous experiences. Core has done this surprisingly well, while also exposing students to ways of thinking and modes of inquiry not normally associated with a subject. It is only half in jest that we suggest that in Core, students not only learn to think about the subject, but also learn to think about thinking about the subject. This approach has provided a back door of sorts into certain areas of learning. The History and Philosophy of Science course, for instance, takes students through important observations and experiments that have defined the scientific tradition, and in doing so provides students with a decidedly non-mathematical approach to thinking about science. Here the verbally talented students find that they may be on stronger footing in reading and understand the ancient scientific texts than their mathematically fleeter colleagues. At the same time, a course like Democracy, Freedom, and the Rule of Law, with its detailed study of the British liberal tradition and the analytical philosophical method, has provided more mathematically inclined students with a comfortable entryway into the humanities.

But even in subjects more conventionally taught at the high school level, both the 'what' and the 'how' of instruction reflect choices made in aligning the SOHS curriculum to the norms of university and professional styles in the discipline. This approach to challenging talented students is a special focus of the SOHS Science Division. SOHS courses and instruction emphasize the process of science, even during the exploration of standard content. In practice, this means engendering a posture of curiosity and questioning among students, supported by the right tools and perspectives for inquiry. To pursue their questions, students need to develop a working appreciation of how to get the data they're looking for by designing and manipulating experimental protocols, and they need to acknowledge, contextualize, and learn from error. Students learn a similar attention to authentic scientific practices, colored by an appropriate regard for uncertainty, in the interpretation and communication of their results.

This same strategy of crafting curriculum and pedagogy around university and professional practices is a natural fit across the disciplines at SOHS. In addition to the thoroughgoing discussion in the chapter on science, it is also a topic in the chapters on mathematics and history, which describe approaches to the conceptual understanding involved in proof and problem solving (rather than simple computational prowess) and the historiographical thinking that are important orientations of these disciplines at SOHS. Our experience has shown that this kind of focus on the methods and attitudes of practitioners is a good fit for talented students. It inspires and rewards them, but not strictly because the material is advanced and challenging; the same approach works among younger students.

All of this points us to an observation made in each of these chapters—science, mathematics, and history—in which the methods are a special focus: the background and role of the teacher are important to the success of the approach. At SOHS, where seventy percent of teachers have PhDs in their field, teachers are well positioned both to model and to show deep enthusiasm for the method and attitudes of the discipline. In addition, these teachers have at their fingertips the questions, examples, and perspective to lead students to a timely historiographical critique of a textbook or make a connection to an advanced field of mathematics. So it is not simply for teaching advanced courses that teachers with advanced academic backgrounds are critical in the project of supporting talented students in a curriculum tailored to them.

We haven't yet said much about a traditional selling point of curriculum for gifted or advanced students—the mechanisms for acceleration. Indeed, the emphasis so far (and more below) on challenging curriculum and live work with teachers anticipates a possible tension with a familiar model of self-paced acceleration. Just such discussions have been a central part of thinking about curriculum and student experience through the life of the school, particularly in subjects like math and language. When courses that are often opportunities for individual acceleration are taught in a group setting, at an established pace, more intentional mechanisms of advancing students toward the upper reaches of the course catalog are called for.

In the Language Division, meanwhile, acceleration is encountered less as a question of how to accommodate particular students seeking acceleration, than it is as a question of the overall pace of the sequence itself. But the story of the Language Division's thinking on how to challenge talented students in a school context points away from a sequence that achieves intensity through a rush to university-level concepts and material. What has been more rewarding to our students is a program centered around an intensity of engagement in a language, supported by frequent class meetings, serious engagement with the cultural context of the language, and robust participation in the class community.

3   Findings about Teaching Online

Stanford OHS's dedication at the programmatic level to live or synchronous teaching, in twice-weekly online seminars (more for languages), is clear already from the introduction to this volume. In the chapters that follow it is clear at a practical level that when our teachers talk about 'teaching online', they are speaking about what goes on in their live classrooms and how they support those class meetings on the flipped model and through other interactions with students. While our teachers do think actively about how to make use of the LMS (Learning Management System) and other asynchronous tools, this is not where the action is at our school. Rather, the focus of attention to teaching online in the chapters that follow is on what happens between the lines—how teachers spend their precious time in class with their students, and how the technology of the online classroom setting bears on those activities.

The story that emerges in the respective accounts of an online class meeting, and that is readily apparent upon setting foot in one, is that what happens there is essentially the kind of thing that happens in a good, seminar-style class anywhere. Students might share reactions and do a close reading in English; a history class will grapple with a particular claim or thesis; and in math, students examine different approaches to a problem. Students progressively take greater leadership roles, formal and informal, throughout their high school careers. Across the disciplines, they move from mere participation to take responsibility for introducing topics, presenting material, and soliciting and fielding comments from their peers. It is in this setting that students are able to practices live and oral communication skills, attend to the concision and topicality of their comments, and monitor their responsiveness to the contributions of others. In addition to the critical, seeding role that such interactions play in creating a healthy intellectual community at our school, what is important in the example of these class activities at SOHS is precisely *that* and *how* they can happen online. The chapters that follow are rich in detail and examples on both points.

The online classroom technology certainly impacts how these activities are conducted. Accordingly, its use is the focus of endless, persistent creativity and refinement by teachers and the entire school staff.

As one might expect, the differing needs and priorities of the different disciplines lead to diverse and nuanced practices. However, some key practices can be isolated in connection with major features of the classroom system. The English and language chapters describe, for instance, a compelling wrinkle to familiar practices of close reading made possible by the collaborative nature of the whiteboard. Several chapters touch on the importance and particular use of 'breakout rooms'—the facility for dividing the class into small groups for independent work. And nearly every division reflects on the potential uses of the text chat that parallels the audio-visual discussion in class. From quick and simultaneous answers in math and language courses, to its uses as a gateway tool for reticent participants, the uses of text chat catalogued in these chapters provides a foothold for considering the ways in which the online classroom and its dynamics might in some cases provide a richer environment for engaging material and students than a traditional brick-and-mortar setting. Of course, these discussions (and those of the chapters on counseling and community in the second section of this volume) are well tempered with honest assessment of the challenges of still-maturing technologies, and of being separated by geography from students and peers. These range from imperfect tools for drawing or freehand input in math, Chinese, and visual arts; to the inefficiency of feedback tools; to more abstract tasks like assessing student engagement and establishing connections among students. But given the importance of these features of teaching and learning, there is also considerable reflection on strategies that usefully address these obstacles. In the best cases, like the at-home lab kits that fill the traditional role of hands-on labs, the strategies meet pedagogical or curricular goals in important new ways.

4   Findings about Teaching in a Community

The importance of live seminars at SOHS, and their success, derive in part from their place in creating and drawing upon the community at the school. Even with ever-increasing opportunities to interact outside of class and sometimes in person, class seminars are still where students make and enjoy the relationships with likeminded peers that they keenly value in the school. And it is evident to both teachers and students that these interactions, in the context of an invested community, are at the heart of the best learning happening at the school. The academic chapters in this volume catalogue some of the central efforts at establishing and leveraging a robust school community, in and out of the classroom.

Perhaps the most dramatic story about seminars at SOHS involves the math division's early transition from its historical model of self-paced material supported by office-hour-style meetings, to the model of seminars then emerging across the school. Chapter 5 characterizes both the rationale and the effects of the change, which was part of a comprehensive effort at building a schoolwide math community. The underlying premise was that students learn math more deeply, with greater engagement and persistence, in the company of their peers, whether in clubs, competitions, or the classroom.

The effectiveness of SOHS seminars depends on participation: not only do students who don't participate gain less by way of the practice that seminars provide in speaking, engaging, and arguing, but they also make more limited contributions to the substance of the dialogue. Chapter 4 details the motivation and effect of the extra emphasis that SOHS English courses place on the schoolwide expectation of consistent participation in class. In these contexts, experience suggests, a baseline requirement of active contribution in each class goes far in fostering more openness, sharing, and experimentation than when students are left to do more self-censoring. While other disciplines cleave to participation policies that recognize their particular objectives in class, widespread participation is clearly essential to other critical experiences at the school. Chapter 8 highlights the contribution that the school's distinctive cosmopolitan community makes to students' perspectives on historical issues, as it does to topics in other disciplines. Students who are comfortable and supported in sharing their diverse perspectives on historical or contemporary episodes, gleaned from their lives and experiences in the different states and countries from which they attend the school, push their peers to consider ideas and perspectives that sometimes diverge from their reflexive outlooks.

5 Conclusion

The disciplines at SOHS have developed in what is in many ways the same context—striving to meet the needs of talented students in an online setting. And both in their own experience and through collaboration, they've found their way to a common set of practices and priorities. They've settled on productive ways to use the technology, to draw on the academic backgrounds of their teachers, and to cultivate community in their classrooms. But they have also pursued their own distinctive opportunities and responded to their own distinctive pressures. The innovation described in the chapters that follow reflects these considerations. The philosophy Core has carved out a curricular purpose and pedagogy suited to high school students, in the absence of any tradition along these lines. English and math, far more established disciplines, have contributed to the understanding of how to accomplish online their rigorous practices. History and languages meanwhile, in addition to their own pedagogical adjustments, reflect in their chapters on the initiatives in their courses and course offerings in response to student needs. And science, confronted by some of the most tangible logistical hurdles in virtue of teaching online, has addressed these challenges in keeping with a division-wide emphasis on scientific thinking. Our school and our students have benefited from this diversity of innovation.

3

Philosophy Core

Karen Kenkel and Jeffrey Scarborough

1 Introduction

The experience of philosophical reflection and dialogue can have a transformative effect on all aspects of students' lives.[1] It can help them integrate their developing selves into their rapidly changing worlds thoughtfully, or differentiate themselves from those worlds in meaningful ways. It can help them reflect critically on assumptions or beliefs that guide their—and others'—behavior and thinking. It can help them learn how to think carefully; provide exposure to, and practice in, different ways of thinking; and—if a consistent part of the curriculum—help create reflective and rigorous habits of mind in a variety of disciplines and contexts. And perhaps most importantly for our contemporary world, it can help a diverse body of individuals learn how to discuss and develop important ideas collaboratively.

2 Pedagogical Aims in Core

The Core program in philosophy at Stanford OHS, henceforth referred to simply as 'Core', is designed with these aspirations in mind. The four-year high school sequence, required of all full-time students, provides students a systematic introduction to different kinds of thinking in a range of disciplines, including science, math, politics, culture, and

---

[1]Many thanks are due to our colleagues in the SOHS Core Division. Their creativity and care in teaching philosophy to high school students is an ongoing source of inspiration and pride. We give particular thanks to Will Beals, Joshua Beattie, Tomohiro Hoshi, Heather Walker-Dale, and Jonathan Weil for discussions about the content of this chapter.

Perspectives from the Disciplines.
Jeffrey Scarborough and Raymond Ravaglia.
Copyright © 2016, CSLI Publications.

philosophy itself. The elective middle school course on human nature investigates fundamental assumptions and thought about who we are, why we do what we do, what distinguishes us from other creatures on this planet, and why all of this matters in the first place.

We *require* this sequence of courses of all our full-time students in order for them to develop critical thinking skills in a variety of disciplines in a collaborative community of inquiry. While a science, statistics, or government course may not be able to devote time to a close investigation of the assumptions that underlie the discipline and its methodologies, these are the topics of our concern. In the freshman year Methodology of Science—Biology (MSB) course, students explore together the underlying methodology and theoretical framework of contemporary scientific inquiry through the combined study of biology and statistics. Sophomore year in History and Philosophy of Science (HSC), students investigate the history of scientific thinking, with a particular focus on how 'errors' in scientific thinking over time both foster intellectual progress and shape inquiry, but also reveal the connection between empirical study and shifting world views. Junior year's Democracy, Freedom, and Rule of Law (DFRL) finds our students concentrating on political philosophy in the particular framework of democratic political organization. In their senior year in Critical Reading and Argumentation (CRA), students focus on the discipline of philosophy itself and study its modes of argumentation, examining key areas of philosophical inquiry such as ethics, epistemology, philosophy of religion, free will/determinism, personal identity, etc. Core is the only *sequence* of courses at SOHS that is required of all full-time students, which means that students traverse their high school experience as a philosophical cohort. This adds staying power and a growing sense of community to the model of inquiry, reserving a place where students from all over the world can think and explore together over the course of their high school experience.

While we are certainly interested in students acquiring philosophical knowledge in our Core sequence, we are equally—and perhaps even more—concerned that students learn to develop, articulate, and support their own views about a range of material in a variety of disciplines in dialogue with others. We are convinced that learning to develop and present good arguments requires practice, and collaboration. It is not something a student can learn solely by observing the teacher, much as she cannot learn to play the piano by watching a YouTube video. Because our classes meet only twice a week for seventy-five minutes each (CRA meets for ninety minutes), all of Core class time is intensely focused on discussion and group work. Lectures, required in some of the courses alongside assigned readings, are viewed outside of class. In the online classroom, our instructors are encouraged to view themselves as facilitators of student discovery, guiding students in the development of their own thinking and prodding them to delve deeper in areas of particular importance, interest, or relevance. The goal of every class is for students to develop and practice their thinking skills in dialogue with others. Students must learn how to present their thoughts clearly, to thoughtfully consider the soundness of others' positions, and to productively disagree. Thus, in the most successful SOHS class discussion, the teacher is a highly sensitive facilitator of a student-driven investigation, who listens carefully, and steers the discussion in fruitful directions down paths of student interest. Being a facilitator is by no means a passive endeavor: it demands a lightness of foot, a real interest in one's students, and a passion for the subject matter itself; it requires scrupulous listening and a critical awareness of one's own agenda and views. Most importantly, it requires a carefully considered curriculum to ensure that students are driving the exploration in fertile terrain. Philosophy as a discipline occupies itself with questions which cannot be addressed in any other way but through the type of argument and discussion we engage in in our classroom, and for our program to be successful in its goals, students must stand at the center.[2]

However, the fact that Core is required of all students merely ensures that students are present. To deeply engage them, we need to help students discover how important and relevant philosophical questions are to their day-to-day lives, in fact, to see how many of their existing questions and concerns are philosophical in nature. While for some it's easy to bring them there, for others it requires more craft of the instructor. The aspirations of our learner-centered philosophy program go unrealized if the curriculum is not meaningful to the students. In an end of the year course survey, one student commented enthusiastically that the instructor encouraged students 'to find a way into philosophy that interests them', and thus affirmed one of the key goals of our classroom. Or, as Tom Wartenberg has put it, 'for education to be successful, the student must have a desire to participate in the process of learning itself.'[3] If the students aren't engaged by the material, a lively discussion that deeply explores essential terrain is impossible. What we want is the student who is convinced, as this student was

---

[2] Tom Wartenberg's book *Big Ideas for Little Kids: Teaching Philosophy Through Children's Literature* provided helpful categories for characterizing our pedagogical approach, which follows closely his model of the teacher as facilitator of philosophical discussions in a learner-centered classroom.

[3] Wartenberg, *Big Ideas for Little Kids*, 18.

at the end of their senior year Core class, that 'Even if this wasn't a mandatory class I would ask that everyone takes it. I have grown as a person and a student....' This is the student who sees philosophy as affirming and transformative inquiry.

While it seems self-evident that students need to perceive the relevance of philosophical inquiry in order to engage in the activity required to learn, the means to achieve it are not equally transparent. The difficulty and abstraction of philosophical material can be a barrier to student engagement, as can widespread preconceptions about the general irrelevance of philosophy. It is not unusual in our everyday world to hear someone dismiss a concern or objection with the comment: 'that's just a philosophical question', usually in order to motor the conversation past reflection and into the desired action. This view of philosophy challenges us to develop a curriculum—comprising readings, lectures, assignments, and discussion topics—that students are invested in thinking about, that they *care* about. (This might include investigation of why they *ought to care about it*, given their fundamental values.) When we succeed in this endeavor, we are happy to see the type of learning trajectory that one student described in an end-of-year course evaluation of our philosophy of science course: '...honestly, prior to this course, I thought philosophy an irrelevant field, but now I have gained a great respect for it, and have learned to apply it to some of my other favorite fields of academic study, and to life as a whole.'

How do we discern what our students care about? Of course, most students in our school care about getting good grades and getting into a good college. And this type of extrinsic motivation can be a useful tool to get students to first approach and stick with our challenging—and not always immediately gratifying—subject matter long enough to reap the benefits. However, the desire for good grades will not motivate the type of transformative philosophical engagement that is our ultimate aim. To do so, we need to tap into a 'caring' that runs deeper, that is powered by the energy of our students' fundamental values, goals, concerns, and senses of self. And this engagement is not simply achieved by identifying and focusing on what is of immediate concern to students, as philosophical study itself shows how relevant irrelevance is to living our lives on our own terms, with our consent. To demand immediate relevance of a philosophical topic can tempt facile or even pandering connections with contemporary social or political issues that may not take advantage of the critical distance and productive alienation from one's world—what Nietzsche called 'untimeliness'—that is one of the pedagogical gifts of philosophy.

Besides grades, our students—like all of us—care very much about themselves. Getting to know our students helps us assess what is important to them, and how we can best tap into this most fundamental and intrinsic motivation for learning. And yet, getting to know students in an online school presents unique challenges. Instructors do not have easy access to the insights gathered from casual interactions or observations in the hallway, at lunch, or at the sports event. We are not able to easily read the body language of students in the virtual classroom. It may be difficult to determine whether a student is bored, exhausted, troubled, or merely thoughtful from her postage-stamp sized image on the screen, or from her tone in text chat. There might be antagonism or *amore* between students in the class that flies under the radar of even the most skilled interpreter of online classroom cues. The SOHS instructor's awareness that the virtual environment may obscure important aspects of her students' lives and concerns tends to drive a very concentrated effort in our school to get to know our students as well as possible through the primary means available to us, namely, the classroom and the curriculum. What this means is that our online instructors work hard to integrate our students into the curriculum itself. This effort takes different forms. We try to develop assignments and activities that mine student concerns and interests, to design assessments that require students to integrate philosophy into their lives; and to choose reading and writing assignments that accommodate different learning styles and preferences. In short, we focus on a variety of strategies that both differentiate learning approaches to appeal to varied learning styles, as well as provide freedom for students to develop and express their own approaches to and applications of the philosophical topics under investigation.

Creating a rigorous curriculum that is driven by students' intrinsic motivation involves careful planning and structure, often hidden to students, to ensure that the personal aspect does not derail the desired intellectual inquiry, but drives it. It also involves experimentation, as well as instructor and curricular openness, to determine what works with any particular class of students. There are many different approaches and types of assignments and assessments that can be used to achieve this goal. We have developed several assignments that have proven particularly successful in this endeavor. Among them are the moral experiment project conducted in the senior year course, Critical Reading and Argumentation (CRA); and the final research project in Methodology of Science—Biology (MSB).

In the ethics unit in CRA, students learn about the three canonic ethical systems in Western philosophy: virtue ethics, deontological ethics, and utilitarian ethics. They read Aristotle, Immanuel Kant, and Jeremy

Bentham/John Stuart Mill. In order to understand the fundamental principles of each ethical system, and to grasp their relative strengths and weaknesses, we could ask students to read existing criticism of each system. However, not only does this position students as passive recipients of the work of inquiry rather than expecting it of them, but this approach can lead to cynicism about ethical inquiry per se: if all of these systems are deeply flawed, why read or think about them at all? Rather than providing students critical assessments of each ethical system, the moral experiment project requires students to discover the strengths and weaknesses of an ethical system *by living it for two days.* How does this work?

The project is presented to the students as follows:

> The moral experiment project asks you to critically consider the moral philosophy of your choice (virtue ethics/utilitarianism/deontology) by living according to the chosen ethical system and reflecting on this experience. The final essay will contain a critical summary of the moral philosophy of choice, a reflection upon its applicability in your life, and some conclusions about what you may have learned about the strengths, weaknesses, and limitations of your chosen ethics.

Over several years of trial and error, the project has come to involve four steps. Step 1: After we have read and discussed together each ethical system, the student identifies by which ethics she wishes to live and submits a prospectus. The prospectus has two parts: (a) A careful exposition of the main tenets of the ethical theory, with a particular focus on aspects of the theory that are relevant to how it would be lived in practice; (b) a brief account of concerns facing the chosen theory, including anticipated problems with its implementation in practice. The prospectus allows the instructor to determine whether the student has a good working understanding of the ethical system of choice, and encourages students to imagine what it might be like to live this ethics. Step 2: Students live as closely and as well as they can according to the mandates of the ethical system for two days. Students are required to keep a journal documenting their experiences, which they submit as an appendix to their final essay. Step 3: Using their notes and prospectus, students write a reflective essay, in which they are asked to consider the following questions: In which situations did the ethics work well? Which less well? Were you able to consistently act within the moral parameters of the ethics, or did you find it necessary to deviate (and if so, why did you deviate)? Did the deviations comment on your behavior, your character, your beliefs, your values, the ethics? The moral experiment final project comprises a critical summary of the moral philosophy of choice, a critical reflection upon its applicability in the student's life, and some conclusions about what students may have learned about the strengths, weaknesses, and limitations of the chosen moral philosophy. Students are encouraged to reflect on how they might remedy the weaknesses and limitations of the moral philosophy they lived. Stage 4: Students revise the essay, based on feedback from peers and the instructor, according to a rubric the instructor provides. In the peer-review process, we have found it productive to partner students who lived the same ethics, so that they offer suggestions for improvement in each other's papers from a place of first-hand experience and knowledge. The peer-review process not only provides students input from different readers, but also leads students to evaluate their own essays according to the rubric even as they provide feedback to others.

The best final projects successfully combine the personal experiences of the experiment with critical theoretical reflections on the ethical system in question. In living the ethics, students develop an organic awareness of the limitations of the ethical system, as well as insight into their own ethical commitments as they confront how far they are willing to embrace their ethical system of choice. As they encounter difficulties, they often must decide whether they will live according to the spirit or the letter of the law in their ethical system, which in turn often elegantly leads to meta-ethical reflections on how ethical systems work per se. They are often surprised when the difficulties that they encounter are not the ones they anticipated, as is often the case, and gain insight into their own ethical selves as part of the process. And in living the system, they become invested in making the system work, and are encouraged to do so by the requirement that they consider how they might remedy the shortfalls of their system of choice.

The students are more excited about this experiment than almost any other assignment in the course; and it is astonishing, sometimes even disconcerting, to see how earnestly some follow their chosen ethical path. (The first year we gave this assignment, we did not inform parents ahead of time, and instructors received several concerned—and some deeply amused—emails and phone calls from parents regarding the abrupt transformation of their child.) One student, who chose to live by Kant's duty ethics, spent two days steadfastly refusing to lie, and consequently found it unavoidable to tell an old and close friend that she thought he made very poor relationship choices. This truth-telling caused the collapse of that friendship. The student reflected on how Kant's ethics seemed unable to adequately accommodate kindness, friendship, or loyalty. Another student living utilitarianism decided to foster greater happiness by pursuing higher pleasures, as Mill requires; in particular, he opted to better himself and his companions by listening to classics on tape while driving across the mid-West to a family reunion, much to the on-going and vociferous dismay of his car-mates, who were hoping for more low-brow fare. He also became a vegetarian for the experiment, and found himself picking at wilted lettuce at the meat-laden noontime reunion buffet, while trying to respond to the objections of his relatives that 'the animals are already dead! You aren't going to cause any additional suffering by eating that meat!' Another student, struggling to treat the Starbucks cashier as an end-in-herself rather than as just a means, recounted how her attempt to converse with the cashier as a person and not just a coffee delivery device ended up irritating both the cashier and the people behind her line because it slowed down the process. In her essay, she questioned whether Kantian ethics is compatible with a capitalist economy. Yet another student, pursuing virtue ethics, quite rightly reflected on the fact that the work of his experiment—formation of character—could hardly be accomplished in two days!

In the process of reading and providing feedback on the prospectus, the journal, the draft of the final paper, and the final paper itself, the instructor gains great insight into the rhythm of a student's days, her commitments, friendships, family structure, geographical situation, motivations, and self-perception. All of this is gained by virtue of a highly engaging and self-motivating experiment that applies well-processed philosophical concepts. Moreover, criticism of moral precepts unfolds through rigorous personal experience and reflection (carefully structured by the stages of the assignment as well as the assignment rubric), which in turn leads more readily to an appreciation of the difficulty of ethical behavior and its codification, rather than cynicism about creating a viable ethical system. On the contrary, students often end up viewing themselves as ethical philosophers as they craft their own hybrid systems out of the experiences they have reflected upon. Whether these systems ultimately bear up under closer scrutiny is beside the point; students have developed a deep understanding of the principles, limitations, and difficulties of living an ethical system; become aware of how often they may be inclined to treat themselves as exceptions to their own moral code in their day-to-day behavior; and practiced and reinforced the habit of engaging philosophically in their lives.

A different type of application and personal exploration is involved in the final project for MSB. This project asks students to apply methods and concepts they have learned during the year in order to construct an experiment/investigation of their own choosing, collect data, and obtain a scientific conclusion by interpreting that data using statistical techniques. The subject matter of their study is largely open, although it must be biological, and preferably have some connection to the material students have studied during the year. While open in topic, the steps, procedures, and expectations of the final project are tightly structured. The first step of the project involves the submission of an initial proposal of possible projects and estimates of the time/cost required for each. The second step requires an update outlining a specific project plan, including information about data-collection methods and the statistical analysis to be undertaken. The last step is the submission of the final report, in which students not only present their materials and methods, the data they have gathered and their statistical analysis of it, but also explain why the subject matter of the experiment is interesting, important, and worth pursuing. This discussion includes background information about the subject matter of the project, the purpose and motivation of the project (what they are investigating and why it is interesting), and, if applicable, a hypothesis stating the initially expected experimental results. Perhaps most important, students are asked to discuss and reflect upon their conclusions. The purpose of this reflection is to highlight the most important things they discovered through their experiments, asking them to consider possible sources of error or limitations in their experimental set-up, and to note any new questions the data has raised. Students consider the conclusion(s) they can draw from the statistically analyzed data where applicable, state whether their data supports or fails to support their original hypotheses, offer thoughts about what they would do differently if they were carrying out the same project again (under the same basic conditions and/or with additional resources), and discuss possible future investigations that could expand on the results obtained in their research.

MSB students apply the concepts and methods they have learned over the course of the year as they develop their projects, and become critical investigators of the environment around them in projects largely shaped by their own interests and passions. The openness of the final project, which asks students to look at their environments as investigative scientists with curious and critical eyes, often has a transformative effect on students' performance in the class. In many cases, the final project elicits students' best work of the year—and sometimes some of the best work in the school. One student, in the process of moving from a rural part of Colorado to a more urban part of Missouri, attempted to compare the empathy levels of people living in rural versus urban environments. Based on her personal experience in rural Colorado, she took as her working hypothesis the somewhat counterintuitive claim that rural populations are less empathetic—more do-it-yourself individualists—than urban populations, where closer proximity and interdependence may evoke greater empathy. The conclusion of her study supported her initial hypothesis, while revealing an unanticipated differentiation of empathy along gender lines, which in turn further fueled her curiosity about empathy and demographics. Her personal investment in the project drove a tremendous effort, which resulted in a final project that was not only her best work of the year, but was chosen to be published in the school's highly selective journal *De Novo*.

Free to investigate something she was passionate about, an environmentally engaged student who lives in Australia wanted to determine whether environmental protection was effective in supporting the flourishing of mangroves. She chose to study the dispersion and population size of mangroves in her immediate (unprotected) surroundings, and to compare her findings with data she was able to get from the local government regarding the dispersion and population of mangroves in a local protected area. The goal in the study was to determine whether the results supported her advocacy of environmental protection for the mangrove area near her house. One of the most amazing things about her project was the method she devised, and the time and effort she put into collecting data, both of which bespoke her deep investment in the project. She used a satellite image of the area, divided it into quadrants, randomly selected some of those, and then used GPS to hike, canoe/kayak, or wade out to the areas she had selected on the map. She then physically marked off the quadrants and collected her data on the plants in the quadrants. Her data did not entirely support her hypothesis, but the surprises actually strengthened her case for the protection of the local mangrove area. She completed her project determined to spend her summer writing to local government agencies, using her data to advocate for environmental protection and education. Her final project, which offered freedom within a structured framework and timeline, was, moreover, her best academic work of the year.

The geographical reach of the SOHS student body means that the impact of such open-topic scientific studies in MSB has great global potential, bringing a shared methodology and critical reflection to bear on widely divergent concerns and investigations from all corners of the globe. In addition to the deep engagement with these projects fueled by students' personal investment, students from many different environments and contexts develop as practitioners of invested scientific study.

3   Critical Thinking in Core

So far, we have made the case that the philosophy Core engages and provokes students in a collegial environment driven by conversation and enriched by projects that call forth creativity and application of critical scrutiny to live questions. These are (some of) the conditions under which high school students readily examine their world and our modes of knowing about the world. So in some sense, what we've done is show how the stage can be set for the engaged study of philosophy throughout high school. And we've addressed in part the question of why we expose our busy students to philosophical study in the first place. At SOHS the primary reason we go to these ends to make philosophical study work in our context is that philosophical reflection is uniquely equipped to train students in the project of critical thinking and argumentation. While our students undeniably derive other value from these experiences, stemming from the worth of exploring important questions, the primary motivation for Core was and is the kind of thinkers and writers that philosophical study can make them.

But even once we have identified critical thinking as a central objective of Core at SOHS, we still need to consider what it is about philosophy and in philosophical study that engenders those qualities, and how. Is any philosophical topic that meets the criterion of relevance and is amenable to exploration in collaborative discussion and student-shaped projects appropriate fodder for cultivating the thoughtfulness, precision, and creativity we hope to see in our graduates? To be sure, a holistic approach is unlikely to do any harm. But given the value and rarity of the opportunity to engage students in an extended formation in philosophy, one would hope to do better than that. It's our argument here that it's not simply the exercise of thinking philosophy demands that is most effective in creating students who bring their critical skills into the rest of their thinking about the world. Rather, such skills and habits emerge from philosophical training in concrete, discipline-specific tools, concepts, theories, and foundational questions. In the remainder of this discussion, we focus on the ways in which SOHS Core is designed to support exactly this kind of experience in philosophy.

Philosophers and educators have struggled to characterize the very proficiency that is the target of training in critical thinking. And it is hard to teach, broadly and reliably, what we cannot define. Some initial efforts to employ philosophical practices in critical thinking in the context of a more general education highlighted the potential contribution of familiarity with formal and informal logic.[4] To be sure, public and even more formal reasoning is chock-full of sins that can be readily characterized and discredited with the tools of logic. Similarly, well-

---

[4]R. Ennis, "Critical Thinking: A Streamlined Conception," *Teaching Philosophy* 14 (1991): 5–24.

established patterns of inference and proof can guide the construction of more secure arguments. So an effort to introduce elements of formal logic into the curriculum of non-specialists has much to recommend it, and the SOHS Core indeed does incorporate some training along these lines.

Practice in formalizing arguments, constructing proofs through various strategies, and recognizing modes of inference can be transformational to a certain sort of student who is already philosophically predisposed and now sees everything as an opportunity to apply formal systems. But these lessons can easily have the character of intellectual puzzles confined to the classroom. Important conversations in the wild are rarely decided, for instance, by an identification of the *ad hominem* fallacy. There are several problems at work here. First, faulty reasoning of the illogical sort is more likely to be recruited to the support of bad positions than it is to be the source of them. Rehearsing fallacies like one might in a tidy introduction to logic is not going to change minds, even if it might be a useful bludgeon to wield in an intellectual showdown. And where sloppy or mischievous reasoning is at the root of dubious conclusions, the problem often lies much deeper in one's understanding or conceptual repertoire. Spotting and avoiding errors of this sort might require that we know something—certain things—about a discipline and its native modes of reasoning. A semester course on generalized principles of reasoning is not going to be of much help. Furthermore, we know from the work of behavioral economists like Daniel Kahneman[5] that even conclusions that seem to have been rationally constructed are often mere rationalizations.

Changing minds requires a more systematic and sustained approach than deploying better syllogisms. To situate students to resolve real disputes, to avoid prejudice and preconception, and to constructively assess proposed solutions, we need to equip them to habitually and deeply probe the ideas they encounter from any number of angles. A conviction that the Affordable Care Act imperils personal freedom, for instance, might not turn on a particularly contentious inference. A given argument for this position might have such a fault, but others may not. Perhaps, instead, it is a certain understanding of the nature of individual freedom, one that is not obvious or universally shared, that drives the perceived conflict between freedom and this law. Some will approach the debate with a different picture of freedom—perhaps one that sees access to healthcare as a right or kind of freedom in

---

[5]D. Kahneman, *Thinking, Fast and Slow* (New York: Farrar, Straus and Giroux, 2011).

itself. Uncovering these implicit networks of values takes a good deal of skilled detective work. A logic or critical thinking course might help us conceptualize the disagreement as a dispute about hidden premises. But it will not give us much practical guidance at all in identifying and characterizing that premise from the vast public discourse on the broader issue, or in connecting a given individual's conception of that value to other values she holds, or in deciphering the rules of evidence that have played a role in the formation of relevant beliefs, and therefore how they might be used to support different positions.

To do a better job at this kind of investigation regarding public reasoning about politics, for instance, we need to know about patterns of justification in a political tradition.[6] What are the available views about where 'rights' come from—either rights to goods like healthcare, or the rights that are ostensibly violated by legislative approaches to providing it? Are there common trumps to individual rights, like justice, that might be invoked to mitigate appropriate constraints on individual action? And what are live views about the function of government that might place the provision of healthcare (either as a right or as a conventional good in society) within or beyond the responsibility and prerogative of the government? We need to know about systems of decision making in society. What voice does a minority have in the face of majority consensus? What are the proper limits, beyond individual rights, of democratically expressed preferences? And we need to know about surrounding theories about people and the world that enter into justifications and arbitration of disputes. What are the views about the fundamental unit in society (e.g. individuals, groups, society as a whole) that give weight to whose rights, welfare, and preferences matter? What are the theories of human nature that help us predict consequences of certain policies for human productivity and choices?

The limits of logic for the purposes of argument analysis and formation stem from the fact that the form of an argument is not always, or even often, where the action is when it comes to the kind of reasoning we expect students to do in their public and professional lives. The action—the substance of an argument that determines whether and with whom it holds sway—is at the very least in the network of beliefs, values, theories, and modes of justification that are characteristic of different disciplines and thinking about different subject matter. This is a central reason why SOHS adopted its model of teaching critical reasoning through a sequence of courses denominated by different dis-

---

[6]In the same way that the English courses frequently return to the question of how one writes across a variety of genres, the Core courses examine how one reasons across a variety of disciplines. (Ed.)

ciplines: so that students can amass a competence in critical reasoning through a mastery of the intricacies of careful reasoning in the (roughly delineated) different domains of inquiry.

In addition to these pieces of discipline-specific knowledge, the Core sequence also exposes students to larger theories that play their own role in underwriting students' critical thinking abilities across the disciplines. Philosophy is often derided for its failure to build an accumulating body of knowledge and conclusions, on the model of science. Philosophical theories are endlessly contested; views with their roots in Aristotle are at once still viable, but also commonly rejected; even popular, intuitively satisfying, and explanatorily powerful theories suffer from notorious defects and seemingly unresolvable problems. So when students learn about philosophical theories, they are not developing a semi-settled and universally recognized understanding for modeling and manipulating the world. Still, grappling with theories or theoretical apparatuses like John Stuart Mill's utilitarianism, or John Rawls's account of justice is greatly empowering to students. And it is not simply that these theories provide vulnerable targets on which students can hone and exercise their budding critical thinking skills. While students surely benefit from retracing or discovering anew the steps in well-worn dialectics between famous positions, they can also gain something from the substance of these views, however flawed they may be in the final estimation. This can be the case for a number of reasons. Just as every philosophical theory is subject to a range of objections based on or even built into competing views, so do the theories we study provide grounds for critiquing positions and claims students encounter in a discipline and in public discourse. Learning how to navigate, motivate, and apply these theories to a range of contexts equips students with concrete tools of analysis to use within and often outside of a given discipline or debate.

Some of the theories students work with in the penultimate course in the Core sequence—Democracy, Freedom, and the Rule of Law— illustrate not just the general-purpose practice to be gained from analyzing and applying a theory, but also the content-specific use that theories in these courses bring with them. One of the most robust and broadly applicable theories that Core students encounter—and which they reference years after graduating from SOHS—is the 'utilitarian' system of Jeremy Bentham and John Stuart Mill. At its simplest, utilitarianism asserts that what is right is exactly that course of action which creates the greatest good for the greatest number. This basic principle, which is at the heart of much more elaborate systems of morality, freedom, justice, and public policy, serves ably for the general purpose of introducing students to the nature and role of philosophical systems. In applying the utilitarian standard of the right to such a variety of problems, we are able to see what it means to use a theoretical claim to address specific issues. And students begin to see, in turn, how a question of what we ought to do in a particular problem, even a practical one, can be informed by more abstract claims about what makes an action good. And what is more, we can see how a particular theory like utilitarianism can have very different prescriptions for these concrete cases than do other theories (as, for instance, the deontological ethical system of Kant discussed above).

However, these broad lessons about theories generally are not the limit of what students gain from grappling with particular views like that of Mill. The reason students reference utilitarianism long after they graduate is precisely because it remains relevant to their lives. To be sure, and as we'll see below, utilitarianism admits to staggering counterexamples and other difficulties. Its defects are among the most effective motivators of competing theories—from Immanuel Kant's focus on the rule or intent of an action in moral theory, to John Rawls's system of justice in political theory. But the basic idea that the consequences of an action (in particular, the net pleasure or happiness compared to pain created by an action) are what makes it good or bad remains an incisive tool of analysis for a broad range of issues in public and private life. For students, this metric draws credibility from its clear ties to common (if not always compelling) modes of reasoning in public decision making: vaccination makes sense despite individual objections and real minor risk to individuals in light of its massive overall benefits; the inevitable loss of some innocent life in war can be legitimated by greater suffering spared others; environmental costs and/or (nearly) incalculable suffering to animals outweighs the convenience, savor, and tradition of a hamburger or steak. The next steps in the course of these arguments are often quite apparent: is it always right to burden a few with the cost of the health, security, and happiness of others? Are the circumstances, or the worthiness of the beneficiaries and afflicted irrelevant? These are not simply questions that expand students' minds, that they benefit from thinking hard about once, and that hone their general skills of argument or critique. This is a detailed template of challenge and response to a particular pattern of argument that students would do well to have ready in their repertoire. That is, however much utilitarianism does not issue unproblematic verdicts on difficult issues, students as future citizens and moral agents ought to know how to formulate an argument about right based on consequences, for any difficult issue they encounter. They should have practice in identifying and analyzing costs to humans and other subjects of pleasure and suffering. And then they should know where to look for the faults in such an analysis: they should know to look, for instance, to how the pleasures and pains are distributed, and they should have models or examples in mind to help them consider whether the choices, circumstances, or other characteristics of those involved raise troubling complications. And then, of course, they should have at hand a knowledge of competing theories, that can help them motivate and explore different concerns. In this model, thinking critically relies on experience and mastery of substantive theories, rather than general rules of inference or procedures.

Still, one might think that the know-how we have just described—the know-how engendered by familiarity with utilitarianism and its challenges—is simply a slightly specialized, richer flavor of general-purpose thinking about consequences. More detailed discussion of Mill and modern versions of utilitarianism might make some headway against this challenge. But other, more idiosyncratic theories from the philosophical tradition suggest that a powerful critical thinking repertoire does draw from the unique contributions of particular theories. In the case of the contemporary political philosopher John Rawls, the theory is relatively specialized but yields an important set of perspectives. Rawls approaches questions about the nature of justice by conceiving it as fairness; if fairness requires that individuals not be able to tailor the rules of the game to their own strengths, Rawls argues, a just society has to be built on principles of distribution that are not designed around the characteristics and strengths of the groups that shaped the distributive principles. So Rawls builds a theory of justice on the likely choices of individuals in a situation where the game cannot be intentionally slanted to a given group: he puts his hypothetical designers behind a 'veil of ignorance' about their preferences, talents, and position in society, as well as about the general composition of society. For students, the necessity of this 'veil' is a powerful innovation, highlighting the potential for institutional bias in the basic structure of our economy and institutions. Even if they don't often imagine what a self-interested individual in such a position of uncertainty about herself would prefer in a given situation (indeed, Rawls doesn't recommend this kind of application), students learn how to consider the possibility that particular features of our social and economic order may play to the strengths of the interest groups that constructed them.

What Rawls himself takes to follow from his model of justice as fairness is a particular distributive principle: people selecting principles of justice in their own interest, who nonetheless don't know where they might fall in society, would only permit a deviation from equality when any economic advantages (i.e. inequalities) have a beneficial impact on those who are least advantaged. Much like utilitarianism, this principle (Rawls calls it the 'difference principle') functions as a tool students can bring to bear on the actual distribution of goods in our society, generating a critique of inequalities that do not meet this standard of justification. Students who have read Rawls, even those who disagree, are able to consider whether a distribution that allows great inequalities without benefit to the least advantaged are just, no matter how those distributions came about. Rawls's theory, then, provides not just the skills of approaching and coming to understand a complex philosophical system, and it has a more substantial role than submitting for students' consideration a particular account of what social justice looks like. In addition to all this, the theory equips students with a set of concepts and tools they can use to analyze policies, theories, and actual distributions of social goods. With these very specific tools in hand, students are positioned to be thoughtful participants in discussions drawing on concepts like merit, luck, talent, desert, and fairness. And they are also prepared to scrutinize their own deeply held views on these topics.

Particular philosophical theories, then, despite and even in virtue of their well-deserved caveats, are an important discipline-specific asset to students' critical thinking repertoires. Another tool for critical thinking that emerges similarly from the discipline-specific explorations in the Core sequence falls under the rubric of what philosophers call 'epistemology'—a field of study that characterizes our knowledge of the world. As consumers and creators of claims about the world, about people, and about values, students gain a considerable critical apparatus as they come to appreciate key distinctions and possible sources of limitation in our claims of knowledge.

Foundational questions about the basis and limits of our knowledge have a home in subjects across the curriculum, and particularly in ethics and traditional fields of philosophy such as identity, the self, and perception. But the history and philosophy of science provides a context in which these questions are particularly acute, and therefore relatively stark. So it is in the sophomore-level Core course, History and Philosophy of Science, that students begin to encounter some of these epistemological questions, which they can in turn bring to bear on other topics outside of the sciences. For instance, in their study of Ptolemaic and Copernican models of the solar system and Newton's theory of gravity, students learn the distinction between regarding a theory and the entities it postulates as having merely *instrumental*

meaning and value—helpful in modeling and systematizing the phenomena we observe—and by contrast conceiving these theories and
their objects as having real and straightforward existence in the world.
While somewhat arcane, this distinction between instrumentalism and
realism allows students to think more easily about precisely what is
being asserted in a scientific claim or theory, and therefore what standards to hold it to in assessing its likely truth. But more generally, the
contrast between evaluating a theory or a practice or institution on
the basis of what it does, on the one hand, and evaluating it on the
basis of intrinsic correctness or justice, on the other hand, is a powerful one. Students who have this distinction ready to hand are able
to better identify the nature of the justification that is on offer in an
argument, and are accordingly better positioned to assess its strengths
and weaknesses.

A similarly revealing epistemological concept explored in the History
and Philosophy of Science course is the underdetermination of theory by
data. In its most pedestrian form, this is the caveat that a given theory
is surely not the only one that is compatible with the data. This was precisely the case with the models of the solar system rejected by Copernicus, for favor of his own model: the competing theories were themselves
roughly compatible with the available observations of the movement of
planets. Copernicus had to argue for his heliocentric view on reasoning
other than mere adequacy to the observed data. (An in-principle form
of the concept of underdetermination expands the difficulty to any theory for any set of data: another that is equally adequate to the data
will always be possible.) Awareness that pivotal scientific advances did
not always hinge on the adequacy of the theory to data makes students better consumers of science, and also better experimentalists:
they know how to generate alternate accounts of a target phenomenon,
and also how to design experiments that address or discern among important competing mechanisms. And they can transfer these skills to
other fields of argument, always alert to other possible explanations.

Theories, concepts, and norms of reasoning all have important
discipline-specific components or origins that contribute to students'
critical thinking capacities and resources. But the Core sequence also
focuses on the gradual development of more broadly applicable critical
thinking tools and strategies. In his discussion of the relevance of philosophy for general purposes, Simon Blackburn imagines philosophers
as 'conceptual engineers', skilled in laying bare the connections and relations among concepts, from the everyday to the highly specialized.[7]

---

[7]S. Blackburn, *Think: A Compelling Introduction to Philosophy* (New York:

Prominent in the conceptual engineer's toolkit since at least Socrates is the simple act of drawing apt distinctions among related ideas. This is a skill practiced across the disciplines treated by the Core sequence, but it plays a particularly prominent role in the Democracy, Freedom, and the Rule of Law course. In addition to the distinctions drawn between the 'positive' and 'negative' conceptions of freedom mentioned above, students have the opportunity to identify and flesh out pivotal differences in, for instance, the varying notions of 'representation' at play in the public debate surrounding the ratification of the Constitution. In the context of historical and contemporary politics, students who appreciate the antifederalist vision of representatives who *resemble* their constituents and share their interests both better understand the real clash of political ideology that informed that struggle, and also can discern in modern politics the echoes and perpetual appeal of the 'ordinary Joe' and outsider candidate. But honing the skill of identifying and using such distinctions has a significant payoff as a general skill of thinking analytically and arguing creatively. Students contemplating their own positions on how much government intervention in the conduct of individuals is warranted to prevent harm to others, for instance, often want to distinguish between harm that is likely or well recognized, and harm that is merely possible, as a way of negotiating the line between legitimate constraint on individual freedom and stifling regulation of our every choice. Facility with meaningful distinctions like these allows students to reject attractive but overly-broad claims, and to develop nuanced views of their own that productively navigate popularly entrenched positions.

An equally fundamental skill in philosophy, and in critical thinking more generally, is fluency in counterarguments. Discovering exceptions to a generalization or intuitively problematic applications of a principle can significantly constrain those claims, undermine them entirely, or suggest fruitful further questions or even revisions. The Core sequence offers students endless opportunity to develop a facility with counterexamples and arguments built around them. Readings for the courses are rich in models of effective (and less effective) counterarguments, ranging from the concrete to the hypothetical. The economist and philosopher Amartya Sen, for instance, cites the greater mortality rates of African American men, relative even to low-income men in China and Kerala, India, to demonstrate that economic growth cannot be identified with freedom in the sense of capacities or flourishing: the relative economic development of African American men does not

Oxford University Press, 2011) 2–4.

reliably translate into the robust life expectancy that is the most basic prerequisite of human flourishing.[8] Much less tangibly, in Critical Reading and Argumentation, students consider John Locke's famous imagined scenario in which the memories and consciousness of a prince are transplanted into the body of a cobbler; the compelling claim that it is actually the prince who inhabits the cobbler's body purports to undermine traditional views that take either the body or a soul substance as keys to identity. In the context of models like these, students begin to develop a nose for evidence or scenarios that can be tailored to precisely contradict a target view or claim.

4 Conclusion

For teachers of critical thinking, it is an unfortunate and troubling fact that students commonly leave dedicated critical thinking courses with little effective change in their cognitive practices and behavior. Studies to this effect have pushed theorists of critical thinking to treat it increasingly as a disposition or habit, or even as a virtue, rather than as a simple skill.[9] The key intuition is that the virtue we intend among our students in training them in critical thinking is not simply the ability to think carefully, incisively, and critically, but the disposition to do so when there is occasion. In this light, the SOHS Core sequence represents a fundamental commitment to training the kind of thinkers we look for in the world. Four years of required and focused practice in the elements of critical thinking across the disciplines is precisely the kind of preparation that builds the disposition to engage the world with critical tools and perspectives. But this is not simply because four years entails a lot of practice; in those four years, students get used to doing critical work together, contributing to conversations, holding themselves and their peers to high argumentative standards, and being responsive to the evidence and reasons offered by others.

One of the original ideas behind the Core sequence, and of featuring it as a required, cohort-based experience for graduates, was that it would be an experience that would engender a common intellectual framework and norms for inquiry in the school. In this regard, the Core succeeds to a degree that is still surprising. To be sure, differences of opinion abound and find a natural forum for expression in the Core classes. But students establish, through modeling, acculturation, guidance, and their own sensitivity and experience, a very clear culture

---

[8] A. Sen, *Development as Freedom* (New York: Anchor Books, 1999) 22–23.

[9] E. J. Hyslop-Margison, "The Failure of Critical Thinking: Considering Virtue Epistemology as a Pedagogical Alternative," *Philosophy of Education* (2003): 319–325.

that is supportive of rich classroom discussions. Among the elements of this culture is an expectation of participation, which students take so seriously that they encourage their more reticent peers and moderate their own comments to make room for others. This participation is at the root, in the most successful classes (and increasingly in the later courses of the sequence), of a mentality of collaborative investigation. Students learn the difference between performing in class and contributing to it; they value productive comments and try to build on them; and they don't hesitate to challenge an author, peer, or teacher. Meeting these standards consistently is a project that typically continues throughout high school and into a student's college career. But students' self-policing and gradual acculturation into the norms of seminar discussions at SOIIS does much of the work not only in developing their critical thinking skills, but in integrating those skills into habits and a disposition to take little for granted.

References

Blackburn, S. *Think: A Compelling Introduction to Philosophy.* New York: Oxford University Press, 2011.

Ennis, R. "Critical Thinking: A Streamlined Conception." *Teaching Philosophy* 14 (1991): 5–24.

Hyslop-Margison, E. J. "The Failure of Critical Thinking: Considering Virtue Epistemology as a Pedagogical Alternative." *Philosophy of Education* (2003): 319–325.

Kahneman, D. *Thinking, Fast and Slow.* New York: Farrar, Straus and Giroux, 2011.

Sen, A. *Development as Freedom.* New York: Anchor Books, 1999.

Wartenberg, T. *Big Ideas for Little Kids: Teaching Philosophy Through Children's Literature.* Plymouth UK: Rowman & Littlefield, 2009.

4

English: Engaged Analysis of Texts, Self, and World

MARGARET LAMONT

1 Introduction

It's late in fall semester, and I open class the way I often do, by asking students for their 'General Reactions' to the reading. We have just finished Chaucer's long poem *Troilus and Criseyde* in our Advanced Topics in Literature class and my question is met with an immediate cascade of hands. 'I'm having a really hard time arranging my feelings on this', one student explains midway through her comments, 'because on the one hand I'm so emotional and so upset and frustrated with Criseyde while on the other hand I understand it's just—it's all—it's just Chaucer'. This student's comment beautifully captures the combination of intense gut reaction followed by critical analysis that lies at the heart of English as a discipline, especially when the focus is on literary analysis, as at SOHS. How can a reader 'arrang[e]' her first 'so emotional' and 'so upset' reaction to the text into an organized analysis, to ask and answer: *Why* does Chaucer set up the reader to feel this profound emotional frustration when his character Criseyde finally deserts her faithful lover Troilus, after seemingly endless foreshadowing by the narrator? As our class period begins students from across the country and abroad launch together into a discussion of Criseyde and her interiority, the motivations for her betrayal of Troilus, whether Troilus is a sympathetic character by the end of the poem, how the ending of the poem relates to the beginning, and just how they are supposed to feel about the bewildering welter of emotions at the end

Perspectives from the Disciplines.
Jeffrey Scarborough and Raymond Ravaglia.
Copyright © 2016, CSLI Publications.

of the poem. As I listen to their ideas, their still exploratory reasoning through of their responses to the ending of the poem and what it all might mean, I couldn't be happier as a teacher.

This chapter is about why and how SOHS's English division set out to create classroom experiences like the one described above, and how those experiences contribute to students' development as individual writers and thinkers both inside and outside of English literature as a specific discipline. Because SOHS is an online school, this chapter also addresses what it is like to teach and learn English literature online. The first half of the chapter explains our general principles as a division. This includes why our curriculum has a specifically literary focus and what exactly that means for student reading and writing, as well as how we go about teaching our curriculum. In particular, English division courses at SOHS stand out for the intensity of class participation in our seminar-style classes and for the kinds of writing students complete. The second half of the chapter addresses advantages of our unique online instructional methodology of blended, flipped classes with synchronous seminars, sometimes referred to as our 'online platform' for teaching English literature, which schools and teachers may be able to adopt or adapt through blended learning, and also challenges, which schools and teachers may consider when thinking about implementing online learning.

2   General Principles of SOHS English: Curriculum

The SOHS English curriculum is very deliberately an English Literature curriculum, rather than a composition curriculum. While many of our instructors have taught composition as well as English literature, their training and focus are on literature and literary analysis, and we believe strongly that this focus best allows us to help students grow as writers and thinkers across our curriculum. All of our courses emphasize close reading, so that students learn to attend to the details of a text and recognize how they create meaning, with the ultimate goal of being able to deploy such details in their own writing to achieve their desired effects. Every course also emphasizes argumentation. Students are always asked to explain why the details they have noticed in a text matter and, more broadly, why choosing one potential interpretation of a text over others matters. And of course they write a lot. In addition, our sequence of high school courses introduces students to key theoretical approaches to analyzing literature. Our goal in exposing students to a wide range of literary-critical methodologies is to give them a sense of the benefits and also the limits of key approaches to literary analysis, so that they are able to choose mindfully, when reading something new, among a variety of methodological approaches to finding meaning in a text. As they progress through the sequence of SOHS English courses, students become aware of how different methodologies allow them to ask and answer different kinds of questions, and they are able to formulate and then answer such questions with increasing confidence and sophistication.

A central principle of our division, derived from our basis in English literature as a discipline, is that students have to read challenging material in order to think deeply and to write well. When choosing readings for our courses, we look for works that can reasonably be interpreted in more than one way, so that each reading offers students the chance to explore multiple possible interpretations on the way to finding their own personal angles on a text. For Chaucer's *Troilus and Criseyde*, that means in part arguing over how much sympathy the poem intends readers to feel for the lovers, given that the narrator ends the poem by rejecting all earthly things and exhorting readers to focus on heaven. What happens to the poem if you take that ending exhortation seriously? Can this rejection of the *thousands* of lines that have come before it be sustained? And what, contrarily, are the repercussions of refusing Chaucer's rejection of the content of his work, not only in this poem but also in his retraction to the *Canterbury Tales*? What about the complex emotional attachments readers form to Criseyde and to Troilus (that mixture of affection and frustration my student described)? Students grapple with real interpretive dilemmas, where different answers lead not only to different interpretations of a single text but to different ideas about how to approach the world more broadly. Is human love, though flawed, intrinsically worthwhile? Or is its petty selfishness laughable from a divine perspective? Each text and our thinking and writing about it ultimately asks students to think about the intersection of people with the world around them, and about their own worldview in relation to those of others.

To support students' grappling with these questions, we assign a lot of informal writing that is separate from their formal writing for courses. Informal writing in our curriculum is a place for students' first reactions to a text and for experimentation. Informal writing sometimes begins as simply as 'I can't believe this ending'. It is a place to practice writing quickly, and we usually suggest students spend no more than one hour writing their weekly or twice-weekly informal responses. Most of all, informal writing gives students a place to work out some of their ideas, and to find specific textual evidence to support their points, before class. Informal writing thus serves as a springboard for seminar discussions.

Seminar discussions are just that—students taking the lead in tackling a text, wrestling together as a group with interpretation. The instructor is there to ask questions, to provide factual information when students need it to refine an interpretation or clarify the historical background of a text, and to push students to show where and how they get from the text to their claims. The instructor is also there to make sure everyone contributes—to bring the quieter students into the conversation, and to make sure that louder, more confident students don't dominate the discussion. By hearing all voices in the class, we strengthen our focus on multiple possible interpretations. For younger students—grades seven to nine—seminars are more structured. Students in our eighth grade class, for example, might be asked to find quotations that support a sympathetic or an unsympathetic reading of Madame Loisel in Maupassant's short story 'The Necklace' as a prelude to debating which attitude is predominant in the story, and, crucially, how the answer matters in interpreting the story's ironic ending, where the vain Madam Loisel spends years paying off what turns out to have been a fake lost necklace. Students in grades ten through twelve take on a greater role in shaping the questions being asked in seminar. For example, in our AP English Literature course, one student presents on a scholarly article each week, using the article as a jumping off point for his or her own discussion questions linking the article with the class's shared reading.

All of this reading, informal writing, and vigorous class discussion feeds into students' formal writing. For formal writing, we are deeply committed to critical argumentation through specific textual analysis. Though we do assign creative projects—like writing a fairytale that fulfills the expectations of the genre, or writing about place in the style of E. B. White's 'Here Is New York' or Joan Didion's *Los Angeles Notebook*—we pair these creative pieces with analytical writing. Our focus is very much on English as a methodology of thinking, where close attention to details of language focuses students not only on *what* a text says, but *how* it does so and with what effect. A key goal of such close attention to form and its effects is that students, by closely analyzing different styles of writing and their effects on readers, become more and more intentional in their own writing to achieve their desired effects on their readers.

To foster such close attention to textual details, we require that students in all grades support their formal arguments through quotations from the text they are arguing about; this pushes them into deeper analysis than is possible through paraphrase or general reference. For example, when analyzing the very short story 'Letter to a

Funeral Parlor', students quickly pick up on the humor of the story, which is in the form of a letter of complaint to a funeral parlor after the death of the narrator's father. But only when students dig into the details of the narrator's comparison of the funeral parlor's coinage "cremains" to describe the father's ashes to other coinages like 'porta potti' and 'pooper-scooper' does the sharper point of the story's satire come across.[1] What is offensive is that the term 'cremains' equates the father's ashes with something not only disgusting but also faintly ridiculous in the narrator's mind. This deeper analysis—not just that the story is funny, but *why* it is funny and what its underlying point is—springs from attention to specific details of the text.

Because our curriculum emphasizes complex literary works of fiction and nonfiction that support more than one reasonable interpretation, our formal writing assignments are always argumentative in nature, and require students to stake out and support their chosen interpretations. We expect students at every level to move beyond true statements ('The story is about the narrator's frustration with a funeral parlor's handling of her father's ashes') to argumentative claims ('The narrator's focus on the coinage 'cremains' suggests the disturbing absurdity of the human body after death'). At every grade level, we push students to articulate clear argumentative claims, to support those claims with specific quotations from the text, and to explain clearly how their chosen quotations support their claims.

We also work with all students to articulate what is at stake in the claims they make, what the 'so what?' of their argument is. What is at stake in choosing one interpretation over another? To return to the poem with which this chapter opens, a student might ask: Did Criseyde enter willingly into a relationship with Troilus, or was she forced? Different answers lead to different 'so what?' claims. If she entered the relationship willingly, then the poem can be read as a bitter indictment of false lovers and of the frailty of human love when contrasted with divine love. But if she was forced into the relationship by her uncle Pandarus and Troilus when in Troy, perhaps she was also forced into a relationship with Diomede once she was traded to the Greek camp, and the poem might be interpreted instead as an examination of the constraints placed on women in medieval society or, alternatively, of the inherent tension in the medieval courtly love tradition when more than one knight is in love with the same lady. It's important to note that the same general argument—Criseyde was forced into her rela-

[1] L. Davis,"Letter to a Funeral Parlor," in *Bedford Compact Introduction to Literature*, ed. Michael Meyer (Bedford/St. Martin's, 2012), 486.

tionship with Troilus—can have a different 'so what?' depending on a student's interests and passions, and it is this 'so what?' that we encourage most strongly in our students as the payoff to all of their close, careful analysis of texts.

To support the developing complexity of students' thinking as they progress through our curriculum, we introduce new literary-critical approaches to analyzing literature each year. Our high school English sequence starts with literary-historical approaches in ninth grade, with an American literature survey course in a global context. Students learn to analyze, for example, Puritan poetry and captivity narratives in the context of contemporary religious beliefs and controversies within the Massachusetts Bay Colony community. But they also learn to analyze these works in the context of where they were printed (in Europe) and why there was a market for them there. Through a deep engagement with historical materials alongside literary works, students gain a sense of the changing and contested definitions of American literature from the beginnings of European colonization through the American Civil War. Our tenth grade course shifts gears from a chronological historical approach to a structural and generic one, where students learn principles of formalism and genre when analyzing literature. Building upon the literary-historical approaches in the ninth grade course, the tenth grade course also introduces students to textual networks, groups of texts that interrelate to such an extent that some of the works depend upon the others for their meaning (as, for example, Tom Stoppard's *Rosencrantz and Guildenstern Are Dead*, the final play read in the course, depends upon Shakespeare's *Hamlet*). Our eleventh grade course turns to poststructuralist and deconstructionist approaches, asking students to consider the reasons for challenges to epistemological certainty and structuralist approaches to analyzing literature, particularly in the context of post-WWII society. By twelfth grade, students can choose among several English courses, all of which incorporate scholarly articles drawn from a range of literary-critical approaches.

These literary-critical methodologies provide students with useful approaches to draw upon as they move toward more ambitious structures of argument. By grades ten through twelve our students regularly write essays in which their arguments build (rather than reiterate) from paragraph to paragraph. Rather than making a claim supported by three equally weighted points, students practice structuring their arguments so that point A sets the stage for point B, which could not be made without having first made point A. Such a structure requires students to organize their thinking more rigorously because they have to decide how each piece of evidence they have lined up relates to the other pieces, and to select carefully among all the evidence available to present the strongest and clearest argument for their own point of view. They also have to decide which methodological approach or approaches are most fruitful for their analysis. For example, in an essay on Romantic poetry for AP English Literature, a student first points the reader's attention to key elements of Keats' idea of 'Negative Capability', the idea that a poet is uniquely sensitive to and able to inhabit the world view and identity of others. Having established this poetic ideal, the student goes on to show how it is embodied in Keats' poem 'La Belle Dame sans Merci'. The student then addresses a complication—*all* human beings in the poem are shown to possess this distinctive quality of poets—which allows her to align Keats' ideas with those of his contemporary Wordsworth, who argued that poets are no different in kind from other human beings. All of this leads to her final 'so what?' that poets cannot claim any special moral space distinct from that governing all other people in society. The student thus moves from a very specific claim, grounded in a specific time period (the Romantic era), and specific poet (Keats), to make a larger claim with relevance to continuing debates today over whether the same ethical rules apply to all people regardless of talent or station.

In all of our courses we strive to make such connections between students' reading and writing for class and their lived experience in the world. When we read older texts, we ask students to think about how the ideas within them continue to affect the world today. Students in our AP English Language and Composition class, for example, note that Ovid's cheeky seduction manual The *Art of Love* isn't so different from modern iterations like *The Rules*. Recognizing these connections leads students to think more deeply about the continuing effects of past modes of thinking—especially those that we might want to find comfortably distant or foreign—when they show up in everyday life today.

Some aspects of our approach to teaching English are non-negotiable. Students must support their arguments through specific textual evidence, i.e. quotations, instead of paraphrase or general reference. Students must strive to understand what a text means, or might mean, on its own terms, as well as in terms of their reaction to it and the cultural expectations we bring with us today. Students must be attentive to the repercussions of one interpretation of a text over another, to the 'so what?' of literary analysis.

But we are also deeply committed to variety, so that students of many different stripes can find their own interests and passions within our curriculum. We introduce students to many different genres (poetry, short stories, novels, plays, nonfiction essays, etc.) drawn from ancient through postmodern literature. Just as important, our classes introduce students to different approaches to literary analysis. We provide students many different ways into literary analysis so that they can learn which ones resonate with them and also do some thinking about why some approaches are more attractive to them. They are learning self-analysis as well as literary analysis.

Many or all of these aspects of our approach to teaching English are probably familiar to you. The next section addresses how we make them work in our online classroom.

3   What Works Better in an Online Classroom

Some of the practices we have brought with us from our brick-and-mortar teaching actually work better in our online classroom. We have also developed some new practices that take advantage of the unique aspects of our classroom to do things we couldn't do in a physical classroom.

One of the best things about our classroom is the ability to mark up a passage together as a class in real time, which fosters the close textual analysis that is fundamental to our approach to English. In our online classroom, we have a shared whiteboard, so that everyone in class can see the same whiteboard at the same time. Instructors can give students drawing and writing privileges so that they, like the teacher, can draw on the whiteboard. I'll give two examples of how we use this whiteboard to mark up texts together as a class—perhaps the most fundamental way in which we teach students to close read texts for details and articulate the significance of those details.

For an eighth grade class, the instructor might be working to show students how focusing on different parts of speech emphasizes different aspects of a given passage. How, for example, does the Epic of Gilgamesh establish the greatness of the city-state Uruk? The instructor has loaded a slide onto the shared screen that contains one of the opening descriptions of the city in the poem, and asks students to mark up all the verbs they see:

> See its upper wall, whose facing gleams like copper,
> Gaze at its lower course, which nothing will equal,
> Mount the stone stairway, there from days of old,
> Approach Eanna, the dwelling of Ishtar,
> Which no future king, no human will equal.
> Go up, pace out the walls of Uruk,
> Study the foundation terrace and examine the brickwork.
> Is not its masonry of kiln-fired brick?
> And did not seven masters lay its foundations?

One square mile of city, one square mile of gardens,
One square mile of clay pits, a half mile of Ishtar's dwelling,
Three and a half miles is the measure of Uruk! (13-24)[2]

Because student mark-up on the screen is anonymous, this allows the instructor to do two things. First, she can see quickly whether any students are having trouble distinguishing verbs from other parts of speech, and then she can correct any mistakes and remind students what a verb is without calling attention to a specific student. Once the class members have settled on verbs, they can take a look at what these verbs tell them. 'See', 'Gaze at', 'Mount', 'Approach', 'Pace out', 'Study', 'examine'—all imperatives, telling the reader to marvel at the grandeur of Uruk. Looking through the passage again with a focus on adjective-noun pairs, students note the emphasis on the city's physicality, its 'stone stairway', its 'kiln-fired brick' and 'clay pits', which leads them to a broader focus on the markers of civilization in the poem—walls, stairways, terraces, gardens, bricks—and a discussion of why the poem celebrates manmade things more than natural things.

For AP English Language and Composition, where most of the class is made up of eleventh graders, we use a shared whiteboard to mark up the prologue to Shakespeare's play *Henry V*. The instructor puts the prologue up on the whiteboard, and the class goes through it as a group three times. The first time, she asks students to highlight in yellow everything in the prologue that refers to Henry's majesty. The screen is soon streaked with color. Then the students tackle the passage again, this time highlighting in red everything in the prologue that refers to the horrors and suffering of war. Again, the screen is soon streaked with color as students rapidly highlight relevant words and lines. Finally, the students close read the passage a third time, highlighting in blue all of the references to the theater and performance in the prologue. Then the class steps back to put all three mark-ups together, which tells them some important things. First, the play contains a fundamental conflict in its simultaneous celebration of Henry's military prowess and insistence on the inevitable horror and injustice of war. Second, the play is very much about performance, which alerts students to Henry's own performances for his internal audiences of bishops, loyal and disloyal subjects, and foreign dignitaries within the play. Third, none of these three main themes in the play predominates; references to all three permeate the entire prologue, drawing students' attention to the fun-

---

[2]B. R. Forster, trans., "The Epic of Gilgamesh" in *The Norton Anthology of World Literature, Shorter Second Edition, Volume I*, ed. Peter Simon (W.W. Norton & Company, 2009), 13.

damental ambiguity in the play's portrayal of Henry and, more broadly, to history plays as a (deliberately) morally ambiguous genre in early modern England.

We also use the whiteboard to help share and organize students' ideas and observations about a text. I mentioned at the start of this chapter that we often start classes with 'General Reactions' to the day's reading. This is something that many of us did in brick-and-mortar classrooms before coming to SOHS. In our online classroom, general reactions can be shared very quickly as students post on the whiteboard themes, quotations, or questions that they would like to discuss. In less than a minute, the instructor gets a snapshot of what students reacted to most strongly in the reading. Because we can move text around on our whiteboard, she can also begin to group together related observations and questions. This serves a few purposes.

Organizing the class's general reactions into categories helps model how to organize a scattered list of observations and questions into topics. When reading and discussing the graphic novel *Maus*, for example, the instructor might group students' general reactions on the board into broad categories. Many students note how surprising it is to see a serious subject like the Holocaust and its aftereffects depicted in a comic book format, and the instructor clusters these observations and questions, such as: 'Expectation of form—don't expect serious subject', 'Does the form lighten the content here?', 'Does the form bring in a different readership than usual for this content?'. Clustering these observations and questions leads to a discussion of form and genre as they relate to reader expectations, and also the potential purposes and results of upending the reader's expectations. Other categories drawn from the students' general reactions might include the double time-line of *Maus* and what it suggests about the way the past impacts the present, the question of 'truth' in this narrative, etc. Thus students come out of the 'General Reactions' discussion that opens class with a whole set of specific themes and questions to delve into during the remainder of class or on their own in their papers.

The whiteboard can also be used to help students line up textual evidence in support of one claim or another. The eighth grade class reading 'The Necklace', mentioned above, might be asked to put on the board as many quotations from the story describing Madame Loisel as they can find. Together with the instructor, they might then categorize these quotations into those sympathetic to Madame Loisel, those unsympathetic to her, and those that are neutral. Doing so helps students process their observations into evidence in support of one or another claim, but also helps them notice the existence of counter-evidence that they need to take into account. The instructor might then have the class organize the quotations on the board according to a different principle, such as when they appear in the chronology of the story, to determine whether the portrayal of Madame Loisel changes from the beginning to the end. By working with students to group their observations about the text in multiple ways, instructors are able to model how to organize observations about a text into claims and also to demonstrate that there is more than one productive way in which to do so—to foster a reiterative process of reading and analysis for students so that they ask more questions of the observations that they make.

The shared whiteboard (or, alternatively, a shared notes pod) is also a great way to share and discuss drafts of student papers, either with the class as a whole or in small groups. Again, the key is that everyone can see the same thing at the same time, and anyone can mark up the text on the whiteboard so that everyone in class can see it. (And while one can do this with a physical whiteboard and projector in a physical classroom, so much time is lost with the endless transitioning to and from the board that it becomes practically impossible to do well.) The younger the students, the more focused the draft review might be. In a seventh, eighth, or ninth grade class, the instructor might ask members of the class to highlight the thesis statement in a classmate's introductory paragraph, which will swiftly show the author whether the paragraph currently has a clear thesis or not. (Papers can be shared anonymously or with names, depending on the exercise.) If the thesis is not clear, students might then be asked to suggest how the author might build on some of the ideas that are present to make an arguable thesis.

It's also easier to share the results of group work in our online classroom than it is in a physical classroom, because students can create their own notes or slides in breakout rooms that they then share with the class when the class comes together as a whole again. If, for example, one group of students is tasked with finding quotations having to do with slander in *Much Ado about Nothing*, the group will return to the main room with the list of quotations visible to the entire class, so that everyone can look at and discuss the quotations together.

In all uses of the shared whiteboard, the instructor can decide whether anonymity is preferable for a particular exercise or not, which is another benefit of our online classroom. We find anonymity especially useful in drawing out shyer students, who are often more willing to contribute quotations on the board anonymously than with their names on them. Anonymity can also help instructors get a quick read on the overall knowledge level of a class in a particular area, especially when some students might be embarrassed by their lack of knowledge if asked to identify themselves (as in the Gilgamesh example, where the instructor asks students to highlight all the verbs in a passage in part to ensure that everyone can identify verbs as a part of speech by the end of the exercise). Alternatively, asking students to put up quotations with their names attached can facilitate forming groups in which students interested in similar topics can work together on analysis.

The online classroom also provides some unexpected benefits with regard to creating a vibrant class community in which every student contributes meaningfully to discussion. Text chat is especially useful in creating a seminar community because it streamlines the flow of discussion, enabling us to fit more substantive interaction into each class meeting. In our classroom, students, or the instructor, can ask for elaboration in text chat while someone is speaking. 'Can you point to some specific textual evidence to support your ideas here?' the instructor might ask a student in text chat as the student speaks on camera, prompting the student to add evidence for her claims. The instructor doesn't have to lose time by interrupting the student verbally to ask her to refine or clarify a claim, which allows the class to cover more ground in a set period of time. The instructor can also use private text chat to rein in an overly talkative student gently—'Great point; wrap up in fifteen more seconds so that we can get to all the other hands up'—to make sure that other class members have a chance to be heard without singling out the talkative student publicly. This, too, ensures that class time is used effectively for all students, so that everyone has a chance to contribute meaningfully.

The online classroom can also be a great place for shyer students to find their voices. The instructor might private text chat a shy student to encourage her to enter the conversation—'I noticed you had great things to say about this topic in your informal homework; can you jump in here?' Anxious students can be given advance notice to prepare through private text chat. An instructor might private chat a student, 'I'm going to ask you to share your chosen quotation first, ok?' so that he feels prepared and ready to speak when called upon. Students help create a welcoming atmosphere, too. 'Great point!' one student might write after another has finished speaking on camera. And, because many shyer students feel more comfortable putting their ideas in text chat than they do speaking them on camera, text chat can form a bridge to getting on camera. An instructor might say, 'Alice, you just made a really interesting point in text chat. Can you elaborate on it for us on camera?' With the confidence that her comment has already been deemed worthwhile, 'Alice' is less anxious on video.

These are just some of the ways that text chat helps make the class welcoming to all students and fosters a truly discussion-based seminar. It's also simply the less formal register of class, a place where students can chat idly at the beginning or end of class, where class jokes can be made, and a general shared community built.

4   What's Harder in an Online Classroom

So far I have been focusing on all the benefits of an online classroom for teaching English. But there are some things in English that are harder to do online than they are in a physical classroom, and this section addresses what those things are and how we address them at SOHS.

The biggest challenge is getting a natural flow of conversation in class, rather than a stilted and unsatisfying series of monologues. In a physical classroom, a good seminar leader can see when a student is leaning forward, eager to jump in with a point related to the one being made by whoever is currently speaking, and can simply nod to that student to go ahead as soon as her classmate finishes. Getting this flow is hard enough in a brick-and-mortar classroom, as anyone who has taught a seminar, or participated in one, can attest. In our online classroom it's even harder, because even if all students are present on video (which is possible, but takes up a lot of screen real estate) it's difficult to catch physical cues because the camera may only show the students' faces and necks. The danger in a lot of online learning is that what is supposed to be a dialogue can easily become a series of tangentially related monologues.

Because the back-and-forth flow of discussion and debate is absolutely fundamental to seminar-style learning, we need to use other means to ensure that students are engaging in real dialogue in our online classroom. In our classroom software, students can click an icon to raise their hands to speak, and the program automatically shows the order of hands raised, a sort of electronic equivalent to who is leaning forward most eagerly at the seminar table. But knowing who wants to speak is only the first step to a lively discussion. Instructors also need to know who wants to build upon a comment just made or, alternatively, who wants to raise a question about the last comment or pose a counterargument. In our classrooms, we have various ways students can indicate that they want to respond to something their classmate is saying. Some instructors have students put up a green check mark to show that they want to respond to their classmate's contribution, and some use polls to check for quick agreement or challenges, or open note pods to spur reactions. Text chat also allows students to respond enthusiastically to the speaker in real time or pose complicating questions that drive meaningful debate. All of these systems allow the class to work through students' varied, often conflicting ideas about one topic before moving on to another, so that students are actively responding to one another and building on each other's ideas rather than moving haphazardly through a series of unrelated comments.

A second, related challenge is assessing the energy level in the room and making sure everyone is engaged. In a physical classroom, an instructor can see whether a quiet student is leaned forward, attentive and alert, or leaned back, bored or lost. In our online classroom, it is much harder to get such a read visually, so the instructor has to be more intentional. We keep track of student attention and engagement in our English courses in a few ways.

One of the most important ways is our participation policy in English, which we take extremely seriously. Exact participation policy details vary by grade level and instructor, but, in general, every student must speak on camera every class. Knowing this expectation, and knowing that the instructor may call on any student to contribute at any time, encourages a lively class dynamic. As one student noted in our semester course evaluations, 'I really liked that everyone had to speak every class, as it made the discussion more interesting and kept me on top of the reading for each class.' This policy also, as another student noted, 'prevents the discussion from becoming lopsided by a small group dominating the talking while others are too nervous to talk.' By keeping track of who has spoken in class, and making sure that every student contributes something meaningful to every class meeting, the instructor fosters a community atmosphere in which students know that the contributions of every single class member are valued and necessary. As a third student commented, this policy 'allow[s] opinions on a topic/idea to emerge that consistent participators may have overlooked', explicitly tying greater student participation to wider ranging and more satisfying class discussions. More satisfying discussions, in turn, increase student engagement. (Crucial to this engagement is a supportive atmosphere where students feel that they are working together and not in competition with one another in class—where they feel able to share a partially formed idea, knowing that others will work with them to build on it and shape it more fully.)

Text chat also helps us monitor student engagement, as even quieter students will often chime in with supportive comments in text for their classmates' ideas. Seeing these running responses to the contributions other students are making on camera, the instructor knows that the student whose hand is not up is still actively engaged in class and paying attention.

Group work requires special attention, because when students are in breakout rooms in our classroom software the instructor can't see all the students at the same time to assess which groups are focused productively on their work and which are uncertain how to proceed or simply distracted. Instructors can pass through the breakout rooms individually to check on groups, and confused students can text questions to the instructor, but the most effective method we have found is to have students work together on a group whiteboard or notepad during breakout sessions. The instructor can monitor the whiteboards for all groups from the main room, which allows her to keep track of which groups seem to be moving along well and which, if any, seem to have stalled out and need some individual help. While we adopted this approach as a way to monitor breakout rooms, an added benefit is that groups return to the main room with something tangible to share with the class as a whole.

A third challenge of the online classroom is that instructors and students have to work a little harder to get to know one another, something that we facilitate through class discussions, group work, and peer review (for students), and on camera requirements and office hours (for instructors and students).

By interacting meaningfully in class discussions (where all students contribute ideas) and working in pairs or small groups, students come to know each other well over the course of the year. Anecdotally, we know of students who became friends after being assigned as peer review partners or doing a class presentation together. Because we emphasize the 'so what?' aspect of student writing, students also share a lot of themselves in their writing and speaking for class, and class members come to know the interests and predilections of their classmates pretty well. When students in AP English Language and Composition write and share their own Modest Proposals, for example, environmentalists in the class discover one another, as do political junkies, education reformers, etc. Most SOHS classes also have active student-run Skype groups attached to them, where students share questions and thoughts about the readings and assignments.

Being on camera means that students and instructors know each other's mannerisms, and are familiar with their gestures as well as their inflections when they speak. Everyone's visual identity includes, also, the space from which he or she is logging in, which can lead to small talk. As in a physical classroom, the time at the beginning and end of class is an informal social time where students greet each other, share news, and say goodbye. It might be nighttime for a student in Europe, for example, while it is early afternoon for Californians. If there is a snowstorm in Colorado, a student might show the white swirling outside her window at the beginning of class. And everyone notices when a background changes—whether it's the instructor logging in from a hotel room because she's attending a conference or a student logging in from a cafe during a college visit. New haircuts, new hats, a freshly completed painting—these are all things that students share, informally, over the course of the year. (We've even had students start dating each other, after what began as low key flirtation in text chat before and after class.)

In terms of instructors getting to know students, office hours are crucial. Because our school runs on a college-like schedule, we don't have our students in the classroom every day. Working with students one-on-one or in small groups in office hours to discuss essay drafts or work towards a thesis gives instructors a good sense of students' interests, their habits of thought, and their process when writing. By asking their students questions and listening to their answers, instructors get to know the quirks of their students, from the one who needs help finding a focus within a cascade of ideas to the one who has trouble coming up with even one topic he might be interested in writing about. Instructors learn which students are over-writers who need guidance on when to stop editing and trust their gut, and which students need to be pushed to develop their thinking beyond the first argument they come up with. They learn who has great overall ideas but struggles with anchoring her claims in specific evidence, and who has a great eye for detail but struggles to organize her observations into a meaningful argument. They can help guide students to essay prompts that play to their strengths and, when they are ready, encourage them to take a leap into new modes of analysis.

We don't yet have the means to do every single thing we would like to do in our online classroom. Witty dialogue, for example, poses a problem. The back-and-forth banter of Beatrice and Benedick in *Much Ado about Nothing* loses much of its sparkle in the noticeable delay as the microphone switches from one student to another. As a result, when we do in-class performances we tend to focus on longer speeches, leaving witty back-and-forth dialogues for homework or out-of-class projects. But at this point we have also developed practices—like shared mark-up and text chat—that we miss when we run our short in-person summer classes. We have also found workarounds for many of the challenges, like getting to know students personally, with the result that students and families regularly cite the close relationship between students and instructors as one of the highlights of their experience at the school. And we have other gains as well—like having a student from Hong Kong and one from Maine, a Kurdish refugee in Sweden and a kid on a farm in the Midwest, all coming together to delving into a text together.

5   Concluding Thoughts

There is no one-size-fits-all answer that we are proposing for either English as a discipline or online teaching and learning more generally. We believe in a variety of approaches in the educational landscape to fit the different needs, talents, and interests of different students. But we have created a model in English at SOHS, for both a curriculum and how we share that curriculum with our students, that inspires students to read, think, and write with great depth and ambition. Just as important, our curriculum and classroom methodology inspire a joy in learning that is fundamental to progress in any discipline, academic or otherwise. We know from evaluating our students' development over the course of each year and across our curriculum that they are growing as critical readers, thinkers, and writers, and their very strong performance on outside measures provides further confirmation—consistently high AP, SAT and other standardized test scores, as well as a number of major national essay awards, such as the Scholastic Awards. But we take the most pleasure in the way these results are accomplished joyfully (though with hard work!). Student evaluations are always only part of the story in evaluating a course's success—the improvement in students' skills over time is the real test of whether a school is doing its job—but they do show how students feel about the learning they are engaged in. One of our foundational beliefs as educators is that students learn best when they are inspired to love what they are doing. And so I close with a sample of student comments drawn from English courses across our curriculum: 'I had a lot of fun and keep finding myself analyzing things in terms of the texts we studied', 'useful and interesting and fun', 'This was a beautiful year', 'my instructor inspired me to learn', 'I look forward to future English classes because of this one', 'the class [was] so much fun', 'I had an amazing time in class', '[The teacher] was a true joy to learn from', 'It's been an amazing year!'

References

Davis, L. "Letter to a Funeral Parlor." In *Bedford Compact Introduction to Literature*, edited by Michael Meyer, 486. Bedford/St. Martin's, 2012.

Forster, B. R., trans. In *The Norton Anthology of World Literature, Shorter Second Edition, Volume I*, edited by Peter Simon, 13. W. W. Norton & Company, 2009.

5

Mathematics

GREGORY NUCKOLS

1 Teaching Mathematics Online and Offline

Imagine a typical contemporary mathematics class in a brick-and-mortar school. The teacher first reminds students of their next written homework assignment and the midterm exam coming up in three weeks. Following a flipped classroom model, the teacher has assigned prerecorded lectures, available online, to be viewed before class. The teacher next asks a few brief questions to check students' understanding of the material covered in the lectures. The teacher also solicits questions about the relevant concepts and homework problems. The teacher leads a whole-class discussion of two problems, each initiated by inviting a student to the whiteboard to show steps of a partial solution. Paying close attention to various levels of comprehension among the students, the teacher then divides the class into small groups and gives each group a series of problems to discuss and solve. During this small-group work, the teacher observes each group, asking questions and responding to the group as needed in order to guide students toward discovering their own solution and discussing different possible approaches. Toward the end of the class period, each group sends a representative to the whiteboard to explain the group's solutions, and a rich discussion ensues among all students in the class.

All the elements of such a class are also present in mathematics courses at the Stanford Online High School, where instructors make use of appropriate technology to facilitate discussion and interaction in the online classroom environment. Based on a platform allowing communication via text, audio, and video, as well as sharing of images,

Perspectives from the Disciplines.
Jeffrey Scarborough and Raymond Ravaglia.

interactive whiteboards, and other applications, the SOHS mathematics classroom is in many ways similar to that of brick-and-mortar schools. A shared virtual whiteboard takes the place of a physical whiteboard, and small-group work is carried out in virtual breakout rooms. But the process of discussion, exploration, and discovery is fundamentally the same. At SOHS, we aim to provide a rich experience in the study of mathematics both for students for whom math is one subject area in a general education having its focus elsewhere and for those students having math, or a closely related field, as their primary interest.

We believe that the framework and techniques developed for teaching mathematics at SOHS could be valuable to a variety of other schools and academic programs. Teachers or administrators who are considering, or already exploring, the use of a flipped classroom model for mathematics courses can benefit from what we have learned about using it and the unique characteristics of the SOHS course model. Our experiences at SOHS are especially relevant to designing courses and instructional models for gifted and academically talented students. As will be discussed in detail in this chapter, the goal of providing an optimal educational environment and experience for gifted students has informed not only the content of our mathematics curriculum but also our classroom environment, teaching approach, and mathematics community outside the boundaries of formal course work. This chapter will also clarify our reasons for making live multimedia classroom discussion the cornerstone of our course model. The information provided here could guide others online programs and schools that might be considering a similar move. After explaining the reasons for many unique features of our curriculum, the next section will discuss our course offerings in detail and show how they serve the needs of a high-achieving, college-bound student population especially well. The following section discusses specific features of our teaching approach and our emphasis on live interaction in the online classroom. Such a discussion leads naturally to a more detailed treatment of the implementation of pedagogical techniques in the online classroom, including examples showing how such techniques might be used in specific courses. Although the SOHS mathematics curriculum and teaching approach is not unique in its effectiveness, we have developed a model that could be used in other educational settings, whether online or in person, to optimally instruct students of high ability.

2   The SOHS Mathematics Curriculum

The SOHS mathematics curriculum is designed to serve the needs of our entire middle school and high school population, whether or not they have a special interest or talent in mathematics, and its structure reflects its origins within a university environment. Many of our students naturally move into post-AP level math courses during their high school years, either because they join SOHS having already completed a good portion of the standard high school curriculum or as a result of acceleration during their SOHS studies. We believe that offering such courses, which we categorize as university-level mathematics, is important; indeed, completing courses in areas such as multivariable calculus, differential equations, and linear algebra during high school may provide an advantage to students seeking admission to highly selective universities with an emphasis on science and technology. At the same time, studying such subjects at SOHS—rather than pursuing access to similar courses at community colleges—allows students to continue working with their friends and peers, and to continue to receive age-appropriate support from instructors and other SOHS staff. Furthermore, being situated within Stanford University gives our mathematics curriculum a natural emphasis on academic rigor and conceptual depth. For example, many SOHS university-level courses were initially developed in collaboration with faculty members in the Stanford University Department of Mathematics. To meet the needs of all our students, the SOHS mathematics curriculum offers a full range of middle school, high school, and university-level courses, with many options for appropriate acceleration and a curriculum-wide emphasis on developing transferable skills and habits that will serve students well in college , whatever academic path they might choose there.

The SOHS mathematics curriculum spans courses from the middle school level through courses normally taken by college undergraduates during their junior/senior years. Starting with Honors Prealgebra, the only middle school mathematics course offered at SOHS, our course sequence proceeds with Honors Beginning Algebra (equivalent to courses often named Algebra 1 at other high schools), Honors Intermediate Algebra (equivalent to Algebra 2), Honors Geometry, and Honors Precalculus with Trigonometry. Courses at the other end of the spectrum include Modern Algebra, Real Analysis, Complex Analysis, and Partial Differential Equations. The far reach of these course offerings allows SOHS students with a strong interest in math to pursue its study in great depth, while remaining within the virtual walls of the SOHS and exploring such advanced subjects with their friends and peers. The SOHS math curriculum includes courses generally considered standard requirements for university-study in the hard sciences, including AP Calculus (single-variable), Multivariable Calculus, Linear Algebra, and Differential Equations. Toward our goal of serving the needs of all our students, the SOHS mathematics curriculum also includes AP Statistics and Advanced Problem Solving and Proof Techniques, a course designed for students moving into the study of university-level mathematics. Finally, our university-level offerings are rounded out by Number Theory and Logic in Action, the latter presenting students with a novel introduction to modern mathematical logic.

The structure of our secondary and AP offerings is mostly traditional, with students beginning their SOHS math studies at an appropriate level as determined by their past course work and placement exam results. Courses such as Honors Beginning Algebra, Honors Intermediate Algebra, and Honors Precalculus with Trigonometry have an especially strong emphasis on algebraic skills, which we believe are an essential foundation for students' future work in calculus, higher mathematics, and the sciences more generally. Students may complete Honors Geometry either between Honors Beginning Algebra and Honors Intermediate Algebra, or immediately before Honors Precalculus with Trigonometry. Our AP-level courses include AP Statistics, AP Calculus AB, and AP Calculus BC. One somewhat unusual aspect of the SOHS curriculum is that students choose between Calculus AB and Calculus BC—these offer two routes for the study of single-variable calculus. Students who complete Calculus AB prior to their senior year may then take AP Calculus C. This option provides a single-variable calculus curriculum equivalent to AP Calculus BC but extending over three semesters of study. A final secondary-level course is Advanced Problem Solving and Proof Techniques, which is designed to prepare students for university-level mathematics and in particular for proof-based, abstract mathematical study. This course serves the same purpose as courses, frequently offered at universities, that are designed to help students navigate the transition between lower-division courses and upper-division courses in mathematics.[1] Students learn and practice proof strategies, refine their proof-writing style, and practice problem-solving skills needed for success in the study of modern mathematics. The recent launch of this course is an example of our approach to developing and refining our mathematics curriculum. Responding to the perceived need to offer some students a more gradual transition into university-level mathematics, we created Advanced Problem Solving and Proof Techniques to provide another option following AP Calculus. Students who might benefit from intensive study of the techniques most commonly used in abstract mathematical proofs and exposure

---

[1] Two such examples are Math 74 Transition to Upper Division Mathematics offered at UC Berkeley and Math 101 Sets and Groups and Topology offered at Harvard.

to problem-solving skills required in more advanced courses have the opportunity to gain this firm foundation as a preliminary step. Although such a course is not offered at most high schools, at SOHS Advanced Problem Solving and Proof Techniques provides a bridge to the university-level mathematics courses taken by many of our students.

University-level mathematics courses at SOHS provide students the opportunity to study both lower-division and upper-division undergraduate mathematics subjects with their peer group and in a context appropriate for high school-age students. Although some students might have the option to take such courses at a local college or university, staying within the SOHS to study university-level math offers several benefits. First, students who have completed secondary-level mathematics courses at SOHS and then move into our university-level curriculum continue to learn with their friends and peers. As will be discussed below, we believe strongly in the value of learning in a social context, one that provides opportunities for rich discussion and a shared process of discovery. Studying university-level subjects within SOHS allows continuing students to benefit from the social context they have already developed during their time at our school. Second, students taking university-level mathematics courses at SOHS can rely on the same advising, counseling, and other supportive resources intended to ensure their success. These resources include access to expert advice during the college application process, which can require special care for students who will have completed a significant amount of university-level study before their first year of college. Third, because SOHS university-level courses were inspired and continue to be informed by similar undergraduate course offerings at Stanford University, we believe these courses to be more valuable to highly capable students than what might be found in many junior college or community college settings. Aiming to instill both sharp computational skills and rigorous conceptual understanding, SOHS university-level courses provide a solid foundation for even more advanced study in mathematics following students' graduation from SOHS.

The SOHS mathematics curriculum provides students with many options regarding their paths through the courses we offer. SOHS students have a variety of goals in mathematics, from simply achieving a good grasp of mathematics as part of their general education to obtaining a solid foundation for advanced study in the physical sciences to mastering as much higher-level mathematics as possible during high school. As will be explained later in this chapter, we believe acceleration in the study of mathematics should be approached with appropriate caution. Keeping that perspective in mind, however, there are several points in the SOHS mathematics curriculum at which interested and high-performing students can move ahead in their study of math. When students enter SOHS, they are placed into our mathematics curriculum through an intensive process that includes a placement exam as well as thorough review of each student's past formal study and extracurricular activities in math. Students' placement, then, is based on ability rather than on grade level. This placement process itself can guide ambitious and capable students toward higher-level courses. Within the SOHS math curriculum, there are several options for advancement. Students who perform exceptionally well in Honors Beginning Algebra may choose to complete Honors Intermediate Algebra and Honors Geometry concurrently. We also have begun offering a summer, accelerated version of Honors Precalculus with Trigonometry, which is open to students who show readiness for such an intensive course. As explained in detail above, the AP Calculus BC course provides an accelerated alternative to AP Calculus AB. Thus, for example, a motivated and high-achieving student who completes Honors Beginning Algebra in seventh grade could in principle complete AP Calculus in ninth grade, followed by three years of university-level study in mathematics. Another option frequently selected by students is to enroll in AP Statistics in place of or alongside AP Calculus.

Although the content included in SOHS secondary-level and university-level courses offers students rare opportunities for advanced study in math during high school, our primary focus is not the content of our courses but rather those habits of mind we hope to instill in our students at all levels of the curriculum. The first and foremost of these is the ability to engage in an active process of mathematical exploration and problem solving, both alone and in a community. We believe this to be a key foundational skill for any kind of successful technical or scientific work in today's world. Mathematics does certainly involve learning standard theorems and techniques; more important, however, is the process of exploration that is required when standard theorems don't apply and well-known techniques don't work. Through carefully guiding students as they approach and tackle novel and unfamiliar problems, we hope to instill this habit of active engagement in our students. Furthermore, it is equally important to be able to engage in such exploration in dialogue with others, even when—perhaps especially when— no participants in the conversation have yet discovered a clear solution. Even such a singular and solitary achievement as Andrew Wiles' proof of Fermat's Last Theorem did not truly happen in isolation. In addition to building on the work of a community of researchers spanning several generations, Wiles was able to complete and perfect his proof only when it was presented and explained to his colleagues, who wrestled with the ideas contained in the proof and offered crucial feedback and corrections.[2] Other habits students acquire in SOHS mathematics courses include always keeping in mind or inquiring as to why a certain algorithm or technique might apply to solving a specific problem (in contrast to simply memorizing that a certain technique should be applied to a recognized configuration of expressions or equations) as well as an openness to considering and evaluating a diversity of approaches to problem-solving. To more fully explain these fundamental goals of our mathematics curriculum, we need to discuss the context of student learning provided by the structure of SOHS as a school and the importance of the live online classroom to our pedagogical approach.

3   The SOHS Approach to Teaching Mathematics

As discussed in *Bricks and Mortar*,[3] the context of student learning is considered an essential component of the educational experience offered by SOHS and one that is just as important as considerations such as course content and instructor qualifications. This is no less true in mathematics as in other subject areas. With the exception of a few very advanced courses such as Real Analysis, real and Modern Algebra, students enrolled in a math course at SOHS learn in community, meeting regularly with a small group of peers who follow a shared schedule as they wrestle with and master the content of the course. Both within the real-time online classroom environment and in outside interactions via email, Skype, and other means of communication, students support one another, check on classmates who are absent from section meetings, challenge each other, and together create the experience of a shared journey through the terrain of subjects such as geometry, calculus, and differential equations. Students create informal online study groups in which they support each other both intellectually and emotionally as they face the challenges involved in mastering the content of their courses. Having a shared course schedule makes rich, real-time discussion possible, and it also conveys other benefits. Students know they will be expected to actively participate in class discussion (often to earn part of their course grade), and this provides a strong incentive to view assigned prerecorded lectures, read assigned textbook pages, and/or begin solving assigned homework problems before class. In the first few years of SOHS, however, our math courses were not fully seminar-based

---

[2]G. Faltings, "The Proof of Fermat's Last Theorem by R. Taylor and A. Wiles," *Notices of the American Mathematical Society* 42 (115): 743-746.

[3]Scarborough and Ravaglia, *Bricks and Mortar*.

and frequently offered students a self-paced option. It is worthwhile to consider the lessons learned during these early years that led the SOHS Division of Mathematics to change our approach and offer courses primarily in a seminar-based format.[4]

Arising from Stanford research projects offering computer-based, individual, self-paced mathematics courses to elementary and secondary school students, SOHS math courses initially allowed some students to work at a faster pace and did not require all students to attend regular live class discussions; problems resulting from this approach inspired us to move toward fully seminar-based instruction. The first lesson learned from the early years of mathematics instruction at SOHS is that self-paced courses often do not work well for high school students, even highly motivated students. When students were granted permission to work at their own pace and not attend live discussion sections (generally because they were excelling in their course work), they frequently fell behind and were not able to complete their courses within the regular term or academic year. As anyone who has enrolled in a self-paced course knows, it is only too easy for other commitments to take higher priority, leading one to fall behind and perhaps become completely disengaged with the course. When students did not complete their courses during the regular academic year, they were then faced with the need to finish them over the summer, a difficult task that frequently interfered with other planned activities. Even those students for whom self-paced courses worked reasonably well did not always use such flexibility in ways that best supported their own learning. A student who completed a course in the middle of spring semester might be tempted to rush through a following course in the spring and over the summer, leading to a negative experience in the fall due to incomplete understanding of required background concepts and skills.

Additional observations also contributed to our decision to move away from allowing self-paced work in SOHS mathematics courses. Lack of full engagement was a problem more generally. Students working at an individual pace did not feel connected to their peers, and the class group as a whole did not cohere due to changing attendance from week to week. This was a second lesson: students and instructors alike did not have the opportunity to get to know one another well without regular, live interaction among the entire class. Finally, a third lesson came from student feedback gathered at the end of each term or school year. Although some students may have specifically requested a self-paced

---

[4]For a fuller accounting of the rationale behind this decision see Chapter 1 of Scarborough and Ravaglia, *Bricks and Mortar.* (Ed.)

option, feedback from most students indicated that the structure of math courses offered during the first few years of SOHS simply didn't lead to an enjoyable educational experience. Especially in contrast with SOHS courses in other subject areas, where following a shared schedule and attending regular discussion sections was required at that time, students overwhelmingly preferred the seminar-based format. Our experience since moving to such a format for mathematics courses suggests that this was a positive change. Students report enjoying their math classes more, and instructors get to know their students as they interact with them and observe dynamics in the classroom—something that is especially valuable when writing teacher recommendations for college application and applications to summer programs. Also, the seminar-based format allows students to absorb and master material at an appropriate pace. Additional benefits will be discussed below.

Because SOHS courses meet for live discussion two days per week (for seventy-five minute periods), it is not possible to cover in detail all the material for a given course during discussion sections. SOHS mathematics courses use a modified flipped classroom model. Most commonly, a flipped classroom model might provide students with prerecorded lectures to be viewed at home with class time reserved for individual and small-group work on problem sets.[5] With relatively limited live class time, however, we do not want online class sessions to simply be a virtual study hall in which students carry out assignments that would otherwise would be homework. Instead, students are provided with prerecorded lectures and assigned reading to study before each class session, and they are also encouraged to begin working on a specific set of problems before class. This allows students the opportunity to orient themselves to the material to be discussed during class and to discern which concepts they grasp reasonably well and which are especially challenging. Students have the opportunity to send their instructors questions or suggestions for class discussion, so that live class time can focus on answering questions, discussing examples, or doing small-group practice designed specifically to address the needs of the students in each section. In-class time, then, is intended to be used for interactive and engaging activities that serve as a bridge between students' initial exposure to a topic before class and their further exploration of that topic in completing assignments after class.

Prerecorded lectures are an essential component of the flipped classroom model used in SOHS math courses, and these lectures are tailored

---

[5] See J. Bergmann and A. Sams, *Flipped Learning for Math Instruction* (Arlington, VA: International Society for Technology in Education, 2015).

to the requirements of different content areas and the needs of students at different levels in their mathematical development. Although videos created by textbook publishers are widely available, SOHS mathematics courses use lectures designed and recorded by SOHS instructors. We have found that this practice provides students with material that is more exactly suited to their backgrounds and aspirations. These lectures may include material that goes beyond what is presented in the textbook, or which more closely matches the learning goals set by the instructor. For many courses, lectures have been designed using a team approach and have been recorded by two or more instructors, so that students might view lectures recorded by their own instructor as they learn some topics, but they might see other topics presented by different instructors teaching the same course. Student have offered positive feedback on this approach—they appreciate the variety of lecture styles and the benefit of learning multiple perspectives on the subject matter. Ideally, students are active and engaged as they view lectures. The lectures themselves are kept relatively short (about ten minutes each in most courses), and typically students might have about four lectures assigned every week. The lectures are intended to encourage active work by the student. For example, a lecture might present a new example problem and then suggest, 'Now pause the lecture, try this problem on your own, and then resume the playback to see one way to solve it.' In courses frequently taken by younger students, lectures are designed for less experienced learners of mathematics. For example, lectures in Honors Beginning Algebra are generally shorter and more concrete in focus than lectures for advanced courses. Lectures in Honors Beginning Algebra explain practical skills in an accessible manner and might also mention common pitfalls to avoid in manipulating algebraic expressions and solving equations. In more advanced courses, theoretical material is often presented in lectures, leaving class time available to focus on more practical problem-solving concerns. A lecture in AP Calculus, for instance, might carefully present the statement and proof of the Chain Rule, with class time devoted to its various uses and applications. Some courses, such as Advanced Problem Solving and Proof Techniques, also include material of a more philosophical nature, which can be helpfully introduced to students in lectures. In Advanced Problem Solving, for example, after learning basic material about cardinality of infinite sets, students are presented with a brief lecture introducing them to formal undecidability in set theory and its implications for the philosophy of mathematics. This material forms the basis for rich discussion during a subsequent live class session.

Many SOHS mathematics courses make use of online learning systems which, although not absolutely necessary in the online school environment, are a natural choice for us given that our students already make regular use of other computer-based tools and resources in their classes. These systems are used in courses such as Honors Beginning Algebra, Honors Intermediate Algebra, Honors Geometry, Honors Precalculus with Trigonometry, AP Calculus courses, and Multivariable Calculus. Online learning systems allow students to complete a portion of their homework assignments in an environment that provides immediate feedback on the correctness or incorrectness of their answers and also offers many supplementary resources such as worked examples and conceptual hints. Most often these systems are produced by publishers of textbooks we have adopted, and students are required to obtain access to them. Typically, a regular weekly homework assignment in one of the courses mentioned above might include some problems to be completed within an online learning system along with other problems to be worked out on paper. Students submit solutions to problems in the second category by scanning their work and uploading it to the SOHS learning management system. In this way, students receive immediate but generally less detailed feedback on their work from the online learning package, and they also receive extensive written feedback, focusing on the problem-solving process and its written explication, directly from the course instructor.

During live section meetings, aspects of the online classroom environment along with various auxiliary tools make possible a rich and interactive student experience. Mathematics courses at SOHS typically use the whiteboard feature of the online classroom extensively. The whiteboard allows entering text, which can be helpful during section meetings. For example, for emphasis the instructor might type, 'Remember: whenever we solve an equation involving square roots we must check our solutions!' after discussing a relevant example. But more commonly handwriting is used on the whiteboard to allow both students and the instructor to write formatted mathematical expressions and equations, and to draw accompanying diagrams and geometric figures. Instructors make use of graphics tablets to allow for easier and more legible handwriting on the virtual whiteboard, and most of our math courses require students to obtain and use graphics tablets as well. A typical segment of a course meeting begins with the instructor displaying a prepared slide containing a problem statement. The instructor might then elicit suggestions from students about how to start solving the problem and how to carry out steps along the way, with different students 'called to the board' to write out the expressions or equations involved. Through use of multiple whiteboards, if needed, the instructor could guide students through a discussion of solving the problem by means of various approaches, whose relative strengths and weaknesses could then be reviewed afterward. The online classroom environment facilitates application sharing as well, and this feature allows instructors to use a variety of specialized tools relevant to different courses. For example, a calculus instructor might use an online graphing tool to display slope fields of differential equations or a spreadsheet to display and calculate Riemann sums. Instructors for many courses might use graphing software to display and analyze graphs of functions and equations, and instructors for courses (such as AP Calculus) requiring students to use graphing calculators might use emulators to bring these tools into the online classroom environment.

An especially important feature of the SOHS online classroom is the ability to use breakout rooms to facilitate small-group work during class. Our mathematics instructors use breakout rooms extensively in their live discussion sections. The mathematics education community has strongly endorsed collaborative group work, and the SOHS online classroom allows instructors to organize students into groups in the same way one might in a brick-and-mortar school environment. The technology of the online classroom gives each breakout room a separate whiteboard and text chat window, and it allows students in a given room to communicate via audio and video. The instructor can move about freely among breakout rooms, observing or offering suggestions as appropriate. It is also possible for the instructor to remain outside all breakout rooms but to view all breakout room whiteboards simultaneously, in separate windows, to monitor the progress of all students in the class at once. A typical breakout room segment of a class session might involve giving each room a slightly different type of problem, with the collection of problems as a whole covering those deemed especially tricky among those assigned for that class day. The breakout room segment itself would give each room a chance to discuss, wrestle with, and solve one example problem (or more) in detail. Coming back to the main room after the breakout room segment, the instructor might then ask a representative from each room to explain the problem his or her group solved. In this way all the students would benefit from seeing examples of various types, and students would also gain benefit from the experience of arguing with other students in the breakout room work, asking and answering questions about steps in solving the problem, and succinctly explaining the solution to the entire class back in the main room.

The richness of the online classroom environment makes it possible for instructors to increase their effectiveness through differentiation.

Differentiated instruction based on student readiness, interest, learning profile, and other characteristics is widely considered an essential component of good teaching.[6] Students are not 'tracked' in their study of mathematics at SOHS, and a class such as Honors Precalculus with Trigonometry might include students from many different grade levels and with a variety of aspirations regarding their study of math. Readiness differentiation and attention to differing interests are therefore important goals for instructors. Tools within the online classroom allow instructors to quickly assess differences in readiness for discussion of specific topics. For example, as will be described in greater detail below, an instructor might begin a class focused on trigonometric equations with an example problem, asking each student to solve the equation and privately submit a solution using text chat. Such an exercise gives the instructor valuable information regarding each student's level of understanding and might also provide guidance regarding the most frequent misunderstandings that are hindering some members of the class. Regular use of breakout rooms facilitates differentiation based on both readiness and interest through the technique of flexible grouping. At times, students of similar ability might be grouped together to direct each student toward practice problems of appropriate difficulty level. At other times, an instructor might form groups of mixed readiness, especially to work problems lending themselves to discussion of alternative approaches. Breakout groups could also be organized by student interest, so that, for example, students in a class who are deeply involved in athletics might be given an application problem relevant to this area of interest.

At SOHS, students also engage in shared exploration of mathematics through a variety of extracurricular activities. We believe that our efforts to build an extracurricular math community have further helped to foster excitement and enthusiasm among students for this subject. Recent years have seen a number of SOHS math-related clubs launched and organized by students, including a Math Club, a University Level Problem Solving Club, a Math Modeling Club, a Math Competitions Club, and a Problem Creators Club.[7] These clubs, which generally meet weekly during the academic year, give students a place to follow their own mathematical interests with each other and under the supervision of an instructor. Some clubs also provide opportunities to

---

[6] D. A. Sousa and C. A. Tomlinson, *Differentiation and the Brain: How Neuroscience Supports the Learner-Friendly Classroom* (Bloomington, IN: Solution Tree Press, 2011).

[7] A full discussion of the role of clubs in establishing community with SOHS can be found in the chapter on student life.

participate in math contests, such as the Purple Comet Math Meet and the High School Mathematical Contest in Modeling. An additional long-standing aspect of the SOHS math community is the Problem of the Week program. In this program, instructors in the Division of Mathematics create a set of three problems every week during the academic year. These problems are published and announced to the entire SOHS community, and we encourage individual students, groups of students, families, and homerooms to try the problems and submit solutions. All solutions are evaluated by instructors, and for each set of problems a list of successful solvers and a detailed explanation of correct solutions is provided. Students need not sign up for this program; they are free to solve some or all of the problems in each set as their interests and time commitments allow. Efforts to build community around mathematics have also included our offering one-time live online presentations by expert teachers and researchers in the field. These presentations expose students to cutting-edge ideas and open questions that are currently engaging the best mathematical minds in the world. All these efforts to support the SOHS math community serve to highlight and supplement the interactive, discussion-based aspect of SOHS mathematics classes.

4   Mathematics Pedagogy in Practice

Live, interactive discussion sections in mathematics courses at SOHS emphasize the process of learning and discovery over unidirectional delivery of content or routine practice of standard techniques. Following the flipped classroom model described earlier, students are expected to come to class having already worked actively with material presented in lectures and textbook sections as well as having begun work on assigned homework problems. For instructors, then, the challenge of preparing for a discussion section meeting is to create opportunities for students to be actively engaged in wrestling with those concepts that will lead them to greater mastery of material they have already learned to some degree. Instructors generally invite students to send suggestions before class regarding problems to be discussed or questions to be addressed. In those courses incorporating online learning systems, the instructor might also have the option to review student work-in-progress, within the online system, on the current assignment and use this information to guide class preparation. During class meetings, instructors aim to guide students in their own process of discovery rather than immediately providing an answer or a specific method to obtain an answer. For example, in addressing how to solve a difficult problem the instructor might begin by listing all the different approaches students have used, successfully or unsuccessfully, in attempting it. Ensuing discussion could then explore the process by which some of these ideas were formulated and ways to evaluate them in order to choose a promising method for proceeding toward a solution. Small-group work in breakout rooms provides another means to facilitate student engagement with the material under discussion. At times, the instructor might group students by the level of readiness they have shown with the material and give each breakout room problems at an appropriate difficulty level. At other times the instructor might create groups of mixed readiness levels and guide discussion within each breakout room so that students with a better grasp of the relevant concepts are challenged to use their understanding to help the other students in that room.

Guiding meaningful and interactive exploration with talented and inquisitive students requires deep knowledge of the subject matter. Nearly all SOHS math instructors have advanced degrees in mathematics or a closely related field. Although such a background might seem unnecessary for high school teaching, we believe it is essential to providing the mathematics education we offer at the SOHS. It might be easier to accept that having a graduate-level background in mathematics is valuable for teaching courses at the upper levels of our curriculum. For example, in discussion of vector spaces over the real numbers in Linear Algebra, an inquisitive student might well ask how the resulting theory would differ if the real numbers were replaced by the complex numbers or perhaps by the integers. An instructor with an understanding of fields, rings, and modules could both mention the easy generalization to vector spaces over fields and offer a glimpse of the much greater complexity of module theory and its potential applications. But such an advanced background could also be helpful in teaching even some of our introductory-level courses. In a course such as Honors Beginning Algebra, for example, students work with irrational numbers such as the square root of 2; in a SOHS section, an instructor might guide the students through a standard proof that this number is indeed irrational. It's not uncommon for students to wonder about irrational numbers and even to ask, 'How many irrational numbers are there?' Although it certainly wouldn't be appropriate to attempt to answer this question completely in a first-year algebra course, a knowledgeable instructor could use this as a launching point to briefly explore irrational numbers more generally, the notion of infinite cardinalities, and even the fact that there are many mathematical questions that leading professional researchers have yet to fully explore and resolve. Indeed, we find that instructors with advanced subject-matter expertise can facilitate discussions that both challenge and inspire all our students to think about mathematics more broadly and more deeply.

One specific feature of the SOHS online classroom that has multiple applications to teaching mathematics is text chat. This feature allows the instructor and each student to type text into a shared section of the classroom interface, either to be visible to the instructor and all students (public chat) or to be shared only between one student and the instructor (private chat). Public chat is active throughout each class, with students using text chat to ask quick questions, mention observations in side comments, or even to answer questions posed by other students. (At times, students might use text chat to begin conversations that are unrelated to the topic of discussion or that do not serve to support the learning environment of the online classroom—this behavior must be managed by the instructor.) Public chat could also be used for rapid and effective brainstorming: The instructor might display a new problem on the whiteboard and ask, 'How many different ways can you think of to solve this problem? Answer in public chat.' Students can then quickly generate ideas and see those suggested by other students, providing a written reference point for subsequent discussion of some of those ideas. Private chat can be helpfully used in many ways. For example, many instructors find that checking in with shy students via private chat can help them to join in the discussion. Noticing that a particular student hasn't yet participated in a class session, the instructor might bring up a new problem for discussion and then privately ask that student in text chat, 'Would you like to get us started on this problem?' Private text chat also provides the means for efficient formative assessment during a discussion. To check students' understanding of a topic, the instructor might bring up a relevant problem on the shared whiteboard and then instruct students to solve the problem individually, typing their final answers into private chat when finished. Students could ask private questions using text chat while working on the problem—the nature of these questions themselves could provide the instructor with useful insight into the level of content mastery of the students asking them—and then the collection of private responses, both correct and incorrect, could give the instructor an immediate picture of the class's overall grasp of the topic.

SOHS classes include students from all parts of the United States as well as many international students. In many subject areas, such as history, this diversity of background and life experience might naturally become part of the discussion on a regular basis. Although perhaps less frequently noticed in mathematics classes, such diversity also plays a role in the study of math and can arise in surprising ways. To offer one specific example, in a discussion section for Honors Beginning

Algebra, a student living in Germany volunteered to solve a problem at the whiteboard involving polynomial long division. As it happened, the student had previously learned an approach to carrying out polynomial long division that is commonly taught in Germany and other parts of Europe but which looks quite different in spatial layout from the method taught in this SOHS course and in most US high schools. As the student began solving the problem using the method he had learned elsewhere, an interesting discussion ensued. At first many students simply complained that the student's work didn't make sense, or was obviously wrong—after all, it didn't look at all similar to the method the class had been taught. With the instructor's support, however, the student continued and quickly obtained the correct results for the quotient and remainder. The discussion then turned to an attempt to understand the student's method, which with some effort could be seen to be equivalent to the one more familiar to the rest of the class. The instructor chose to use this unexpected event to challenge the students to think about and comment on the true nature of the subject matter under investigation in mathematics. When recognized as a teachable moment and facilitated carefully, an opportunity such as this can provide students with a sudden glimpse of the concepts truly underlying various ways in which polynomial long division or any mathematical technique might be carried out—an invitation into the deeper conceptual understanding of mathematics that is the goal of all SOHS math courses.

5 Conclusion

Mathematics instruction at SOHS is notable for the fact that it happens entirely online and with live class discussion as a central element, but our approach to teaching math has many other unusual and distinguishing features. The first of these is the far reach of our vertically-aligned curriculum, which extends into realms of university-level study rarely taught in high schools. The second is our focus on interactive exploration as a key learning modality. This focus appears not only in the rich discussion that occurs during formal classroom meetings, but also in the wider SOHS math community through clubs, invited presentations, and the Problem of the Week program. A third distinguishing element is our success in differentiating instruction, both within classes and in our curriculum as a whole, in order to serve the needs of hardworking students with a variety of goals in studying math—some of whom achieve significant prizes in national math contests or might show readiness to engage in their own independent investigations. Future efforts to strengthen our curriculum and continue building a vibrant math community at SOHS may take a number of forms. For example, new courses might be added in subject areas such as the theory of probability or discrete mathematics, depending on student interest. Also, we wish to continue evaluating accelerated courses such as the summer intensive version of Honors Precalculus with Trigonometry—other similar summer courses could be added if we believe that they would serve the long-term learning and success of our students. Finally, the community of SOHS mathematics instructors is itself a rich learning community in which instructors share new ideas for innovative use of the online classroom environment and other specific aspects of our school's online environment as well as current thinking about teaching mathematics in general, and this shared exploration supports ongoing refinement of our curriculum and instructional approach.

References

Bergmann, J. and A. Sams. *Flipped Learning for Math Instruction.* Arlington, VA: International Society for Technology in Education, 2015.

Faltings, G. "The Proof of Fermat's Last Theorem by R. Taylor and A. Wiles." *Notices of the American Mathematical Society* 42 (1995): 743–746.

Scarborough, J., and R. Ravaglia. *Bricks and Mortar: The Making of a Real Education at the Stanford Online High School.* Stanford, CA: CSLI Publications, 2014.

Sousa, D. A., and C. A. Tomlinson. *Differentiation and the Brain: How Neuroscience Supports the Learner-Friendly Classroom.* Bloomington, IN: Solution Tree Press, 2011.

6

Sciences: Thinking Like a Scientist

Kim Failor

1 Introduction

As would be expected at Stanford Online High School, the science curriculum takes a rigorous approach.[1] From the inception of the school, science instructors have trained students to think like scientists. This heavy emphasis on the ways of scientific thinking reflects important developments in science education, as demonstrated by the recent publication of the *Next Generation Science Standards* by several prominent national science organizations. Across the SOHS science curriculum, specific pedagogical approaches foster the skills necessary to think like a scientist including student inquiry-based activities, lively class discussions, and engagement with science beyond the textbook. Upon this foundation, students learn many of the same physical, chemical, and biological concepts as their peers at brick-and-mortar schools, but are able to expand their breadth and depth of knowledge.

2 Scientific Skills to be Taught Anywhere

The unique foundation of the SOHS science curriculum is a commitment to training students to think like scientists. While national organizations and publications devoted to science education increas-

---

[1]Many, many thanks to my colleague Dr. Gary Oas for his significant contributions to this chapter with respect to middle school and university-level physics. This chapter also would not be possible without the enlightening and invigorating conversations with every instructor in the SOHS Science Division. Their passion for teaching, their insights into the uniqueness of SOHS, and their numerous examples of student successes and failures were inspiring and invaluable.

Perspectives from the Disciplines.
Jeffrey Scarborough and Raymond Ravaglia.
Copyright © 2016, CSLI Publications.

ingly emphasize skills of scientific thinking, this approach doesn't always come naturally to teachers. To be fair, most science instructors themselves were not taught in this manner in their K-12 education. But if we accept that the goal of a science education is to cultivate genuine interest in and enthusiasm for science, the best way to do this is to teach students to understand science not as a set of facts to be memorized, but rather as something that can be *done*. And in order to *do* science, one must be able to think like a scientist. Whether discussing historical examples, hypothesizing about complex concepts, or conducting their own experiments, SOHS students develop the skills used by practicing scientists. These key scientific skills were identified by the school's science instructors through their own professional science experience designing and conducting experiments at the lab bench and communicating their results.

While these skills can and should be taught anywhere, SOHS students are in a unique position to learn them. As described below, SOHS courses have many engineered opportunities to develop the ability to think like scientists which can be implemented at any school. However, due to the online nature of courses, students do not always have the watchful eye of their instructor immediately available which allows some novel opportunities to emerge. Students grapple with concepts on their own, carefully formulating questions for class, office hours, or email, or finding other reliable resources for explanations. Students need to be able to troubleshoot and occasionally develop non-obvious solutions to problems that arise with their lab work.

2.1 Asking Questions

A defining characteristic of nearly any scientist is curiosity that is fueled by observations of the natural world, discussions with colleagues, and an inherent desire to explore. This curiosity naturally leads to asking questions about phenomena, some of which yield fruitful experimentation. A scientist asks questions and seeks knowledge in nearly any situation, and these habits of mind can be inculcated in students. They can be encouraged to generate their own questions both in and out of the classroom. In class, it can be as simple as giving the students a challenging graph related to the day's material. Prompted to describe and explain the graph, students can begin to ask a wide variety of questions. What does that unit of measurement on the x-axis represent? How were these measurements taken? How does this relate to what I already know? Why did this pattern emerge from the data? What else might I like to know that is not represented on the graph? Through repetition of this short exercise, teachers can build on students' disposition toward inquiry, first establishing the expectation each time a graph is presented, then applying it to graphs that the students produce with their own data, and finally extending the skill to information presented outside of graphs. Outside of class time, these skills can be taught through the pedagogical tools of assessments and lab work. Both can cultivate curiosity when they are open-ended and allow students to explore their own interests. For instance, a lab assignment might require students to test a defined set of variables to become familiar with equipment and protocols, while also calling on students to explore a variable or two of their choice.

2.2 Manipulating Protocols

Requiring students to define and test their own variables necessitates an ability to manipulate a known experimental protocol so that it can be adapted to test the novel variables, another skill that trained scientists possess. There are a variety of approaches that practicing scientists use in conducting experiments, from meticulously following established protocols to creatively designing new assays. Regardless of a particular scientist's style, she knows the purpose of each step, which parts of the protocol are flexible, and how to string protocols together to fully test a hypothesis. The SOHS science curriculum is designed to get students to think about *how* they generate useful data. This is done in a number of ways, from asking them to design their own methods for testing a hypothesis to assessing their understanding of particular steps in a protocol through summative lab assessments. On occasion, circumstances such as missing or unavailable lab materials require students to consider a suitable substitute. Regardless of the motivation for examining the procedural steps of an experiment, students are invariably surprised to find that there is more to science than learning the concepts and making observations. The skill of examining and changing a protocol is something even practicing scientists often don't encounter until working in an academic or professional lab.

2.3 Understanding Error

A key component of understanding a protocol is accepting that error and uncertainty are inevitable and inherent to the methods of measurement. Students can often define the terms 'accuracy' and 'precision' and will include 'repeat experiment' in a diagram of the scientific method, but a scientist knows from experience the impact that these concepts have on the interpretation of data. In fact, a significant percent of published scientific research can't be replicated in another lab, demonstrating the variability of data, the influence of unknown factors on experiments, and the need to test concepts innumerable times before being certain of the conclusions.[2] Unfortunately, students often assume that science is a set of facts embedded in clear, if complex, relationships. The content of textbooks represents the product of decades of work testing hypotheses in countless ways. Even the most thoroughly tested ideas can come under scrutiny, yielding the splashy exceptions that lead the media to declare 'they'll have to rewrite the textbooks'. In addition, there is a large gap between relatively well-established textbook science and research science that is filled with uncertainty about how the experimental data fits together to create a coherent picture of a phenomenon.

Incorporating uncertainty into one's learning of 'facts' is in some ways in tension with the too-familiar task of rote learning itself and so is inherently difficult. Psychologically, it is often easier for us to learn when the facts feel solid and there aren't too many exceptions to juggle in addition to the new knowledge. Nonetheless, an appreciation of uncertainty yields a deeper understanding of science and has benefits beyond the classroom.

It is easiest to teach this kind of appreciation of error and uncertainty in the context of experimentation. Scientists often refer to uncertainty as error in experimental data, describing the statistical error inherent in data collection. However, this terminology often leads the novice to think that she has done something wrong in performing the experiment. 'I wasn't careful enough measuring the volume of liquids I added', or 'I didn't seal the tube tightly enough'. Mistakes in following a protocol can certainly contribute to a lack of certainty about data, but there are also factors inherent to the experiment itself. A measuring device can only be so accurate. The environment of the lab can only be so tightly regulated. Factors beyond our recognition may influence the outcome. When an experiment is repeated by another group or by the same person, the results will likely differ, and that is to be expected. It is important to make a distinction between mistakes and statistical error so that students understand the limitations in improving the accuracy or precision of results.

One starting point for training students to appreciate uncertainty is changing the way we talk about experimental data, including this differentiation between mistakes and statistical error, and combating the notion of the 'correct outcome' of an experiment. At every opportunity, students should be reminded that the data they recorded are the facts

---

[2]J.P.A. Ioannidis, "Why Most Published Research Findings Are False," *PLoS Medicine* 2 (8): e124, 2005.

that must be accounted for. While mistakes may have occurred, that should not be the first explanation for differences in results. Students should be encouraged to consider the lack of precision or accuracy inherent to how data were generated and collected. For instance, the human eye cannot distinguish between sufficiently similar hues. This results in a natural limitation to interpreting results from an experiment that yields a color change. The student isn't performing the experiment incorrectly; the imprecision of the results are due to an inadequacy in the methodology itself. To facilitate students' understanding of the variability of data, they should compare their results with others in the class. This can initiate a conversation about how differences in data arise and what happens when experiments are repeated, even in the absence of calculating statistical error.

Just as the data of professional scientists aren't immune to statistical error, neither are students'. It is therefore useful to bring published data into class when applicable. Gregor Mendel's monohybrid cross in pea plants didn't yield a perfect 3:1 ratio of dominant and recessive phenotypes. How can we be certain of the *laws* of inheritance that his work generated? Any graph that incorporates error bars can be used to demonstrate statistical error in published scientific research and is a useful extension of the graph analysis exercise described above.

2.4   Translating Among Representations

In addition to graphical representations of information, working scientists need to be able to understand ideas in multiple forms including text, figures, and equations. Each of these forms is utilized when original scientific research is published. Students may be most familiar and comfortable with a textual or verbal explanation of a new idea, but learning in science often has the added complexity of a large and specific vocabulary used to explain concepts. When ideas can be explained visually through figures, graphs, tables, and direct observation, the difficulty of mastering the vocabulary can be temporarily set aside. For instance, a video model of the inner workings of a cell, especially without a voice over, allows students to appreciate the elegance of biological mechanisms. Students can easily visualize how internal cargo is transported on a network of cytoskeleton, and upon that understanding, teachers can add the ideas of directionality and powering the movement along with the vocabulary of tubulin, kinesin, and dynein. Animations can also be helpful in specifically training students to move between different representations, especially when graphs are generated with a time component. Students can see that a bouncing ball results in a sinusoidal wave when its motion is graphed with respect to time.

2.5 Drawing Conclusions

After a scientist has built up a body of observations and data, he can begin to infer or deduce larger patterns and explanations that are the foundation for further experimentation. Generating conclusions based on the data is not an end, but rather a pause to evaluate how the data informs a broader understanding of the topic. That pause may also result in a reevaluation of past conclusions, attempting to fit the pieces together with an understanding that the scientist might not yet have all of the information needed. When beginning to describe the world, students have difficulty separating their observations from the conclusions. If you drop a ball and ask students to describe what they observe, they might say 'I see a ball being pulled to the floor by gravity' instead of 'the ball moves faster and faster as it falls'. Similarly, students also have a natural inclination to state that a single experiment 'proves' some phenomenon. While experiments in school often do involve thoroughly tested concepts, students should still appreciate the level of uncertainty in their data that certainly exceeds the threshold that disallows proof.

2.6 Collaboration and Communication

Of course, the conclusions that a scientist reaches aren't useful until they are shared. Sharing one's work not only allows it to be a foundation for future research, but can also inspire others. New ideas are often fostered through collaboration, especially when experts with different strengths find connections and interdisciplinary overlap. Just as in any discipline, students should be encouraged to collaborate with one another and to communicate their work through a variety of media. At SOHS, our focus is on clear communication that builds into forms authentic to the field of science. It's useful to consider how assigned presentations and lab reports mirror the formal communications of scientists at meetings, conferences, and in publications. When possible, students should be introduced to examples of such communication from professional scientists, whether in readings of primary research papers or classroom visits from scientists. There are a variety of outreach programs that can connect scientists and educators in just such a way.

3 Middle School Curriculum

At the middle school level, the SOHS science curriculum begins to build the foundation of scientific thinking. This approach involves challenging the students in a multitude of ways: they are required to actively engage with peers through inquiry, restructure assumptions about specific topics such as energy, and physically explore their world through experimentation. Each of the scientific skills described above is featured in the middle schooll science courses, so they can be refined during high school.

3.1 Inquiry-Based Approach

An inquiry-based approach, especially in the middle school year, capitalizes on students' natural curiosity and youthful enthusiasm and challenges them to ask deeper and more careful questions. On a basic level, inquiry can be incorporated into traditional assessments by asking students to synthesize the information they've learned. In order for students to connect ideas that were previously disparate in their minds, they must ask themselves the right questions to fit the pieces together, thus also demonstrating deep understanding of the ideas to the teacher. However, an inquiry-based approach is most effective when it utilizes hands-on experimentation and collaborative discussions with classmates.

The first segment of the seventh-grade inquiry-based physics course is primarily discussion-based and employs very little mathematics. This low-stress introduction allows students to form a sense of community and to feel comfortable with stating their views, even if ultimately deemed incorrect. As a result, there are far ranging discussions on topics from the nature of space and time to the limits of human perception. In addition, this first segment includes an exercise to assess and enhance students' mathematical abilities, giving them a chance to arrive at a common ground. One of the first in-class exercises in the seventh-grade inquiry-based physics course asks students to arrive at categories of concepts pertaining to science. How would one categorize an atom? A force? Temperature? This lively discussion generally takes about two weeks with a continued intense debate about the nature of core concepts throughout the year. Eventually the students themselves settle into the fundamental set of entity, property, interaction, and process.

The challenge of instituting an inquiry-based model within an online course is obvious. The approach undertaken in Inquiry-based Physics is to examine very simple phenomena that students can view via video conferencing and also examine physically in their home location. Much of the inquiry is through classwide and small group discussions. More quantitative analyses (experiments) are performed individually by students locally, while general results are discussed in the class setting.

3.2 Challenging Assumptions

Some concepts in science are far from intuitive and resist ready explanation; students can often form persistent misconceptions simply by making assumptions about the gaps in their understanding that are left unexplained. If these misconceptions aren't rooted out, they can last a lifetime. Rather than reserving such a task for upper-level courses, misconceptions can be confronted in the middle school years when they are easier to counteract. In some cases, it is possible to avoid the misconception altogether through foresight and careful explanation. As described above, the first activity in seventh-grade Inquiry-based Physics is to categorize core scientific concepts. This task arose out of experience with textbook errors, discussions with students in SOHS university-level physics courses, and even conversations with doctorate-level physicists who seem to not have a thorough comprehension of the fundamental structure of physics. A prime example is the concept of energy. A search of the standard set of introductory physics texts shows that the definition of energy is never precisely given. The standard statement that 'energy is the ability to do work' is opaque and prone to develop misconceptions.[3] Students, and professional scientists, often think of energy as a 'kind of stuff', that it has an ontology in and of itself rather than being a property of something else. I have not yet encountered in an elementary physics textbook the statement that energy is a property and is not an entity that exists on its own. Students in the SOHS university-level physics courses are advanced for their age and often are quite adept in calculating in the context of physics. However, often due to their rapid advancement, some have profound gaps in their general understanding of the structure of physics. It is in anticipation of this need that one of the core missions of the seventh-grade Inquiry-based Physics course is to have students arrive at the most basic understanding of the structure of scientific theory such that they have a solid framework in which to place concepts such as energy.

3.3 The Scientific Skills

An important component of the middle school science courses, as with all SOHS science courses, is bringing students' conceptual understanding into the physical world through experimentation. The process of science is complex and at this stage the focus is on procedure and data representation. Each week of the eighth-grade interdisciplinary science course includes lab work and each of these labs asks students to do some combination of designing the procedure individually and considering how their data is communicated. These skills are scaffolded throughout the course so that students gain confidence in their ability. A critical component of becoming confident in these skills is communication with

---

[3]T. Hsu, *Physics, A First Course, 2nd Edition* (Appleton: CPO Science, 2012).

their classmates. Student work is highlighted in every class, and students are encouraged to post pictures and videos of their experiments as they complete them.

The middle school science courses also particularly focus on skills that students are assumed to have when they enter high school level courses but aren't always explicitly taught including creating, reading, and interpreting graphs beyond a basic level; abstraction of phenomena to various representations; and visualization skills, including dimensional reduction (e.g. inferring the shape of an object from a two-dimensional image). The seventh-grade physics course has enumerated these detailed skills, and has incorporated other concepts from the Physics Education Research (PER) community. Students are scored on their mastery of these skills using Standards Based Grading (SBG). The assessment structure allows students to see clearly which skills they are mastering and to concentrate on those they may not be mastering. The philosophy in this course is that students will arrive at mastery at different rates and students should have the ability to return to previous topics and reassess their mastery.

4 High School Curriculum

The SOHS high school level science courses build on the middle school curriculum with a continued emphasis on student inquiry and lab work. Throughout the curriculum, students are challenged to solve complex problems through engagement with their peers so they can appreciate alternative approaches and common missteps. In doing so, they continue to develop the skills necessary for scientific thinking as explained above with ample opportunities to ask questions about the natural world, and to describe concepts verbally, numerically, and graphically. These skills are also fostered through students' at-home lab work, which becomes more sophisticated in high school courses, including hypothesis development and more careful data analysis. The lab work is designed to drive students to understand and design their own scientific methodologies, including processes for testing hypotheses, selection of variables, and authentic and individual presentation of data.

SOHS science courses cover the broad spectrum of sciences, including physics, chemistry, biology, environmental sciences, and astronomy. In general, the curriculum is designed to offer students flexibility in their science course sequence based on their interest and ability. The only strict requirements are that chemistry be taken before biology and students must have adequately mastered prerequisite material before enrolling in Advanced Placement courses. Flexibility allows students to tailor their science education to reflect their progression through mathematics, their interest in pursuing advanced work in a particular scientific discipline, or their overall coursework balance. The most common path through high school level courses includes the Core course Methodology of Science—Biology (discussed in the chapter on Core) concurrently with Honors Chemistry in freshman year, followed by Honors Physics in sophomore year and AP Biology in junior year. This sequence alone would meet the SOHS graduation requirements, although many students opt to take an additional AP science course or post-AP elective (described below).

Between the rigorous coverage of advanced high school level science content and development of real-world scientific skills, the SOHS curriculum asks a lot of students, and thus it is critical that students remain engaged. Relevance is an important tool in this project: science courses incorporate the most recent scientific research as frequently as possible, promoting scientific literacy while tracking students' experiences and interests. Student engagement is also maintained by relating the various fields and sub-fields of science with one another by referring to concepts learned in prior courses, thus also reinforcing that learning.

4.1 Scientific Literacy

Everyone encounters science in adult life, whether it is through media consumption, interaction with scientific and medical professionals, or participation in the debates that shape our society. We read headlines about recent scientific breakthroughs (gravitational waves!) or reports on what is healthy to consume (coffee?). We visit doctors who suggest different daily habits or treatment options for serious conditions. We hear friends, family, and colleagues discuss the relative merits of sustainable living practices and see politicians engage in international debate about climate change. While we can't predict what scientific revelations are to come within our students' lifetime, we do have an obligation to give them the foundation of knowledge and skills necessary to understand and evaluate the new science they encounter. After completing the SOHS coursework, for example, any graduate should feel comfortable with the basis of the new CRISPR-Cas9 gene-editing technology including the nature of genes and enzymes, be able and willing to ask questions about how it works, and engage in a discussion of the boundaries of ethical use.

To facilitate students' scientific literacy, some topics that are relevant to societal discourse are directly incorporated into SOHS classes. For instance, the Honors Environmental Science course devotes most of the spring semester to topics of local, regional, and global environmental impacts, climate change, and sources of energy. Through classroom discussion and activities such as calculating their own carbon footprints, students become more aware of their own environmental impact and the domino effect their choices have. This activity holds particular significance at an online school where students are geographically dispersed and pursue substantially diverse lifestyles. One class of students might include a student in Vermont who doesn't travel much, has a vegetarian diet, and avidly gardens, alongside a competitive international athlete who is always on the go and is more active than average. These two students would have dramatically different carbon footprints, which leads to an interesting discussion that is all the richer because the range of footprints are exemplified by people you know. Beyond this activity, students engage with the scientific data that informs individual decisions, recommendations from scientific bodies, and government policy. Students are encouraged to ask questions, such as how was this data generated and how is it used?

Beyond activities and classroom discussion, scientific literacy is built through deep engagement with the same topics that society grapples with. Continuing with the example of climate change in SOHS Honors Environmental Science, students thoroughly examine the myriad sources of energy used today including fossil fuels, alternative energy sources already in use, and experimental alternatives. As part of this unit, students prepare a written argument about alternative energy sources based on two scientific articles. They are responsible for finding two primary research papers regarding either wind, solar, or algae-based power, and they develop a thesis around what they've learned. For instance, a student might argue that breeder reactors are more sustainable than traditional fission nuclear reactors. In addition to researching the topic, developing an argument, and writing a short paper, students then present their work to their peers in class. This multifaceted project not only allows students to learn about alternative energy sources generally, but to engage in detailed analysis of the same information used by professionals and thus to be more informed when discussing these ideas outside of school.

This research project highlights another important component of scientific literacy–encountering the latest research in class. Generally, introducing scientific research in class takes the course material beyond the textbook and into related topics that are making headlines. Nearly any scientific advance that can be simplified enough to make headline news can easily be incorporated. The discovery of an Earth-like planet that orbits Proxima Centauri could lead to an interesting discussion in a physical science classroom about how such discoveries are made, while a life science classroom might explore the conditions necessary to make a planet habitable. Emerging diseases such as Zika can be worked into the study of viruses, fetal development, or the nervous system in biology class. Including headline news in class allows students to see how what they are learning is actively leading to new advances in knowledge, while modeling good practices of scientific literacy.

While the science that appears in the biggest headlines may be the easiest to bring into a class, numerous sources on modern scientific research are adaptable to coursework. Science news aggregators publish a large number of relevant articles in relatively accessible language and science journals themselves increasingly provide online resources for educators and articles summarizing important research, without the formal language of the primary research article itself. In AP Biology, students are frequently asked to read a recent news article written for a scientifically-interested audience, or to find and evaluate their own. For instance, when learning about the regulation of gene expression, students read about how a slight change in the regulation of a specific gene results in the variation of beak sizes seen among the finches of the Galapagos Islands. (Any mention of Charles Darwin or the Galapagos Islands instantly gets the attention of students.) This particular bit of research is also useful in that it highlights the intersection of many areas of biology including genetics, animal development, the relationship between beak structure and function in determining preferred foods, ecology, and evolution. This research is too current to be found in a biology textbook, despite its utility as an example. In addition, it is written at a level appropriate for advanced biology students and puts the vocabulary and concepts they are learning to practice.

4.2 Connecting Concepts

Frequently science courses are divided into units that progress from basic ideas on a topic such as stoichiometry to deeper understanding, culminating in some major summative assessment. This structure encourages students to think of the concepts they've learned as belonging to one silo or another, a tendency that is exacerbated across courses in different scientific disciplines. Ask students in a biology course to use the molecular weights of the components of a buffer solution to generate a recipe for the buffer, and they may appear perplexed by the task because they don't associate what they've learned in chemistry with concepts being investigated in biology. Whenever possible, SOHS science courses point out connections between units in a course, between courses, and to real-life examples.

In AP Biology, study of the digestive system particularly demonstrates such connections. Digestion falls under the animal physiology unit of the course and thus highlights many of the general themes of the unit including the function of different tissues and the specialization and coordination of organs within the system. However, the digestive system also provides an opportunity to review material that students learned months earlier regarding the molecular constituents of life, such as proteins, carbohydrates, and fats. Animals must break down each of these molecules in order to make use of them, so students must recall how these large molecules are composed of smaller subunits. Since chemical digestion is performed by enzymes, students must think back to the experiment in which they investigated the optimal environment for enzyme efficiency. Particularly relevant is the acidity of the stomach and the need to neutralize that acidity with buffers in the small intestine. And all of these processes can be connected with real-life examples given that we consume and digest all manner of foods every day. Why can't we digest fiber? Are there any animals that can? What is the biological and chemical differences between us and them?

5   Advanced Courses in the Sciences

At SOHS, some students complete AP-level courses as freshmen and sophomores and are interested in continuing to pursue advanced work within a scientific discipline. SOHS offers multiple university-level physics courses including Modern Physics, Light and Heat, and Intermediate Mechanics. In biology, students have the option to take Advanced Topics in Biological Research. Due to the advanced nature of the material and the sophisticated experiments required to demonstrate the concepts included in the curriculum, these courses do not have a lab component, although the focus is still on developing the students' scientific skills at a deep level.

5.1   Advanced Topics in Biological Research

Advanced Topics in Biological Research is a course for students who have successfully completed AP Biology and are interested in continuing their study of biology. Many of the students may be considering a career in biological research or medicine and some have already done sophisticated research independently or in a local research lab on topics including cancer, bioengineered enzymes, ecology, and plant biology. The course is styled after a university-level research seminar in which students read, present, and discuss primary research literature. The instructor chooses the papers for the year from the full range of biology topics, including both seminal and cutting edge works. Given that each week reflects a new topic, the curriculum is flexible such that emerging topics can be easily included. The objective of the course is to build skills in learning science through primary research papers, in addition to introducing students to the ways of thinking and modern techniques that they will encounter in college and beyond.

Until this point in the science curriculum, students have often relied on textbooks as part of their learning. The textbook may provide an organizing principle for a course but also serves as a comprehensive resource for reading course material, completing practice problems, and accessing online ancillary materials such as animations. Textbooks are designed to facilitate a systematic understanding of the discipline, and also must be relevant for years. For all of these reasons, textbooks focus on well-established knowledge and are not positioned to cover emerging topics. But when students are ready to engage with the leading edge of science, they need to learn in a different way. Primary research is not written solely to facilitate learning and often assumes a large body of prerequisite knowledge. Scientists themselves, of course, are not learning from textbooks; they learn through experimentation, keeping up with the latest published work, and engaging with colleagues. This course trains students in the latter two approaches.

In order to bridge the gap between textbook and primary literature, students need to develop several skills. The first is how to approach a paper in a field they are unfamiliar with. While students will have encountered the human immunodeficiency virus (HIV) and the basics of virology in their previous biology courses, for example, they aren't familiar with the techniques used to identify the molecular mechanism that allows HIV to enter human cells. In order to understand a paper that elucidates this mechanism, students first need to recognize the context and goal of the paper. This can often be achieved by first reading the paper's abstract and discussion, and then the introduction and results. Once students have a broad understanding of the paper, they can begin to dig into the technical details and jargon. Through experience, they learn which new vocabulary terms to look up and which can be overlooked given the scope of the class. Each student develops her own approach to understanding the bigger context and specific terminology and techniques of research papers.

Another habit that often needs to be unlearned at this level is making broad conclusions based on specific data. Students are quick to say that a single experiment proves the hypothesis is true, probably because that has been their own approach to conducting classroom-based lab experiments, which are often intended to demonstrate broad concepts. However, research scientists are careful to break down an argument into small components, each with its own supporting data. A careful scientist attempts to preempt questions about the validity of her claim through careful experimental design and by testing hypotheses in multiple ways. In reading primary research papers, students must be prompted to consider the purpose of each sample and experiment so they can begin to appreciate the logical structure of the argument that the scientists present. One particularly useful approach to facilitating this process is discussing each figure of the paper and having students consider how one sub-figure builds on another throughout the paper as a whole.

While one goal of the course is to introduce students to exciting modern biological research, a useful way to initially build the skills needed to read modern scientific papers is to choose a paper regarding an experiment they are already familiar with. Matthew Meselson and Franklin Stahl's 1958 paper on the semi-conservative replication of DNA is a particularly effective example.[4] Many biology courses cover classic experiments from the 1950s regarding DNA. Advanced students have almost certainly encountered a cartoon representation of Meselson and Stahl's work in their textbooks. When students read this paper at the start of Advanced Topics in Biological Research, they are already familiar with the larger context of the research and are therefore able to focus on how to decipher the technical jargon and the step-by-step process of the authors building the logical argument favoring semi-conservative replication of DNA.

This technique of revisiting specific experiments can also be used when the prerequisite course is designed to include modern research. In SOHS AP Biology, students are asked to read a news article about the molecular underpinnings of the evolution of Darwin's finches on the Galapagos Islands. Students learn that a small change in the regulation of a developmental gene that controls beak size results in the variation between cactus finches and ground finches. In Advanced Topics in Biological Research, students delve even deeper into the same research by reading the primary source. For students who have this earlier encounter, there is an exciting 'a-ha' moment as they recall discussing the connections between genetics and evolution in a familiar example. However, in this more advanced course, students can see how researchers reached the conclusion that this particular gene is necessary for the variation in beak size. Because students are already familiar with the conclusions of the research, they have an easier time reading the more sophisticated treatment of the topic and can thoroughly exam-

---

[4]M. Meselson and F.W. Stahl, "The Replication of DNA in *Escherichia coli*," *Proceedings of the National Academy of Science* 44 (7): 671–682, 1958.

ine the methodology. What are the experimental steps in establishing the rational argument? Was the sample size big enough? What limits the sample size? Are model organisms useful in the study and are the findings applicable?

Another important component of learning beyond the textbook in Advanced Topics in Biological Research is engaging in the same collaborative learning process as scientists. To this end, students are given the responsibility to lead the seventy minute discussion of a paper in class. In the presenter role, students dive deeper into a topic than they would week-to-week. Depending on their interests, they learn about the lives of the scientists who conducted the work, they investigate how the work fits into the much broader field of research, or they consider the difficulties that come in applying the research in practice. They are also on the spot for understanding the paper in its entirety so that they can correct their classmates' explanations if necessary and focus the discussion to proceed in the allotted amount of time. When in the participant role, meanwhile, students are compelled to contribute to class in a way that doesn't always happen when the same adult instructor is leading–they want to support their friends and classmates, and they are invested in contributing to sustain a collegial investigation. This practice of continual engagement in class fosters a sense of classroom community in which students feel more comfortable failing in an explanation.

Of course, this is not to say that the instructor is not involved in the class. The instructor provides each student presenter with significant support prior to the day of class. This process ensures that the student has the correct interpretation of the paper and individual figures. Student and instructor discuss how best to facilitate conversation, which figures can be omitted from the discussion, and how to achieve the learning objectives for the particular paper.

5.2 Advanced Topics in Biological Research–Writing Option

In addition to the course as described above, students in Advanced Topics in Biological Research can also include a writing option. In this supplement, students evaluate a variety of forms of scientific writing and engage in their own long-form project to write a scientific review.

Through the study of different styles of science writing over the course of several weeks, students gain an appreciation for the process of science and outside factors that influence that process such as regulation and funding. In Advanced Topics in Biological Research, students evaluate cutting-edge research through primary sources, research review articles, and scientific journalism. For instance, the class might read about and then discuss CRISPR-Cas9-mediated genomic engineering through each of these writing forms. This is a technology that first gained attention in the scientific community in 2012 and is far too recent to have found its way into introductory biology textbooks. Students first learn the history of the research leading up to the breakthrough discovery through a scientific review. The review also details the mechanism by which genes can be edited and explores potential applications. A scientific review is the equivalent of a textbook in this instance, although in discussing the paper, students begin to consider the ethical implications of genomic engineering. Should scientists be allowed to engineer human genomes? Perhaps only if it results in the elimination of deadly disease? What about non-fatal diseases or cosmetic issues?

Following this introduction to CRISPR-Cas9, students explore how the technique can be applied in a specific instance by reading a primary research paper. They discuss the intricacies of the experimental design including the importance of controls. They appreciate the narrow conclusions and consider them in the context of the review article. The results of this one study are just a very small piece of an exciting whole.

Students next consider the technology from the point of view of scientific journalism. At this stage, it is easy for them to notice the lack of technical detail, the colloquial language, and the personal touches. After the thorough examination of the research paper, one student noted of an article from a popular magazine, 'It seems like it was written for children'. What isn't immediately apparent to the students is that through this form of writing, they can gain a fuller appreciation of how science is conducted. In this example, the popular article highlights the struggle for patent rights. Who has these rights? Who *should* have these rights? Why does it matter? The conversation steers itself to the economics of research. The class also revisits the topic of the ethics of genomic engineering which precipitates a consideration of the mechanisms for controlling scientific research. The conversation then moves to the economics of research once again, in addition to the regulatory agencies with a say in how research is conducted.

Through study of varied sources and student-led discussion, students gain an understanding not only of the scientific topic, but also of how science is conducted, from the design of a single study to the economic and political forces that can shape the work and its application. They also become prepared to engage responsibly in the important conversations we have as a society about the possibilities that arise due to scientific progress, such as those now available through genomic engineering.

After engaging with a variety of scientific writing forms, students embark on their own journey of writing an in-depth scientific review of twenty or thirty pages in the second semester of the course. This is a scaffolded process that occurs over an entire semester. Students can choose any topic within the broad field of biology, although it must be specific enough that they can dig significantly deeply into the scientific literature. Students then spend six weeks researching their topic, compiling notes, determining a purpose for the review, and refining or refocusing their topic. In the process of writing their papers, they produce several drafts that undergo instructor- and peer-review. When producing such a long paper, students encounter new challenges that don't typically come with a shorter form of writing. Some stumble with defining their topic, some with organizing their thoughts, and some with finding the research they need. In the process of becoming better writers, they also become deeper scientific thinkers. They witness first-hand what it is like to immerse oneself in a very specific topic and also gain a better appreciation for what remains unknown in the field and where it may be heading next.

6 Teaching Students to Think Like Scientists *Online*

From the discussion so far, one might consider the SOHS science curriculum to be distinct because of its rigor, depth, and systematic focus on developing scientific skills, but otherwise not all that different from what is possible in a bricks-and-mortar setting. However, one question always emerges when educators discuss the possibility of teaching science at an online high school—how do the students do their lab work? Lab work is a critical component of the SOHS science curriculum just as it is at any other school, and special attention is given to providing students hands-on experience with concepts and scientific skills. The majority of experimentation is done at home with materials around the house, acquired locally, or provided as part of a designed course kit. On occasion, at-home lab work is supplemented with virtual labs and online simulations. There are some obvious differences between doing experiments at home and doing them in a classroom laboratory, but it has been our clear experience that many of those differences can be turned to our advantage.

6.1 Conducting Lab Work At Home

When the focus is on training students to think like scientists, even experiments with simple materials can present fascinating and challenging opportunities to learn. In the middle school course Foundations of Science: Energy and Matter, one focus is on the difference between potential and kinetic energy. Students think about this difference experimentally by building and 'launching' a geyser with Mentos candy and cola. This lab can be performed anywhere that you don't mind having a sticky mess and uses materials that are easily accessible nearly anywhere in the world. But the experiment goes beyond following a straightforward set of steps and making observations. In order to calculate the velocity of the cola erupting from the bottle, students must know the maximum height of the geyser. This part of the protocol is not provided to students. In fact, part of the challenge to them is to devise two different ways of taking the measurement, thus giving them an opportunity to practice the skill of formulating and manipulating protocols. These young students are immensely creative in their approaches, standing on ladders in an attempt to catch the peak, dangling strings over the bottle and measuring how much gets wet, marking the length of the shadow on the ground, and even attempting to collect the data with a drone. Students repeat the experiment and get a sense of how precise (or imprecise) the data can possibly be and are asked to report on how trustworthy they find their measurements to be, reinforcing their appreciation of uncertainty in science. Finally, the students must communicate their findings in both written and verbal forms. They clearly write out their method for determining the height of the geyser such that any of their classmates would be able to repeat it. In addition, students submit a photo or short video of the experiment in progress. The instructor creates a compilation to watch together at the start of class, and everyone shares in each other's fun and inventiveness, contributing to the creation of a community of scientists who are comfortable sharing their successes and failures and providing thoughtful commentary on the work of others. Later in the year, students are asked to repeat the experiment, this time asking a different set of questions. Will the geyser still erupt if you use a different flavor or brand of candy? Why or why not? What about the flavor or brand of soda? What is the relationship between number of candies and height of the geyser? A simple experiment based on an internet sensation becomes an enriching experience when you ask students to think like scientists.

Many of the SOHS science courses, especially the physics and middle school courses, conduct their at-home lab work in this way. Labs are designed to make use of items that are easily acquired—a meter stick, a kitchen scale, any ball students have at home, and free software for collecting and analyzing data such as Audacity. Students are encouraged to get creative, which plays a unique role in opening their eyes to the world around them. Some courses require more specific reagents that can't be purchased in sufficiently small quantities or relatively uncommon equipment such as graduated cylinders and pipettes. For these courses, especially chemistry and biology, students obtain a prepackaged kit of supplies. Even with an assembled kit, the focus of lab work is on developing the skills of a scientist.

Lab kits nearly always come with a manual of protocols to follow, making it easy for students to slip into the relatively mindless task of following instructions word for word. While protocols are an important aspect of conducting scientific research, a scientist is able to choose and modify a procedure to meet the desired objective. She understands how the experiment will test the hypothesis and which steps of the experiment must be done precisely. Often substitutions can be made or incubations prolonged. In order to promote the students' ability to understand the protocol deeply, teachers need to actively encourage students to question the procedure they are performing. This can be as simple as requiring students to respond to questions related to the actions they performed. For instance, in the SOHS AP Chemistry course, students are required to complete a lab quiz with each lab assignment that tests their understanding of what they did. In one experiment, students determine the rate of a chemical reaction by measuring the time it takes a tablet that bubbles in water to float. Students test the variables of tablet size and water temperature. After conducting the experiments, students must explain potential sources of error in the measurement. In addition, they must design an experiment based on the original to test the relationship between tablet size and an additional variable. In considering how the protocol can be used to yield data for a different purpose, students must first understand how the protocol was used to meet the original purpose.

Whenever possible, students are encouraged not only to design related experiments, but also to conduct them. This can sometimes be difficult with a prepared kit of materials designed to give a student just what he needs and no more. Students need to supplement with materials from around the home, reuse an apparatus, or substitute one tested variable for another. Nonetheless, it is possible and desirable for the curriculum to include student-developed investigations so that they can feel ownership over the scientific process and ask the questions that interest them. As an example, students in AP Biology investigate osmosis by putting cut potato samples in water with varying concentrations of salt. Students first conduct the experiment using potato and prescribed salt concentrations. From the data, students calculate the concentration of solutes inside the potato and then repeat the experiment varying some other condition, such as substituting a different fruit or vegetable for potato or a liquid other than water. With this freedom to ask their own questions, one student flipped the protocol entirely and chose to use the potatoes as an indicator of water quality and the concentration of solutes in water from various sources including tap water,

water filtered at home, and distilled water. With encouragement to go beyond the lab manual provided in the kit, the student was able to ask questions about his own physical environment just as a scientist might.

In addition to protocols, kit-provided lab manuals often provide students with empty data tables to fill in as they go. This practice can lead to the same lack of attention to what information is being presented and why. Students can fall into habits that reduce the clarity of their communication. If someone other than the student (or even the student herself a month later) looks at the data table, will they know what 'tube #1' was? It is useful therefore for students, even in the middle school years, to consider how they present data to their audience. Having students construct their own data tables or graphs with minimal instruction also provides the class an opportunity to compare. Which representation of the data helps the audience to reach a conclusion about the results? Are there different ways to construct a data table? Could anything be added to this graph to make it clearer? In looking at the data as represented by classmates, students can judge for themselves what is helpful to include and how to improve their own practice.

6.2   The Advantages of At-Home Lab Work

When the SOHS science curriculum was originally developed, there was no question that lab work was a critical component, and indeed it has been a challenge. SOHS science instructors continue to improve the lab component of the curriculum every year as new resources become available and the collective experience of instructors and students is considered. That experience has been invaluable and has clearly shown that there are immense benefits to students conducting labs at home. The experience is not the same as in a bricks-and-mortar setting, but at-home lab work may actually produce stronger scientific thinkers. Because the instructor is not present to make observations during the experiment, students need to conduct their work with much more independence and creativity, although it also opens opportunities for the instructor to be creative in developing lab assignments as well.

We've considered how the SOHS science curriculum is designed to provide students with plenty of opportunities to understand and manipulate protocols as a scientist would. Occasionally, there are unexpected opportunities to do the same. Sometimes a critical component on an experiment is missing from the prepackaged kit. If students didn't take a thorough inventory of the hundreds of items in the kit when they received it, they may not realize the omission until it is time to do the experiment. The first piece of advice from the instructor is always 'is there something else you can use in place of it?' Students are prompted to consider the function of the missing component in the protocol. Is there something else around the house that can be used instead? Could the apparatus be set up in a different way? Can the reagent be obtained elsewhere? In an extreme example, a student was missing a necessary reagent, and through his internet research discovered it was a common component of diapers, used to wick away liquid. He proceeded to purchase a pack of diapers and disassembled them to get what he needed. In a more common scenario, a chemistry kit might be missing a test tube stopper needed to assemble an apparatus. The stopper must allow a tube to pass through, but otherwise prevent air or liquid from leaving. Any number of things could be substituted depending on the creativity of the student and materials available on hand. One student used children's putty as an inert seal.

At-home lab work sometimes demands that students be creative, but it also requires that they clearly communicate what they've done. A student in AP Biology was attempting to melt agar in order to make blocks of gelatin for an experiment regarding diffusion. After heating the agar in the microwave for close to ten minutes (eight minutes longer than the suggested time), she contacted the instructor. Since the instructor was not present to oversee precisely what was going on, it was incumbent on the student to describe clearly what she saw. After some back and forth, the student made the critical observation that the agar was received in powder form rather than a gelatinous solid as expected. A simple modification of the protocol got the student back on track. Clear communication is also required in explaining the results of an experiment, especially when students design a part of the investigation. Beyond the watchful eye of the instructor, it is the student's own report that is the sole basis for understanding and assessing the student's experiment.

Students are also challenged by at-home lab work when they don't get the results they expect. A student's first encounter with this sort of outcome often results in panic stemming from the assumption that the grade depends on the accuracy of the results obtained. While it is true that many of the experiments students perform have been done thousands of times before, this is a unique opportunity to learn that there is no 'right answer' in science. The student obtained the results that he did, and nature is not attempting to obfuscate the truth. As a teacher, it is almost more satisfying when the students don't get the expected results: when expectation and acquired data don't align, the student has to grapple with how the data reflects on their understanding of the course material and the experiment itself. Why doesn't the data support the hypothesis, especially when the hypothesis seems reasonable given what the student has learned in class? Indeed this is a question that scientists struggle with as well. There are any number of explanations that students can consider. Perhaps the student realizes that the apparatus was set up incorrectly in a way that affected the results. But students are quick to blame themselves and should be encouraged to think about other possibilities. Maybe the methodology is inaccurate, as in a chemistry experiment that results in color changes that are difficult to distinguish. In such circumstances, students can become more comfortable with uncertainty and understand that not all experimental approaches produce precise and easily interpretable results. Students should also consider that there may be unknown factors influencing the results. In one biology lab, students measure the breakdown of various sweeteners by yeast. Naturally, they hypothesize that substances like sugar and corn syrup will cause the yeast to be very active, but artificial sweeteners will not. However, they are often surprised after completing the experiment to find that the yeast respond to the artificial sweeteners, sometimes as much or more than sugar. Those students who go beyond assuming that their own work was faulty do some additional research and learn that many artificial sweeteners contain some amount of sugar, just below what is still considered zero calorie. This experiment helps students understand that scientists need to continue to consider confounding variables even when they think they know precisely what they're doing.

In addition to the valuable challenges encountered through at-home lab work, SOHS students face a uniquely enriching lab experience in virtue of their geographical dispersion. The local environment and availability of resources can lead to variability in the data that can be taken advantage of in the classroom. Some experiments are not even possible unless students are situated in different locations. For instance, in a global school, one can measure the diameter of Earth using a method developed by Eratosthenes in ancient Greece. By measuring the length of the shadow of a stick at local noon on the same day at distant places on Earth, students can use some relatively simple geometry to do the calculation. With dozens of students hundreds of miles apart, it becomes possible for a class to work as a group to recreate this historical data measurement. When the answer isn't precisely what they expected, there's a valuable discussion to be had about uncertainty in data and alternative approaches to answering the same question.

Doing experiments in different locations also introduces local variables that can lead to insights and fruitful discussion. Student-generated data can be brought back to the classroom and compared. Students find that even though they all followed the same protocol, and maybe even used the same reagents from a prepackaged kit, they can have vastly different results. In an example from a SOHS chemistry class, students performed an experiment with a compound that readily absorbs water from the air. While that wasn't an intended variable of the experiment, students in different locations found a pattern in their data that suggested that students in humid climates, such as Florida, had less reliable data than those in drier climates. Together the students proposed a revised protocol in which the powdered reagent was dried in a low temperature oven just before use. The student in Florida repeated the experiment and demonstrated that the class had successfully deduced the source of variability. This once again demonstrates that an unrecognized variable can have a substantial impact on the outcome of an experiment, and it was the collaborative work of the student scientists in different locations that uncovered it.

6.3 Supplementing the At-Home Experience

While as much lab work as possible is done at-home, there are still a few unavoidable limitations. Students cannot perform experiments that are dangerous enough to require careful disposal protocols, professional supervision, or special equipment such as fume hoods. They also don't have access to expensive or sophisticated equipment such as a torsion balance apparatus to measure Coulomb's law in physics. In such cases where students would benefit from lab work that utilizes one or more of these requirements, SOHS provides multiple options from online resources available to all students to on-campus summer lab courses.

Online resources are continually expanding and becoming more sophisticated, and SOHS science instructors are always on the lookout for useful new tools. Simulations are a basic way of providing students with a substitute for in person lab work. The University of Colorado–Boulder provides PhET interactive simulations for a variety of disciplines, most notably in physics. Students can easily manipulate the variables and observe the outcome for gravity, electromagnetism, and kinematics. In chemistry, simulations are useful in manipulating the variables of the ideal gas law. For biology, the Howard Hughes Medical Institute hosts BioInteractive, which is a rich resource of virtual labs, data from primary research literature, animations, and more. Beyond simulations, online resources can be used for virtual lab work. The ideal virtual lab is a 'sandbox' in which students can manipulate the equipment, choose their own variables, and make mistakes, rather than just clicking through the experience without deep engagement.

Some students also choose to participate in the lab courses offered through the SOHS Residential Summer Program. These courses offer a two-week lab experience on the Stanford University campus in the teaching labs. In this intensive two-week program, students have access to the sophisticated equipment, reagents not safe for home use, and expert instructional oversight. In the biology labs, students make ample use of compound microscopes and gel electrophoresis equipment. For chemistry, students can run reactions in the fume hoods and generate antimicrobial nanoparticles. The physics lab encourages students to answer questions in any number of ways using their creativity and a lab full of supplies. In one lab, students are asked to measure the speed of sound. A group of ten students developed four different methods, utilizing PVC pipe, Arduino sensors, video and audio capture technology, and more. While students are excited to be with one another, in a lab class setting and using research equipment they don't usually have access to, the emphasis is still on developing the same science skills that they work to refine during the academic year.

7 Conclusion

Throughout their time in the SOHS science courses, across all of the activities they engage in, students are developing the skills to think like scientists. They are conducting hands-on experiments, engaging in living discussion with their peers and teachers, and going beyond the textbook through their assignments. Each of these approaches to learning has the skills of scientific thinking at its root. Students are continually prompted to ask questions, be creative in finding answers, reinterpret data and facts, and be comfortable with uncertainty. Whether they take just one course or more than six, students gain the ability and confidence to participate in scientific inquiry and have become life-long learners of science.

References

Hsu,T. *Physics, A First Course, 2nd* Edition. Appleton: CPO Science, 2012.

Ioannidis, J.P.A. "Why Most Published Research Findings Are False." *PLoS Medicine* 2 (8): e124, 2005.

Meselson M. and F.W. Stahl. "The Replication of DNA in *Escherichia coli.*" *Proceedings of the National Academy of Science* 44 (7): 671–682, 1958.

7

Ancient and Modern Languages

KATHRYN BALSLEY

For philology is that venerable art which exacts from its followers one thing above all—to step to one side, to leave themselves spare moments, to grow silent, to become slow—the leisurely art of the goldsmith applied to language: an art which must carry out slow, fine work, and attains nothing if not lento. For this very reason philology is now more desirable than ever before; for this very reason it is the highest attraction and incitement in an age of 'work': that is to say, of haste, of unseemly and immoderate hurry-skurry, which is intent upon 'getting things done' at once, even every book, whether old or new. Philology itself, perhaps, will not 'get things done' so hurriedly: it teaches how to read well: i.e. slowly, profoundly, attentively, prudently, with inner thoughts, with the mental doors ajar, with delicate fingers and eyes....

–Nietzsche, Preface to *Daybreak*

1 Introduction

When I first started the Latin program at SOHS in 2006, I never anticipated meeting any of my students in person.[1] I most certainly did not anticipate flying to southern California to chaperone a large group of them for a weekend of togas and test taking at the annual California Latin State Convention. But this is the power of languages at SOHS. Our students are willing to fly across the country, to share a hotel room with classmates they have never met in person, and to spend a weekend in matching t-shirts making bad Latin puns with their Latin

---

[1] A great deal of thanks is owed to Laura Barletta, Lauren Bickart, Jenny Nadaner, and Anna Pisarello for all their help and input with this chapter.

Perspectives from the Disciplines.
Jeffrey Scarborough and Raymond Ravaglia.

teachers. For however much our group may have differed from other Latin clubs at convention (we probably had the only group of students jetlagged from east coast flights), where they did not differ from those around them was in their engagement with the weekend activities, in their pride in their school, and in their excitement to be spending time with friends outside of the classroom. Indeed, the lengths our students went to just to be together for a weekend of a shared academic pursuit demonstrates that online language courses can, and should, foster this kind of community.

This level of engagement and community, which may seem unusual for an online school, is the reason we think students seek out language study at SOHS. Learning a language depends upon interaction, whether between students and instructors, between classmates, or between cultures. Our division uses the online nature of our school to foster and deepen these interactions, drawing upon innovative instructors and curriculum to examine continually the nature of intensive language study. The goal of the Ancient and Modern Language Division at SOHS is to provide students with an engaging and intensive study of language and culture one which demands of them their full attention and participation, and we believe this can best be achieved through the unique environment of our online classroom.

In this chapter we will explore how our division approaches intensive language courses for gifted students in an online environment. We will discuss first the ways in which we define intensive and how we build a program and a curriculum to implement this understanding of intensive language study. We will then look at the online classroom itself and the advantages and disadvantages of this environment for language instruction. Finally, we will discuss community building within and outside of the language classroom and the real and potential challenges for developing a community of language learners who are online.

2 How Do We Define Intensive?

Beginning a discussion of language study at SOHS by analyzing, etymologizing, and redefining a word, especially one as simple as 'intensive', is perhaps a little too on the nose. Intensive is a word, though, that deserves some reflection, especially since it is often used to describe language instruction. So what is an intensive language? Does intensive refer to the frequency of meetings? To the level of the textbook used? To the speed at which concepts are taught, or the speed at which they are mastered? Should intensive language courses be exclusively immersive? Does intensive language study look different when it is online?

When the language program at SOHS was first developed, the word 'intensive' was characterized by teaching university-level courses as part of the sequence. The goal of language instruction was to give students an education in a language that would prepare them for upper-level university language study. Latin 1 and Chinese 1, the first languages offered at SOHS, were accelerated courses, typically covering two years of high school language instruction in one year. In this first iteration of language instruction, students reached the AP level in their third year of language study, which was beneficial since most of our students began language study only in their sophomore or junior year. Our first language courses followed the model of other courses at SOHS, meeting twice a week in a seminar-style classroom, with the bulk of the teaching done through prerecorded lectures, textbook readings, and regular homework assignments, all of which were done outside of class time. The pace was rigorous, often using a university-level textbook, and class time was largely dedicated to in-class grammatical drills, pronunciation, practicing sentence patterns, and conversation.

This definition of intensive as university-level coursework generally worked well when the school first began, but it proved to have weaknesses when our student population grew larger and younger. As SOHS expanded to include a ninth grade, we now had students who were significantly younger and had different goals for their language study. Ninth-grade students were not in such a hurry to reach AP by junior year. Moreover, the growth of the school also introduced a wide range of ages in any given language course. Since grade levels at SOHS are not determined by age, and since our courses were open to all grades, students in a single course could span in age from eleven to eighteen. Intensive for a seventeen-year-old is much different than intensive for a twelve- or thirteen-year-old, regardless of their native abilities in languages.

The other weakness in our definition of intensive was the balance of work done in class and out of class. While we followed the pacing of university languages, we did not follow the frequency of class meetings. Most language courses at the university level, be they beginning or not, typically meet five times a week. We were meeting twice and hoping for the same results. For many programs, intensive language study is defined by its frequency of meetings, with some intensive language courses meeting as much as two hours a day, five days a week. Our two hours of class time each week simply were not sufficient for the kind of language instruction we wanted to achieve. We needed a new understanding of intensive and how it applied to teaching ancient and modern languages to our heterogeneous student population.

As we thought about language instruction at SOHS as part of the larger SOHS curriculum and in line with the goals of the school, we found that focusing on engagement was the most important aspect. This shift actually gets us closer to the original meaning of the word intensive, which comes from the Latin verb *intendere*, meaning 'to direct one's reach toward' or, more simply, 'to direct attention'. If we look at the word in that sense, intensive does not mean a struggle or even something highly concentrated; it simply means something you pay attention to or focus your mind on. As our good friend Nietzsche reminds us in our opening quotation, philology, the study of languages, 'will not get things done' so hurriedly: it teaches how to read well, that is 'slowly, profoundly, attentively, prudently'. An intensive language course, then, should be a course that requires a student's full attention, and full attention comes from full engagement. This became the goal of the language courses at SOHS: to present something that would fully engage students and demand their attention.

Defining intensive as something that requires a person's full attention may, at first, seem straightforward. Students must (of course!) pay full attention to the language they are studying. This undivided attention, though, does not come readily in language courses at all schools. Language study is, first of all, treated in many schools as an elective. The student has their 'regular' classes and then, if they can, they squeeze in a couple years of languages. In this framework, languages are not always taught in a rigorous or serious manner because they are an extracurricular, not meant to take up much of the student's time. Language instruction also often requires regular rote memorization and drills, and the necessary repetitiveness of language study does not leave much room for independent thought or problem solving: a student has flashcards and must review them; the student has a verb conjugation and must conjugate it; the student has phrases to hear and repeat. While these things can be challenging, they are not always mentally stimulating or fully engaging. Finally, there can be a tendency in some language courses, especially in the first year, to infantilize the material and by extension the student. Students are necessarily limited by their understanding of a language's grammar and vocabulary, and this limitation can, at times, result in dialogues and exercises whose topics are irrelevant to a high school student, especially a gifted student seeking out new challenges. It can be difficult to take seriously a language course that is not taking the student or itself seriously.

We knew as we were building our language program that we wanted to do things differently, and different did not just mean being online. We wanted meaningful and engaging classes, we wanted something that was academically rigorous and serious for our gifted students, and we wanted to create a model where language courses were not treated as an elective. Achieving all of these things required looking at the outer administrative framework of the division, the classroom in which we taught, and the community we created for our students.

3 Building an Intensive Language Program

The logistics of the language division at SOHS are essential to our success. As we will see, these logistics—the framework we developed as a division around our individual classes—are the first important piece of creating a program that will engage our students as fully as possible, and our division-wide decisions about requirements, placement, course frequency, and curriculum all play a key role in who we are as a division and how we teach the things we teach.

3.1 Requirements

Language study at SOHS is not an elective but a requirement; students at SOHS are required to take two years of a language in order to graduate. Our division, though, designs our program and our curricula with the assumption that students will take four years of a language with us. Our courses are therefore thoughtfully planned out, with each year following directly on the previous year, and our instructors are in regular dialogue about textbooks, course topics, and major assignments in their courses. We are already discussing the third and fourth years of the program in our first-year classes and bringing our new students into a language community which we anticipate them being a part of for their entire high school career. A student's decision not to take more than two years of a language is something we take seriously, and we will meet with students to discuss why they are not continuing and assess as a division ways of maintaining student enrollment through all four years. When we take this four-year approach to language study, our students see us as invested in their language learning, and they, in turn, invest themselves in the program.

While the hope and aim within the languages division is for students to take a language course each year they attend SOHS, this goal can be a challenge. Students should, ideally, always have a language option for each year they are at SOHS, but when students join us already at an advanced level in languages or when younger students stay with us for longer than six years, it can be difficult to have enough courses beyond the AP level for each student. We have begun offering different kinds of advanced courses in the Spanish program (e.g. Directed Study, Conversational Spanish, and Spanish 5) to help us determine the best ways to expand each of our languages beyond a four-year sequence as need for such courses grows.

3.2 Placements

Correct placement into a language course is essential for student engagement. If a class is too hard or too easy, a student quickly becomes disengaged. Language courses at SOHS require a placement exam, and our placement tests are designed and redesigned each year to ensure proper placement for students.

One of the biggest challenges we face with these placement exams is the results themselves. Many students receive a placement lower than they anticipated, and this lower placement can often discourage students before they have even started the course. These lower placements happen not so much because our courses are so advanced but because they teach language in a scholarly and academically rigorous way. For example, a student may have studied Latin for two years, but may have never encountered, or been taught the names for, certain grammatical constructions. Or a student who can speak Spanish may have never written a literary analysis of a piece of Spanish literature in Spanish. To help set student expectations, Ancient and Modern Languages as a division now makes available mastery lists, documents detailing all of the grammatical topics and cultural themes we cover in a given year, for students taking our placement tests. We also work with our Advising program to get the message to families that our language courses are just as involved and engaging as all other SOHS classes and that a lower-than-expected placement is meant to give students a positive experience at the school. This trend in lower placement has also sparked a division-wide conversation about renaming our courses in order to move away from a model of 1, 2, 3 and AP as course descriptions. This could liken us to other divisions at SOHS where course titles like Textual Analysis and Argumentation or Democracy, Freedom, and the Rule of Law do not have an obvious level attached to them. For example, a course titled Latin Prose and Poetry, and not Latin 3, may still sound like a good course option for a student who has already studied Latin for three years and who may not want Latin 3 appearing twice on a transcript.

3.3 Frequency

As discussed above, we realized that our initial model of biweekly class sessions was simply not sufficient for meeting our goals in the languages. Language courses at SOHS currently meet three to four times a week. This class schedule is more frequent than other courses at SOHS, and we have found the additional class time requisite for successful language instruction. In some courses students still watch lectures, completing a significant portion of the work outside of class, but the increased class time means more time for engagement with the language, especially for our modern languages where students need more time practicing oral/aural communication skills in a real-time environment. Few people can learn to speak a language or understand it without the practice and confidence built through interaction with other people. This class schedule, as we have found, is the right balance between the seminar style of SOHS and traditional language instruction that meets on a daily basis.

3.4 Curriculum

Curriculum is more than just the textbooks we choose—it is the standards we have in class, the teachers who teach the class, and the respect we afford our students in the work we assign them. When we look at the curriculum of languages courses at SOHS, there is our over-arching goal of active learning and serious engagement with a language, one that is often tied to a strong integration of a cultural component. The curricula go beyond what is often seen in a traditional online course and, in many cases, what is seen in independent schools as well. What is key across all languages at SOHS is that our courses are more than chapters from a grammar book. Students are given assignments and taught in such a way that they must pay full attention to what they are doing. Intensity at SOHS does not come from the amount of work itself but from the amount of thought and care a student must put into the work. This in turn comes from the thought and care instructors put into designing each course. Ours is not a plug and play model where any instructor can step in and run through premade PowerPoints to accompany a textbook and review workbook answers. Each course is unique, altered and developed for the specific group of students in a given class. The uniqueness of our program is the uniqueness of our students; each language class is community based, both in terms of the community built in class and how students engage with the community around them or other communities (ancient, modern, local, international).

For the sake of brevity, we will look in this section at the Latin program but many of the pedagogical and curricular approaches taken in Latin apply to Spanish and Chinese as well.

The Latin program at SOHS has a four-year high school sequence as well as a two-year middle school sequence. We offer at the high school level Latin 1, Latin 2, Latin 3, and AP Latin. For middle school students, the first year of Latin is spread out over two years, and students begin with Latin 2 when they enter the high school. Students typically spend the first two years of Latin working through grammatical concepts and practicing with adapted Latin passages. The third year of Latin marks the transition to unadapted Latin prose and poetry, with students translating a rotating list of authors, including Caesar, Cicero, Ovid, and Catullus. The fourth year of Latin is then the AP year, and students read Vergil and Caesar in preparation for the AP Latin exam. The curriculum itself is driven by an emphasis on grammar and translation, building confidence each year in grammatical terminology, vocabulary, and translation. All students are translating unadapted Latin by the third year, and they have had a strong exposure to extended passage translation and narration throughout the first and second year.

SOHS Latin takes a grammar-based approach to Latin instruction. The instructors in the program largely come from a university background, having pursued advanced degrees in the Classics and having taught at the undergraduate level. SOHS Latin sees a value in formal academic training and preparing students to be contributing members of a scholarly community. For us this is as much about having students join a dialogue around Latin and Roman studies that has been occurring for a thousand years as it is about giving them the framework for Latin translation. We achieve this level of engagement in several ways: emphasis on textbooks and instruction that is grammar driven; teaching students not only how to translate but the terminology and vocabulary for grammatical constructions; clear movement towards the translation of unadapted prose and the ability to understand and use commentaries; incorporation of secondary criticism and literary analysis into upper levels of Latin. We are teaching students not only the Latin language but the language we use to talk about Latin, giving them a confidence and comfort level with the way scholars engage with the study of the language and its culture.

A unique aspect of the SOHS Latin program is the separate culture curriculum offered each year. We have found this culture curriculum to be essential for student engagement with the course. For some students, Roman history or mythology are the reasons they chose to study Latin in the first place, and offering dedicated time to explore these topics allows students to see how the language and culture go hand-in-hand. Students have dedicated textbooks on history and culture, and both topics appear on all assessments. There are also projects each semester that require a blend of historical and cultural research and prose composition, often with amazing results. Latin 2 students, for example, have produced a Twitter account for Cicero (in Latin, of course), a Facebook page for supporters of the plebeian cause (modeled on the Arab Spring), and YouTube reenactments of Roman banquets with family members (in togas!) reading from a student-produced Latin script. Our Latin program now comes with a disclaimer to families that they will, at some point, end up on camera in a toga before their student's Latin career with us is over.

The culture curriculum in the Latin program is also a space where students have numerous opportunities to research independently and then share collaboratively their research with each other. I often learn most about my students as people through their engagement with the culture curriculum. A student living in the Philippines, for example, cut papyrus from his own backyard to make into paper. His video included a fascinating, and unintentional, tour of his house and garden as he made his paper. Another student, who was studying music and pursuing his own career as a violinist and conductor, researched Roman music and then wrote an original composition based on the notes possible on ancient instruments. These projects were not students trying to show off; rather, they were opportunities for students to make connections between the ancient world and their own and to share their diverse backgrounds and interests with each other.

Finding time for this curriculum is a challenge, especially when Latin classes meet only three times a week. Much of the culture component in Latin classes happens through outside reading, prerecorded lectures, and class discussion boards. Each week, for example, students will have a 'culture challenge' to respond to, using a shared Edmodo or Tumblr page for the rest of the class to see. The challenges vary depending on the course level: Latin 1 students will be asked to find a depiction of a particular myth in art and discuss something they found striking about the depiction; Latin 2 students will find foundation myths in other cultures similar to the Roman story of Romulus and Remus; Latin 3 students are asked to use Caesar's cipher, described in their Suetonius reading for that week, to create a coded message (in Latin) to share with the class; AP students are asked to comment on a scholarly essay, listing two points they agreed with and one they disagreed with. These class forums provide a way for students to engage with the cultural curriculum in a meaningful way, while still leaving valuable class time for critical activities like on-camera translation or vocabulary drills. Moreover, they support the idea that classroom engagement and community does not need to stop when students exit the classroom. Indeed, for our students, these online forums are the places where some of the most meaningful engagement happens.

4 Language Instruction in the Online Classroom

We have seen how the outer framework of the language division at SOHS can promote student engagement. We have a clear language requirement for graduation and we design our program for four years of language study; we properly place our students to ensure engagement in a given course; we have our students meet more frequently so they get the exposure and practice they need in language learning; and we offer a curriculum that taps into the expertise of our instructors and the diversity of our students. All of these aspects of our program, though, could be replicated in a brick-and-mortar school. The next aspect of the language division at SOHS that we need to examine is the online classroom itself and how and why it is the best environment for us to do what we do in language instruction.

First and foremost, the diversity and talent of our students are hallmarks of the school itself and these students enrich each course and discipline in their own ways. We could not have the students we do, in one class, were we not online. Each of our courses find ways to take advantage of this student diversity and have each student's unique background be a contributing part of the class. For some of our students the online nature of our classes allows them to travel to the country where the language they are learning is spoken; other students may already be living in a country that speaks the language they study. The inherent globalness of our classroom community only further solidifies the importance of language study. Students also bring widely different perspectives to class, informed by their own upbringing, experiences, geographic location, and educational background. Our classroom community is automatically a global community.

Secondly, our online classroom allows for something unique and essential to our language classroom: consistent and meaningful participation throughout a class period. Traditional language classes can involve a lot of waiting: waiting for a turn to speak, to translate, to ask a question, to write on the board, to share an opinion. In our online classrooms, students can always be engaged and involved with the course, whether they are on camera speaking or not. As we will see, the various tools within our online classroom that supplement the persistence voice and video conferencing features—text chat, a collaborative whiteboard, breakout rooms—give language students at SOHS the ability for simultaneous participation at any point during class. An SOHS language student does not need to 'wait to be called on' in order to participate deeply and meaningfully in class, and this is essential for a community of students who are both gifted and online.

Finally, our online classroom gives our students multiple avenues for support that can, in turn, build confidence and promote course engagement. Language classes have an important and necessary performative element; students are often required not only to listen and comprehend but also to come on camera and speak or translate. In a traditional classroom there is no real alternative to this performative element of class: if you are called on, you must speak. As we will see, our online environment gives language students numerous ways of lessening the anxiety of being on camera and speaking in a new language. This is particularly important for gifted students, some of whom are more inclined to perfectionism and may feel they must be 'right' before they can participate. We are able to ease students into their language study by using our online classroom to our advantage, giving all students ways to participate and engage with a new language that will build their confidence and reduce their anxiety.

4.1   Text Chat

A component of our video conferencing environment, the text chat feature is a unique and integral part of our school, and our language courses have been designed to take full advantage of text chat. The benefits of text chat for language instruction are so great that one of our Spanish instructors has given a conference paper on the advantages of text chat in the Spanish classroom, and her own findings, bolstered by secondary research, show that text chat in the language classroom allows for increased:[2]

- meaningful communication—better/faster processing of what the L2 student hears;
- control of pace of interaction—for example, a student can 'interrupt' to ask the instructor a question which may lead to slowing down the pace of the discussion or an explanation of a related-topic grammar and/or content-based;
- negotiation of meaning—for example when the instructor asks the students in class what they think a vocabulary word means and to provide a definition in Spanish or a synonym in Spanish, the students collaborate in text chat offering their ideas in Spanish on the meaning of the word;
- noticing without interrupting instruction—one such example would be when a student make a written comment in text chat noticing

---

[2] J. Nadaner, "A Closer Look at Corrective Feedback in Synchronous CMC: The implications of L2 Spanish high school student-designed feedback for CALL," Eurocall conference at the University of Padua, Italy, 2015.

the similarities between the conjugations of the present subjunctive and the formal imperatives in Spanish;

- focus on grammatical and lexical forms—when students or the instructor type into text chat and a student, aided by the visual written text, is able to recognize and make a comment about a particular grammatical form or vocabulary word used;
- corrective feedback—the instructor is able to write into text chat corrections to mistakes students make while speaking;
- oral proficiency—by writing out their thoughts, the students are more inclined to speak up in class; and
- use of prompts—when the instructor writes a question or topic in text chat to stimulate class discussion.

A common theme in this list is the use of text chat for corrective feedback in a way that is nondisruptive and efficient. In a traditional classroom, a student would have to interrupt the teacher for this kind of clarification; in our classroom, a student question can go in text chat and be responded to at an appropriate time. Likewise, other students can respond to a question posed by a student, giving them immediate feedback. This open channel for questions and comments fosters an environment of support and collaboration for students, all of which help build confidence in language study. Our text chat also has a private text chat option, allowing students to ask questions or submit answers that classmates cannot see; this feature again removes potential hurdles for students seeking and receiving help.

4.2 Whiteboard

Even though the shared whiteboard is an invaluable tool in all courses, I have seen its value most readily in the Latin program. Collaborative work is difficult in Latin, especially in the higher levels of the program where a good deal of class time is spent having students translate out loud, one by one. Thanks to the shared whiteboard, students in AP Latin can view a specific passage together, collectively mark up the text, and add notes and comments before one of their classmates comes on camera to translate. While one student is translating, other students can answer grammar or context questions on the board or offer vocabulary hints to assist their classmate in their translation. The student who is translating on camera can explain their translation, marking up the text for everyone to see. For each individual student's turn translating, every student in the AP Latin class is still engaged with the text, whether they have been called on to translate or not. This kind of collaborative work cannot happen in such a simultaneous way in the brick-and-mortar environment. The whiteboard can even allow for anonymous participation, a chance for all students to put an answer on the board without other students, or even the teacher, knowing who wrote it. Some of my favorite teaching moments are when I put a topic or question on the shared whiteboard and ask my students to 'attack the board' with their thoughts. The screen magically fills with text, and even though I do not know who is writing, I know that there is a collective understanding happening and my students can all take pleasure in the group knowledge they see on the board.

4.3   Video and Audio

Integrating video or audio clips into language study is already a common occurrence in most language courses. What is different about using these elements in the SOHS language class is the ability for students to react to the video or audio collectively and in real time. In a Chinese class, for example, students watched a video about public transportation in China and a student commented in text chat, 'Are the buses that crowded all the time?' This comment, which was not disruptive, allowed for an extended conversation in text chat about transportation in China. Students who lived in China, or had visited, could add their own personal experiences and students living in other cities could discuss crowding in their towns. In the brick-and-mortar class this kind of comment, and subsequent conversation, may not be acceptable as the video is playing. Moreover, once the video ends in a traditional classroom, a student may no longer want to ask the question or the opportunity for this kind of extemporaneous conversation has passed. The real-time feedback, live texting as students watch videos or listen to audio clips, fosters a more natural flow of engagement and participation.

4.4   Breakout Rooms

Breakout rooms are the last piece of the online language classroom and perhaps the most necessary for the language division. These rooms are places for students in the modern languages to work with speaking partners, practice their oral and aural skills, and generally build confidence in a low stakes environment among their peers. With the teacher removed, students can ask each other questions, get explanations and clarifications, and generally benefit from peer to peer interaction in a way very different from the larger classroom. In the Latin courses, the breakout rooms are a place for small group work on a specific text or even a single sentence, and this close collaborative work again allows for simultaneous participation and peer to peer teaching and questioning. In all of our language courses, breakout rooms are essential for how we teach.

4.5   Challenges to Online Language Instruction

Our courses are dependent upon the technology to work in order for our classes to happen. The oral and aural element are two of the most important elements in modern language courses: a student needs to be able to listen and respond, in real time, in a way that is clear and intelligible so that instructors can give appropriate feedback. While in some courses a student is still able to actively participate even without a working microphone and webcam, in the modern language courses these tools are absolutely necessary. Students need a strong connection and to be able to be heard clearly each time they speak. Our reliance in language courses on working technology can mean class time is taken up by waiting on a student to get a microphone or webcam to work. Connected to this, students also need to hear instructors clearly, a requirement which can be compromised by connectivity issues. Our modern language instructors continue to discuss ways of using an immersion approach with their instruction that is successful for our students, and the biggest hindrance we face to immersion teaching is our technology.

Our online classroom, and varying connection speeds, also means that students cannot 'speak in unison' successfully. Since rapid-fire call and response and choral responses cannot happen regularly, students must give individual oral responses in class. While this kind of individualized speaking allows for individualized feedback, it also limits how often students can speak in class and can add a greater pressure on students to be correct when they do speak. The instructor's job in designing lesson plans is to create as many opportunities as possible for students to have practice with speaking in a way that is beneficial to the student but also does not detract from class time. Instructors have also introduced ways of managing this potential limit on oral engagement, including additional office hours only for speaking or using software that allows students to record themselves speaking for feedback. The Chinese classes, for example, have used a program called VoiceThread that allows students to record videos of themselves talking; the instructor or other students can then give feedback on the video.

These additional meetings and programs for assessing oral and aural understanding can be a time-consuming process for instructors. One-on-one meetings with students require thoughtful scheduling to accommodate the busy schedules of SOHS students; it is not as simple as grabbing a student after class for a five-minute conversation. Moreover, spoken language exams, to some extent, must be given in phases: a written portion with a proctor and then an oral portion with the instructor. This adds to the time students must spend on a given language class, outside of the scheduled class time, and adds to the schedule of the instructor.

5 Creating a Community

Our curriculum and the online classroom all create opportunities for engagement, for an intensive course that demands a student give the class their full attention in class and out of class. The creation of a community is central for success within languages and for the language program itself. We naturally face an additional hurdle at SOHS in creating and maintaining this community for students who are online, of varying age, and of diverse demographic backgrounds. What our students do have in common is their decision to attend SOHS and to learn languages in our unique environment; our job in languages is to draw on this commonality to help strengthen our students' connection to the program and the school.

5.1 Community within the Classroom

A strong classroom community enhances and elevates student engagement. This is not about making all of our students friends with each other but it is about making sure every student knows that their presence in class is necessary and important. It is also about creating a space for students where they feel comfortable and confident to participate. As we have noted, language classes can be especially challenging for some students because of the performative element, and having a positive relationship with fellow students can help ease this challenge. This familiarity is all the more important at an online school where students need to know that their classmates are real people, equally as engaged with the course, and that their own presence is vital to the success of the class.

Language courses fortunately offer many opportunities for students to engage with both the material and each other. Frequent in-class presentations and projects give students the opportunity to share their own interests and learn about one another in a way different than what they do in other courses. Indeed, students in language courses are often called on to speak about themselves, to share their personal interests or their daily life with one another as part of their oral practice. From where they live to how many siblings they have to their favorite music, getting to know students better is typically built into the language curriculum. We also have the opportunity in language courses for frequent one-on-one interactions between students, whether through conversational exercises or peer review of written assignments. In upper-level language courses students engage more frequently with each other through class debates and other group work that helps build strong relationships. Even the simple task of having students do peer review in courses like Spanish 1 and AP Spanish can be extremely beneficial for our students, who need added interaction with each other and the opportunity to see each other's work.

The language program, finally, has smaller section sizes than most other courses at SOHS, and our upper-level courses are typically only one section. This means that students not only get to know their classmates better but they have the opportunity to take a language class with the same group of students for all of their time at SOHS. The intimacy formed in these classes can be a powerful thing, and we often see strong camaraderie develop in our courses over the years as a core group of dedicated students return each year to resume study with each other.

5.2 Challenges to Classroom Community

A challenge we face in language instruction and building a community within a class is the wide range of ages and experience we can have in a given class. When our language courses first began, we did not need to worry about grade or age requirements, but as our school grew to include first a ninth grade and then a middle school, we began to see increasingly younger and younger students in our first-year language courses. At first we did not see any issues with allowing these young students to take our high school courses, but it soon became clear that these younger students, while no doubt gifted academically, were not yet socially or emotionally ready for the demands of a high school language course. We also faced issues with having such a wide range of ages in a single course: finding material engaging for both thirteen-year-olds and seventeen-year-olds is quite the challenge. The level of discussion or simply the maturity in text chat would vary. Moreover, the background preparation of students also varied. Upperclassmen may be better at basic time management, handling outside assignments and on-time submission without issue. Younger or new students often struggled with being prepared or remembering to turn something in.

We also found that as students advanced in their coursework those who began a language too young had issues when they reached the upper courses. Students in the third and fourth year classes are asked at that point to engage in sophisticated literary criticism and analysis, writing, in the case of Latin, formal essays on Augustan propaganda and Caesar's 'othering' of the Gauls. In Spanish they may be asked to read literature meant for an older audience, and in Chinese they may be discussing the problems of population aging or looking at differences between Chinese immigrant parents and their second-generation children, all topics better managed by older students. The writing and analytical skills of our younger students were not yet on par with their older classmates, and we increasingly found that a student in the languages needs to be on track with their humanities courses and formal training in English and history to successfully engage with the material we presented in the upper levels of language study. Too wide a range of ages and background in humanities was affecting the quality of both the classroom community and the quality of classroom discussion.

In response to these challenges, and in the hopes of continuing to build a strong community within the classroom, we have made two major changes to the language program: the first is new restrictions on the age and/or grade level of students entering our high school courses; the second is the creation of a middle school Latin program. All incoming seventh and eighth graders are now given Latin 1A as their default language option. Latin 1, Chinese 1, and Spanish 1 are open only to high school students. Interested middle school students may submit a petition—and in some cases take a placement test—if they want to be considered for a high school language course. These grade restrictions are, not surprisingly, tricky and we are still working towards having the best options for our younger students who may be academically ready for advanced language study but still need another year or two at the school to be able to fully and deeply engage with an advanced course. Heritage speakers or students from an immersion school are especially challenging: we do not want these students to take a year off from a language they are pursuing but we also know that our high school courses, especially our more advanced courses, would not be a good fit.

5.3   Community Outside the Classroom

The growth of languages and the division itself at SOHS has been remarkable. Language instruction at SOHS began with three years of Latin and Chinese, both of which were accelerated, college-level courses for upperclassmen. Now we have three languages, offering courses from the middle school level to post-AP, and a community, in many cases student led, has risen up around these courses. We have active clubs for each of our languages, and we have been offering summer travel opportunities for SOHS students for the past four years. This external community provides numerous outlets for students to stay engaged with the language they are studying in a way that feels less high stakes, and allows for deeper and more concentrated study in something a student enjoys. This is a place where we, as an online school, borrow from the model of traditional brick-and-mortar schools and their language programs to bolster our online community.

As instructors we are always looking for ways to help our students engage with each other and the community around them in meaningful ways. Our student-run clubs certainly offer opportunities for students to be with each other and pursue topics and activities of interest to them, but we are always looking for new ways to push our students out into the larger community of high school students studying language or into the communities themselves speaking the languages our students are studying. Latin and Spanish students, for example, take the National Latin Exam and the National Spanish Exam, annual exams made available to all high school students and for which our students can earn medals and, in the case of the National Latin Exam, receive scholarships for studying Classics in college. The Spanish program has also been exploring various ways of integrating Social Emotional Learning and Service Learning into the courses by finding ways for students to learn about their community, contribute to their community, and practice Spanish in a real-life setting. Students in AP Spanish and Spanish 1, for example, are tasked with finding someone in their community with whom they can have regular conversations, and this experience allows them to interview a person on a variety of topics, learn things from their perspective, develop a friendship, and practice their Spanish. Our summer travel opportunities are also aimed at helping our students engage not just with each in person but with new cultures or communities. While these summer travel opportunities are open to all students, instructors in Ancient and Modern Languages have played a large role in researching, curating, and chaperoning these travel options. These trips bring together all of our division goals of exposing students to other languages and cultures, building connections between students, and offering learning opportunities that are wholly engaging, whether that be on a service-oriented trip to Panama or a historically-steeped sightseeing trip of Italy.

While these sorts of activities may seem extraneous to language instruction, they are in many ways the heart of it. Contests, clubs, and travel create an identity for each of the languages, show students they are a part of something, and, most important, they re-enforce the idea that students are part of a much larger learning community. Learning language at SOHS will not in any way keep them from a part of language study that many consider the most enjoyable.

6 Conclusion

The Ancient and Modern Languages division at SOHS has worked hard to move out of the shadows of elective language study. Perhaps more than other divisions, we face a real challenge of enrollment numbers. Students not only have other languages they can study, but they can also study the languages we offer in a variety of different ways. Online language instruction is itself a booming business, and we are fighting in some ways for a part of that market. What sets us apart, and what makes us a part of SOHS, is the level of engagement and intensity our program offers. Enrollment in our classes is not a given, and we must work each year—and each day—to show our students the value of our individual course and our language program. We offer what other online language classes cannot—a unique community of engaged students and instructors, a unique curriculum that takes advantage of our community, and a unique teaching platform that gives our students a myriad of ways to participate in class and interact with their classmates.

As we look towards the future of language study at SOHS we continue to examine and discuss what growth looks like for our division. Growth could mean offering more languages or it could mean offering more courses within our current three languages. Would our student community be better served by a French program or a middle school Spanish course? By Japanese 1 or Chinese 5? Whichever direction we choose to go, we do so confident that our existing framework and the tradition of intensive language instruction we have created and refined over the past decade will allows us to grow and engage our students in a way that is unique and wholly consistent with the mission of SOHS.

7 Afterword: Middle School Language Options

When we decided to expand our course offerings into the middle school—and restrict access to high school courses to our high school students—we agreed as a division to pilot Latin first. Our aim with the middle school Latin program was to offer a place for our middle school students, both with and without prior language experience, to be introduced to the SOHS approach to teaching languages, and we believe that Latin provides a solid foundation for all language study, whether that be ancient languages, Romance languages, or Asian languages.

First and foremost, Latin gives a great primer on English grammar. Any language study will help students understand English grammar better, but the logic of Latin and its consistent approach to grammar will make this process all the easier. Seventh- and eighth-grade students are developmentally at a point where they both need a refresher on English grammar and can handle more advanced and nuanced discussion of grammar. Latin provides the best framework for this 'othering' of English grammar and the curriculum is built around unpacking and understanding English grammar as much as Latin grammar. The Latin program will also introduce students to key terminology in both Latin and English grammar (and language study in general). Students will understand main clauses, subordinate clauses, relative clauses, prepositional phrases, participial phrases, conditionals, and indirect statements in both languages, and they will understand very clearly how nouns, adjectives, verbs, adverbs, and pronouns differ from each other and when they are used (or not used).

Latin is also a language that requires the highest attention to detail. Students cannot rush through Latin and they cannot 'fake' an understanding of the language; it requires slowness and exactness, a great skill for students to learn in middle school. SOHS students, in particular, who are accustomed to associating being 'fast' with being 'smart' will benefit from finally having to slow down and demonstrate mastery through diligence. Memorization is also necessary for success in Latin, and, by starting with Latin, students will develop tools and skills for memorization that work for them and that they can carry into their other language courses. Latin grammar is a very pattern-based grammar with lots of repetition and lots of logic; students won't be memorizing for the sake of memorizing but will instead begin to see and understand patterns and reasons for what they are memorizing.

Middle school is, finally, a time when many students are first encountering epic poetry, mythology, and a more formal study of history. The Latin sequence provides a way for students to go deeper into these topics and move beyond a cursory understanding of the ancient world. The middle school Latin program gives students some of their first opportunities to think about how we study ancient cultures, how Roman approaches to government and philosophy impacted the Founding Fathers of America, and how mythology is more than entertaining stories explaining natural phenomena. At this stage in their academic development, middle school students are ready to think more critically about these topics with which they are already familiar.

References

Nadaner, J. "A Closer Look at Corrective Feedback in Synchronous CMC: The implications of L2 Spanish high-school student-designed feedback for CALL." Eurocall conference at the University of Padua, Italy, 2015.

8

History: Teaching History at the SOHS

MICHAEL SLETCHER

1 Introduction

The origins of education can be traced back to prehistorical times with human cave paintings and oral traditions. One of the biggest developments in the history of education occurred with the introduction of writing and literacy, which led to humans recording their customs and beliefs in different parts of the world. In the western world, historians of education might begin their study of modern education with the cultural and scientific accomplishments of the Mesopotamians and Greco-Romans. For centuries, Europeans inherited ideas about education from these civilizations, yet it was only during the late Middle Ages that the idea of the university emerged and, together with the combined influences of Judeo-Christian and Greco-Roman learning, established our modern concept of education with the so-called medieval liberal-arts curriculum (i.e. *trivium* and *quadrivium*). The university itself emerged from earlier European institutions, like monasteries and cathedral schools, which meant that the scholastic schoolmen of the Middle Ages focused largely on theological pursuits. Of all the arts and sciences, the most important pursuit of the medieval schoolmen was the study of theology. Logic, music, and geometry were also important, but they served as handmaids to the more important study of theology, otherwise known as 'the Queen of the Sciences'.[1] With the

[1] T. A. Howard, *Protestant Theology and the Making of the Modern German University* (Oxford: Oxford University Press, 2006), 56, and Michael Sletcher, "His-

Perspectives from the Disciplines.
Jeffrey Scarborough and Raymond Ravaglia.
Copyright © 2016, CSLI Publications.

introduction of the university, it was not long before grammar schools dotted the European landscape, serving the purpose of preparing talented youth to study at one of the universities. It was this dual model of grammar school and university that established our modern concept of western education—i.e. that secondary school served the primary purpose of preparing youth for the rite of passage to higher education and, respectively, adulthood.

Although the main objective of this dual relationship between grammar school and university was largely theological at the beginning, the university soon began to produce civic-minded graduates, like government administrators (trained in Roman and Common law) and physicians (trained in physics).[2] Accordingly, European universities and grammar schools moved gradually to a more civic-minded curriculum that produced careers in government, law, medicine, and education itself. These professions and others were solidified during the nineteenth century with the creation of professional schools and research universities, most notably in Germany and the United States. The modernization of the university and secondary education in a growing and complex industrialized world in the twentieth century belies a fundamental point about the development of education in a now post-industrialized world, the belief that we have progressed or surpassed the medieval pedagogical framework.

During the Middle Ages, the instructor would read a lecture from an original source and students in the lecture hall would take notes on the lecture. This established the pedagogical framework for the university and secondary education for centuries. Despite the movement from passive to active learning in the twentieth and twenty-first centuries, there still remains a heavy emphasis on the lecture at the university-level, especially at large research universities where class sizes are large and high faculty-student ratios make it difficult to utilize different approaches to active learning. For lecturers, who see the classroom as a platform to diffuse years of research and study, they, too, are reluctant to replace the lecture method with active learning in the classroom. In fact, the reliance on the lecture as the central pedagogical device in university learning today remains so prevalent that the old adage about higher education—often attributed to Mark Twain—still rings true: 'College is a place where a professor's lecture notes go straight to

---

torians and Anachronisms: Samuel E. Morison and Seventeenth-Century Harvard College," in *History of Universities, XIX*, ed. Mordechai Feingold (Oxford: Oxford University Press, 2005), 188–220.

[2] M. Sletcher, "The Rise of Civic Humanism and Civic Education in Seventeenth-Century Old and New England" (PhD Diss. University of Cambridge, 2003).

the students' lecture notes, without passing through the brains of either'.[3] This adage does not apply so much at the secondary level, where more developments have taken place regarding interactive lecturing and active learning. In the average secondary classroom, which usually does not contain more than twenty-five or thirty students, technology has allowed more interaction between instructors and students, whether the class is designed around interactive lectures or 'flipped teaching' (i.e. the exclusion of lectures during class time).

Technology is not a recent phenomenon in human history. It has existed from nearly the beginning of human events with the invention of tools, agriculture, and art. What is new regarding technology, however, is the possibility to educate in real-time across a vast space in what we might term the 'virtual classroom' or 'online education'. Although the idea of online education had its origins in earlier inventions that stem back to the second half of the nineteenth century with the utilization of electricity and the subsequent twentieth-century inventions of the transistor, integrated circuit, microprocessor, personal computer, and, of course, the Internet, in more recent years, the idea of massive online education—otherwise known as 'Massive Open Online Courses' (MOOCs)—has filled the public imagination, largely as the result of publicity by both the media and entrepreneurs. Much of the hype has revolved around the idea of a magic bullet to create affordable education for the masses and, perhaps equally important in tech and entrepreneurial circles, the next phenomenon or multibillion-dollar company in Silicon Valley.[4]

Interestingly enough, the idea of massive open education is not new; it has existed in various forms in the second half of the twentieth century. For educational administrators and national boards of education,

---

[3] Attributed to Mark Twain, quoted in: D. Koller, June 26, 2012, "Massive online education: Daphne Koller at TEDGlobal 2012", *TEDBlog*, accessed June 16, 2014, http://blog.ted.com/2012/06/26/massive-online-education-daphne-koller-at-tedglobal2012.

[4] For Sebastian Thrun of Udacity admitting that his MOOC courses are often a 'lousy product', see Schuman, 'The King of MOOCs Abdicates the Throne: Sebastian Thrun and Udacity's Pivot toward Corporate Training', http://www.slate.com/articles/life/education/2013/11/sebastian_thrun_and_udacity_distance_learning_is_unsuccessful_for_most_students.html and Max Chafkin, 'Udacity's Sebastian Thrun, Godfather or Free Online Education, Changes Course', http://www.fastcompany.com/3021473/udacity-sebastian-thrun-uphill-climb. For a more recent declaration of the MOOC failure by Stanford University professors John Mitchell, Candace Thille, and Mitchell Stevens, see Dan Stober, 'MOOCs Haven't Lived Up to the Hopes and the Hype, Stanford Participants Say'. http://news.stanford.edu/news/2015/october/moocs-no-panacea-101515.html.

this usually took the form of recorded lectures and exercises on cassette tapes, video (Beta or VHS), CDs, and DVDs. It also took the form of live local television broadcasts of university lectures with the expectation that students would audit or receive credit for the televised course after they successfully submitted their course assignments and completed the final exam.[5] For educators in different parts of the world, the idea of education outside of the brick-and-mortar classroom simply meant a supplement or addendum to the traditional classroom; in no way, did it suggest the idea of replacing the brick-and-mortar classroom with a new or better model. In fact, western nations often revealed more about themselves—their social and economic challenges regarding education—than achieving a universal model of education as an alternative to brick-and-mortar education. In Canada, for example, learning off campus or online is still associated with 'distance learning', revealing more about Canada's large geography and sparse population over such a large landmass. In geographical terms, Canada is the second largest nation in the world. Of its nearly thirty-five million residents, a significant number live in regions making it physically impossible for them to attend brick-and-mortar campuses or schools. Consequently, the country has associated online education with the problem of distance. In recent years, Canadian universities, like Athabasca University in the province of Alberta, have developed online education courses, but still prefer to associate online education with the concept of 'distance learning'.[6] Unlike Canada, Britain does not have the problem of such a large landmass in relation to its population. Yet it does have a long history with social tensions and conflicts stemming back to the Industrial Revolution and the establishment of a large working class. Consequently, it is no surprise that online education in the UK is often associated with the idea of openness or leveling the playing field

---

[5]Like the great lecture series on cassette tapes, CDs, and DVDs at many public libraries, university television courses also had the purpose of providing education and even entertainment to a larger public who lived in the environ and surrounding environs.

[6]The one exception I have found while looking at online programs at Canadian universities is Acadia University in Nova Scotia, which calls its program, 'Online Learning'. Acadia, however, places the online program under the university initiative 'Open Acadia', an obvious reference to the British idea of online education as an extension of the 'Open University'. At the secondary level, Canadian schools have made more of an effort to move beyond the idea of distance education (e.g. the Virtual High School in the province of Ontario), but like many other online schools in Canada and the USA, the classes are asynchronous (i.e. there is no live video instruction where students and teachers interact in real time). This is the most important feature that distinguishes SOHS from other online schools and makes it the best model for achieving high quality education.

for the British working class. With the establishment of the 'Open University' in 1969 by the British Labour Party, the idea of part-time and off-campus learning spread to different parts of Britain, and with the emergence of online education during the 1990s, the two concepts merged into one. In a society where one's education and accent establish social and economic standing, online education has become synonymous with 'open education'—i.e. those, who for various economic and social reasons, could not attend Oxbridge or one of the major British universities and, instead, attended the Open University.

It is harder to define the emergence and direction of online education in the United States, namely because it has taken more than one direction and because individual states often influence the direction of educational policies and curriculum. Overall, there have been a number of directions in the area of online education across the country, some being more successful than others. When it comes to innovation, technology, and education, the United States has taken a lead role and nowhere is this more evident than on the campus of Stanford University, where, in 2005, the founding of the Stanford Online High School (SOHS) by Raymond Ravaglia established a new model of education that would provide an online alternative to the brick-and-mortar school while maintaining and expanding upon the high standards of both secondary and higher education.[7]

If massive open education is not a new concept, neither is the idea of online education. It has existed since the invention of the Internet, yet, in recent years, there has been a major technological advancement that has allowed high-quality online instruction like that given at SOHS to become possible. This recent change in technology is the high rate of speed by which electronic data is now able to travel through bandwidth on the Internet, thus making it possible for live-synchronous video interaction between students and instructors. This latest technological development has allowed SOHS to establish an educational model of the virtual classroom, a seminar-style class that is live, interactive, and retains much of the same features of the traditional classroom, what might be termed a 'virtual Harkness table'.[8] In so doing, SOHS has created the only model of online education that provides synchronous online instruction to students at the secondary level. Moreover, it has incorporated the recent pedagogical trends towards flipped or inverted

---

[7] Scarborough and Ravaglia, *Bricks and Mortar*, xi.

[8] Scarborough and Ravaglia, *Bricks and Mortar*, 83. I prefer to call it the 'Virtual Oxbridge Tutoring Model', for I see the 'Harkness Method ' as a pedagogical method based largely on the Oxbridge model of tutoring individuals or a small group of students in a seminar setting in the tutor's office.

classrooms, but the underlying goal of the school has been to facilitate 'a far more traditional model of seminar-style coursework common at universities and some independent schools'.[9] Using this model, SOHS has created a paradigm shift in education, in which technology is used to build on the foundation of modern education and retain the best features of brick-and-mortar schools—in so many words, SOHS has not created a paradigm shift with the idea of dismantling or changing the traditional classroom, but rather to incorporate their best features in another format while providing further technological options to students both in and outside the classroom.

The study of history at SOHS is similar in many ways to the study of history at other independent brick-and-mortar schools. History instructors use many of the same pedagogical techniques to interact with students, whether in a seminar setting or in a one-on-one situation. In addition to other courses, they teach a set of core history courses in their area of expertise. Besides teaching these courses, they are homeroom teachers; they supervise school clubs; they participate on administrative committees; and they hold biweekly office hours for their students to discuss their classes or simply to discuss theories or questions about the study of history. If there is one main difference between the study of history at SOHS and other brick-and-mortar schools, it is the platform by which they teach—i.e. they teach online. While emphasizing the similarities between SOHS and traditional schools, this chapter will look at the challenges and benefits of teaching online in the section 'Pedagogy and Technology'. It will then look at the SOHS History Curriculum, showing the diversity of courses offered by the school, and conclude with a synthesis of SOHS's place in the online world of education—that is to say, its unique position in the changing world of education and the advantages and challenges this model provides for teaching history and other disciplines online.

2   Pedagogy and Technology

2.1   Asynchronous and Synchronous Learning

Recent interest in online education has focused largely on the idea of an educational revolution, in which millions of students from around the world would have access to high quality education at a low cost. This MOOC model was touted at a 2012 news conference announcing edX, a joint partnership between Harvard and MIT to teach courses online, and received a lot of media attention. University leaders at the time spoke enthusiastically about reaching a mass body of students

---

[9]Ibid., 105.

and some hailed online education as 'revolutionary', the 'single biggest change in education since the printing press'.[10] The belief was that one Nobel laureate professor could teach millions of students replacing expensive labor with cheap technology and increasing productivity.[11] This business model has since become less attractive to both educators and entrepreneurs, but still there were some important points regarding online education at the news conference. Besides the benefits of the flipped classroom, which included recorded lectures to be watched outside of the class, there were other engaging formats to present course content to online students. As John E. Chubb, former president of the National Association of Independent Schools, and Terry M. Moe of the Stanford Hoover Institution reported in a *Wall Street Journal* op-ed:

> Online technology lets course content be presented in many engaging formats, including simulations, video and games. It lets students move through material at their own pace, day or night. It permits continuing assessment, individual tutoring online, customized re-teaching of unlearned material, and the systematic collection of data on each student's progress. In many ways, technology extends an elite-caliber education to the masses who would not otherwise have access to anything close.[12]

Although Chubb and Moe envisaged online education as asynchronous and teaching the masses at a low cost, they did touch upon some of the benefits of using this asynchronous technology. Since its founding, SOHS has utilized this asynchronous technology, but the school has gone much further than this by implementing synchronous learning as the cornerstone of its online platform. In so doing, it has addressed a number of concerns about online education that might be of especial concern if SOHS did not use a synchronous platform, such as the ability to cheat on exams, tests, quizzes, and assignments without the presence of an instructor or exam proctor in the classroom or in real time.[13]

For history instructors at SOHS, there are a number of asynchronous and synchronous pedagogical formats outside of the class to assist students in learning the class content and developing critical, creative,

---

[10] J. E. Chubb and T. M. Moe, "Chubb and Moe: Higher Education's Online Revolution," *Wall Street Journal*, May 30, 2012, Op-Ed Section.

[11] Ibid.

[12] Ibid.

[13] D. Newton, "Cheating in Online Classes Is Now Big Business," *The Atlantic*, November 4, 2015. This asynchronous assumption about online education is so pervasive that one often encounters it not only among journalists and the general public, but among professional educators and academics. For example, see Srigley, 'Dear Parents: Everything You Need to Know about Your Son and Daughter's University and Don't.'

and problem-solving thinking skills. Like brick-and-mortar classrooms, students receive syllabi, course outlines, and documents about school policies. They access these handouts using a Learning Management System (LMS), which provides instructors with the electronic capability of 'handing out', 'turning in', and 'handing back' assignments, essays, and research papers, as well as conducting adaptive tests, quizzes, and exams. The LMS 'course schedule' provides a more detailed weekly breakdown of each course than the course syllabus and outline. Moreover, it provides online links and interactive course content designed by each history instructor to facilitate learning in an online environment. For SOHS history instructors, this includes embedding interactive maps, charts, documents, and databases in their LMS 'course schedules'. In courses that look at the social and economic developments of the Roman Empire for example, instructors might include the interactive mapping tool, 'Orbis: the Stanford Geospatial Network Model of the Roman World',[14] which allows students to evaluate costs—both in time and monetary value—of communication and transportation in the Roman Empire. As a dynamic, interactive tool that deals with variables like different types of shipping vessels, seasonal conditions, and multiple modes of travel on both land and sea, history instructors can pose social and economic historical questions to students who, in turn, solve them while considering environmental conditions and constraints that contributed to the movement of people, goods, and information.[15] In an online environment, students are able to solve these problems synchronously (as a spontaneous question in class) or asynchronously (as an out-of-class assignment) while, at the same time, generating historical data and information.

For history instructors, LMS links and interactive tools are designed to engage students more directly with the course material by linking both primary and secondary sources, interactive maps and charts, online databases, library resources, video documentaries and clips, recorded lectures with video and PowerPoint slides, PDF files, and other asynchronous tools for students to learn in a flipped and non-flipped classroom environment.

---

[14]http://orbis.stanford.edu

[15]Questions instructors might ask students, whether synchronously or asynchronously, 'What was the fastest way to travel from Rome to London during the winter?' 'What was the cheapest way to travel from Rome to London during the winter?' And questions that might relate to real historical events: 'If Octavian had to march his army from Spain to Egypt during the summer, which was the best means of travel for him and his army?'

Although SOHS places a premium on synchronous learning, it also makes use of a variety of other technological tools that enhance the asynchronous learning experience. These include recorded lectures, chat or discussion boards, email, and Skype study groups. With recent pedagogical trends towards flipped teaching, recorded lectures now play a crucial role in disseminating information to students when they are not in class. History instructors at SOHS practice the flipped classroom approach by recording a series of video lectures that cover major topics and themes for each history course. Students, in turn, watch these lectures on their own time and use them to prepare for upcoming class discussions. Among some of the benefits of recorded lectures is that students are able to watch course lectures at a time and location that suits them. In some cases, students might find it easier to watch lectures on their mobile devices while at home or traveling between locations. Another benefit to recorded lectures is that students have the ability to rewatch lectures before classes, tests, and exams; they also have the ability to stop and replay difficult or critical concepts of the lecture, so that they fully grasp the course material.

When it comes to lecturing, history instructors possess their own idiosyncratic styles. In the traditional classroom, styles can range from the formal to informal, from participatory to performance. Recorded lectures, however, do not allow for real-time participation. History instructors, therefore, rely on them to disseminate important historical knowledge, whether in a formal or informal lecturing style, and expand on the course material and historical scholarship. During the synchronous seminar sessions, they might choose to engage in the participatory style of lecturing to clarify or expand on certain historical topics and themes. This is done sparingly, however, and instructors use it more as a pedagogical device to provide historical understanding and context when students stray too far afield and need to be brought back to the main point. By engaging students in a participatory style of lecturing during live seminar sessions, history instructors are not simply asking students historical questions, but attempting to point them in the right direction. Typically this means they are engaging students with the Socratic Method of lecturing; in a brief and *ex tempore* manner, they are using the participatory style to direct class discussions, create transitions between topics, and, in few instances, push the reset button and begin the discussion anew when students stray too far afield.

If there is one capability about online classes at SOHS that clearly differentiates it from brick-and-mortar classrooms, it is the text chat feature. This is a unique and invaluable resource, serving multiple functions besides the most obvious—i.e. another medium of direct communication between instructors and students. In text chat, students have the ability to ask brief questions or request clarification while the instructor conducts the seminar, allowing the instructor to respond immediately, bank the question for the next phase of discussion, or even change the direction of the discussion based on student inquiries and observations. Students also have the ability to ask and respond to instructors' and fellow students' questions using the text chat feature. This capability, together with the audio-visual discussion, serves as a useful gauge of class engagement and comprehension of the material. 'In this environment', Scarborough and Ravaglia explain in *Bricks and Mortar*, 'it is easy to tell when students have energy to pursue a line of discussion further, when a topic strikes a chord with a particular student, when a transition is appropriate, or whether a student is expressing confusion or is pondering a possibility'.[16]

During live seminar sessions, history instructors have the ability to use the text capability to ask brief questions to see the students' level of understanding and engagement. This requires short-answer and fill-in-the-blank questions, or simply questions of interest that are designed to enhance students' engagement in the subject matter. For example, when covering the 1960s in AP US History, the instructor might pose a trivia question related to the section on the Origins and Rise of New Conservatism: 'Which person in national politics today do you think was a "Barry Goldwater Girl" in the 1960s?' Students do not encounter the question or answer in the course reading material, lectures, and slides, but they do become more engaged by historical anecdotes, questions, and trivia, especially when they are relevant to the present or their own lives. Unsurprisingly, many students fill the text chat with the names of prominent female politicians today and, yes, most guess the correct answer: 'Hillary Clinton'.

Students' comments in text chat allow SOHS history instructors to see who is paying attention in class; they also allow history instructors to simply ask students to provide 'yes' or 'no' answers if they agree or disagree with a statement. Although video-conferencing software provides instructors with the ability to create in-class polls and questions, to which students respond during class time,[17] in a more informal setting, instructors might choose to conduct polls or pose short-answer questions related to the course content or class discussions using the text chat feature. Text polling during history class

---

[16]Scarborough and Ravaglia, *Bricks and Mortar*, 93.

[17]Students also have the ability to respond to audio statements or questions by clicking 'agree' or 'disagree', which appears next to the student's name in the class's 'participants list'.

is not only a useful way to measure the students' level of engagement, it also engages students as participants of history and allows them to express their opinions on both historical and contemporary events and issues as they emerge spontaneously during class discussions. For example, the instructor might pose some of the following historical questions in text polls while covering historical events, themes, and issues related to human evolution, early human civilizations, the history of philosophy, legal or constitutional history, ethnic studies, civil rights, the environment, etc: Who agrees with the 'Out-of-Africa' thesis? Who agrees that culture is learned and not innate? Who agrees knowledge is learned and not innate? Who believes the American colonists had a legal right to separate from Great Britain? Who believes Andrew Jackson's administration was responsible for genocide during the Indian removals (i.e. the 'Trail of Tears')? Who agrees with any part of the Dred Scott Ruling, and if so, which part of the ruling? If you were president during the Harry Truman administration, would you have dropped two atomic bombs on Japan? Who believes that the Civil Rights Act should apply to private property? Who thinks gay marriage should be legal? Who believes that climate change is happening today and is caused, in part, by human beings? Students, of course, will analyze the questions in more depth based on the material covered in class and elaborate on their answers. This inevitably leads to further class discussion, but, in the end, text polling is a way to engage students in class and measure participation; moreover, it measures students' views on important historical events and contemporary issues and provides history instructors with a frame-of-reference of how to proceed in class. Do students understand the historical material? Are they able to connect the material with bigger historical themes and ways of thinking, and do they understand historical context when discussing the material in relation to contemporary history? Instructors can see if students understand historical context when asking a question as simple as, 'should gay marriage be legal?' Most students will answer the poll in the affirmative, and expand in text chat on why it should be legal, usually on moral grounds. When they see American polls as late as 2004 and earlier showing that a majority of Americans thought gay marriage should be illegal, they are forced to explore—sometimes with the help of the instructor—why most Americans within a generation thought so differently than they do? Such polling questions extend to a variety of historical themes and topics, including race, class, and gender. And, as a side note, they reveal something important to all history instructors: not only do they reveal what millennials, the next generation, think about the past and present, but, consequentially, what will be the future.[18]

In addition to asynchronous online tools, like prerecorded lectures and text chat, history students at SOHS attend synchronous seminar-style classes that meet biweekly for seventy-five-minute sessions. During these sessions, students interact in real time with their instructors regarding the course content and material while also having access to a shared whiteboard, text chat facility, among other communicable devices. In all our SOHS history classes, the educational objective of live, interactive seminar-style classes is not simply to convey the course content, but to develop students' abilities to think critically and question the material among peers, and even to question the instructors' knowledge and reasoning of the material.

> The primary function of the discussion seminar is. . . to engage students in the material in a variety of ways that deepen understanding, develop skills of criticism and argument, and enliven the topics. In the humanities [i.e. history], this can mean. . . delving into an analysis of the views at issue by, for instance, working collaboratively to extract the logical structure of an argument and then submitting it to criticism, electing competing views from students who must then defend those views against the probing of teachers and fellow students, and both illustrating and evaluating the implications of classical positions by applying them to contemporary circumstances.[19]

Consequently, the ability to remember dates, places, names, and basic facts is not so important in the study of history at SOHS. More important is the development of the students' cognitive and analytical abilities so that they develop skills of criticism and argument, and that they reflect on historical phenomena and not pedantic facts and

---

[18]Text chat not only gauges the participation level in class, it also has a private-texting feature, which allows students and instructors to text privately or openly in class. This feature allows instructors to communicate directly and privately with reticent or loquacious students, helping one, in a gentle way, become more loquacious while perhaps helping the other, if dominating the discussion or straying from the key points, become more reticent during class. Students also use the text chat feature to discourse among themselves, allowing instructors to see another medium of discussion during video-audio discussions. If students stray from the key points or subject matter during these text exchanges, which seldom happens during engaging classes, the instructor pulls them back with audio or text warnings. SOHS instructors, to a large extent, encourage these text exchanges, or as one *Los Angeles Times* reporter observed during a SOHS discussion section on Democracy, Freedom, and the Rule of Law, 'It's like students passing notes in class, except that this is sanctioned—mostly.' Mitchell Landsberg, 'More Clicks than Cliques: Love of Learning Propels Students from Around the World at Stanford's Online High School'; Scarborough and Ravaglia, *Bricks and Mortar*, 92.

[19]Scarborough and Ravaglia, *Bricks and Mortar*, 87.

trivia. In so doing, students learn to approach larger and more complicated historical problems by asking, for instance, why certain historical
events or phenomena occurred and, equally important, what were the
effects: What led to the Agricultural Revolution around 10,000 BCE
and what effects did it have on the world? Why did the Roman Empire
Fall? Why was there a Revolution or Civil War in North America in
the last quarter of the eighteenth century? Why was there an Industrial
Revolution and what effects did it have on Europe, the United States,
and the world? What were the causes and effects of World War I and
World War II? Why did the Soviet Union collapse? Why did al-Qaeda
attack the United States on September 11, 2001? The date of the final
question does not matter so much;[20] what does matter is that students
develop critical-thinking skills and the intellectual capacity to analyze
and understand historical phenomena over time and space, including
an understanding of contemporary issues and events.

In order to do this, students have to learn to analyze historical questions, like those in the above paragraph, by using social, political, economic, religious, and cultural intellectual frameworks. They might also
use other intellectual frameworks, like the environment, philosophy, science and technology, and law, depending on the subject or a particular
historical phenomenon. For example, when looking at the effects of industrialization in the world, students learn to analyze the economic
changes that took place, like the shift from a largely agricultural and
mercantile economic system to a modern capitalist economy; the social
and demographic changes, like the shift from largely agricultural and
rural settlements to urban manufacturing centers with large populations and the creation of a new middle and industrial working class;
cultural changes that are reflected in literature and art, like the realist
writings of Charles Dickens, Emile Zola, Honore de Balzac, and Fyo-
dor Dostoyevsky, and the realist paintings of Gustave Courbet, Jean-
Francois Millet, and Honore Daumier. Other intellectual frameworks
might include the environment and how the landscapes changed as a
result of the industrialization, as well as the emergence of new philosophical writings, like the writings of Adam Smith, John Stuart Mill,

---

[20]The date does have historical significance if we look at the Great Siege of Malta
(September 11, 1565), the Battle of Vienna (September 11, 1683), and the Battle of
Zenta (September 11, 1697). In the mind of modern jihadists, including members of
al Qaeda and ISIS, these three historical events, especially the Battle of Vienna, represent Muslim defeats against the West in what has been an age-old epic struggle between Muslim believers and non-Muslim infidels. Therefore, it is no coincidence that
the former leader of al-Qaeda, Osama bin-Laden, chose September 11 as the date to
launch a terrorist attack on the United States. J. Matusitz, *Symbolism in Terrorism:
Motivation, Communication, and Behavior* (Lanham: Rowman & Littlefield), 36–7.

Charles Fourier, Robert Owen, and Karl Marx; and the advancements in new technologies, like steam-powered engines and boats, and new theories in science, like germ theory and natural selection.

Typically, there is never one reason or one overwhelming framework to explain historical phenomena in a particular region or the world, but students learn to analyze historical phenomena from different perspectives and present their own reflections and conclusions in a seminar-based setting with both peer review and instructor feedback. Not surprisingly, the history instructor's pedagogical focus becomes more a reflection on teaching students *how* to think rather than *what* to think. For example, when students learn about the economic growth and industrial output of Great Britain and the United States in the nineteenth century, it is not uncommon for students to associate economic growth with improvement in the standard of living or quality of life, or to associate the process of industrialization with historical progress. If students move in this direction during a seminar discussion, the instructor is able to interject with a question of whether students would prefer to live in preindustrial seventeenth century or nineteenth-century industrial England or North America? Some students might associate progress with industrialization or simply with the idea of time (i.e., the later the period, the better), but others will inquire further about social conditions like race, class, and gender. This exploratory process is a way to get students to think about different historical perspectives, the multiple narratives and points-of-view that fit into a larger narrative about industrialization. During this process, the instructor might provide historical examples or documents to create a social or socioeconomic intellectual framework to underscore the effects of industrialization on different parts of the population. By understanding the social and cultural changes of a largely agricultural society—where many peasants and yeoman farmers worked and lived next to family members and by the rhythms of the seasons—to a largely industrial society—where many laborers worked long hours doing repetitive work, lived in crowded and squalid housing conditions, and structured every minute of their daily lives around the clock with no time for leisure, including weekends—students begin to understand the intellectual framework of analyzing the effects of the Industrial Revolution from a social perspective (and not simply an economic interpretation), and to question assumptions about historical progress in relation to technological advancements or materialism. In so doing, they can relate the social effects of the Industrial Revolution to other historical revolutions or technological advancements. In a seminar-class setting, the intellectual links and class discussions can go in many directions. SOHS instructors

are experts in their fields, and, as experts, they are continually impro-
vising, depending on the dynamics of the class. One real-time scenario
that might play out with regard to helping students think about historical phenomena from a social perspective is the following question: 'Are
you and your parents better off as a result of technological innovations,
like email, the Internet, and smart phones?' The irony of asking this
question in an online setting might come up as part of the class discussion, but what is more important is that students begin to think about
a pre-internet society and what were some of the social advantages and
drawbacks of these recent technological innovations. Developing students' analytical skills, like social, economic, and political intellectual
frameworks of historical phenomena, relies heavily on the experience of
live, interactive seminar classes and expert instructors, or as Scarborough and Ravaglia explain it: As 'the educational goal moves beyond
foundational mastery of basic concepts to an emphasis on developing
an ability to engage in a time-extended process of critical reflection,
real-time feedback and interaction is essential.'[21]

SOHS history instructors develop their students' creative, critical,
and problem-solving thinking skills during live seminar-class sessions
and biweekly office hours, which are also conducted in a synchronous
forum of live, video interaction. They also make use of a variety of
online resources and tools, but equally important from a pedagogical
perspective is the talent, ethos, and diversity of the student body. While
placing an emphasis on serving a talented and passionate student body,
SOHS has the unique position of serving a multinational and multicultural student body from across the globe.

2.2   History Instructors and Student Body

After the founding of SOHS in 2005, the first students to matriculate
were talented and bright youth who excelled in an online environment.
Since then, SOHS has continued to attract these types of students—
students who are intellectually curious, mature, and self-motivated. In
order to do well in the SOHS history program, these qualities are
necessary, especially since SOHS students are expected to approach
and discuss complex historical subject matter, including historiographical analyses of their secondary sources, as well as possessing the self-
discipline to watch lectures and do historical exercises and assignments
outside of class.[22] In addition to these qualities, it has been apparent

---

[21]Scarborough and Ravaglia, *Bricks and Mortar*, 82-84.

[22]If students lack these qualities in the online environment, they are probably
better off in a brick-and-mortar school where instructors can consistently monitor
their body language and their engagement level.

since the school's founding that small seminar classes or the blended, flipped synchronous-seminar approach to learning worked well with a diverse and talented student body, a great majority of whom craved individual attention from faculty members and peer feedback from classmates. In history classes, individual attention from professional historians helps students to develop essential critical-thinking methods while also learning to analyze texts and events in their proper historical contexts. In order to do this effectively, class sizes (or faculty-to-student ratios) do matter. Indeed, in the history program at SOHS, small class sizes have provided students with the ability to receive one-on-one and small group instruction while developing their historical knowledge and critical-thinking skills. Yet, it is still the quality of the student body that makes SOHS a success, or as Scarborough and Ravaglia explain it, the curricular and pedagogical approach has been largely designed around a dedicated and gifted student body:

> Our experience bears most immediately on curriculum and pedagogy for gifted, passionate students. As it stands today, SOHS reflects a view, acquired in work in gifted education prior to the [founding of] SOHS as well as during its conception and early years, that the optimal academic environment for talented and dedicated students is one in which they engage difficult material *with* similarly situated peers and teachers who have the academic background to inspire and challenge them. . . SOHS, its seminar setting, and a curriculum focused on courses sufficiently challenging and finely targeted to our students, are designed to make such an approach to education for talented students possible.[23]

Since its inception, SOHS has targeted passionate and talented youth. At the same time, it has targeted a dedicated and gifted faculty who inspire and challenge students with the highest academic standards and goals, in addition to cultivating the emotional and intellectual capabilities of individual students.

At SOHS, students studying history are bright and motivated; they typically take a leading role in their own education, pushing the boundaries of their learning by discussing advanced historiographical and historical subjects. SOHS history instructors often introduce them to university-level material, such as the analysis of historical texts, including course textbooks, and ask students to explain their historiographical significance in relation to the course content. In so doing, students are expected to analyze the course material at a much higher and critical level than most high school history classes, including advanced-placement history courses. The expectations of introducing SOHS stu-

---

[23]Scarborough and Ravaglia, *Bricks and Mortar*, 4.

dents to university-level material and concepts involves the employment of highly trained and skilled history instructors who can teach a variety of historical subjects in a specialized field, including self-critical historiographical analysis of the course material. For example, when teaching World History, the instructor might introduce students to the course by asking them why they are studying world history, or put another way, why is world history part of the SOHS curriculum? The question itself puts the students in the position of thinking not only about the curriculum at SOHS and other schools, but why they are taking the class in the first place—besides the obvious answer of earning another credit on their transcript. For more advanced students, like those at SOHS, they typically explore the complexities of the question, and even though the great majority of them will have little to no experience with historiographical thinking, they begin to develop critical reasoning skills about the course and textual content. That is to say, students learn (either on their own or by the Socratic Method) that 'World History' is essentially a new course in the history curriculum in the United States and the Western World; that if they had taken the equivalent of a 'World History' class when their parents and grandparents were attending either a secondary school or college, they would have taken a 'Western Civilization' class. In order for students to hone their historiographical thinking skills and understand why they are now studying 'World History' instead of 'Western Civilization', the instructor might urge class to discuss the world in which their grandparents and, in some cases, their parents grew up. In so doing, students discover a completely different world than their own, when a Cold War between the West and Soviet Union shaped historical writing and the school curriculum. In both the United States and the Western World, history texts and school courses reflected this world order; oftentimes, they included a subtext or an underlying theme that the West, with its democratic political structure and capitalist economic system, was the better of the two, or definitively the best form of civilization throughout western history. This underlying theme typically played out in history classes across the United States with an emphasis on the West and also drawing comparisons and contrasts between certain civilizations— ancient Athens and Sparta or ancient Greece (i.e. Athens) and Persia, one representing the ideals of the West (democracy, individualism, private property, and freedom of speech); the other representing the ideals of the Soviet Union (totalitarianism, collectivism, and censorship). The underlying message, though sometimes hidden in the subtext of the historical narrative, is clear: the West is the best.[24]

Once SOHS students understand the underlying message of many 'Western Civilization' textbooks, the instructor is then able to ask them to identify some of the major changes that have occurred in the last twenty-five years. Through class discussion, students identify the collapse of the Soviet Union and the emergence of 'Globalization' as a new historical phenomenon—i.e. as the new world order. Together with advancements in technology, namely the Internet, students begin to understand the dramatic changes that have occurred in recent years: that the world has become more interconnected through travel, commerce, and technology; that the world is now more multicultural and multinational.[25] From this historical shift, students begin to learn that schools and universities have begun to reevaluate their curricula and one of the changes that has taken place in history or social studies departments across the United States is to replace 'Western Civilization' with 'World History', a course that has more relevance to students living in the modern period of 'Globalization'.[26]

In addition to asking SOHS students why are they are studying world history, the history instructor might ask them to analyze their history texts throughout the year and provide historiographical interpretations of the present. In recent years, students have provided a number of criticisms of the world history texts, which include the lacunae of certain historical subjects and periods in Japanese, African, Polynesian, and Oceanic history. These criticisms are small when considering the full breadth and scope of writing any world history text from beginning to

---

[24]It is hard to find a 'Western Civilization' textbook that does not contain all or part of Pericles' 'Funeral Oration' speech, which sums up the differences between Athens and Sparta from an Athenian perspective. The same applies to Herodotus' 'Histories', which portrays the Persians as barbarians and unfree while the Greeks are portrayed as civilized and free. In filmology, there are similar examples of historiographical thinking, like the movie '300', which used the Herodotus model to portray Greeks as free and civilized and the Persians (i.e. Iranians) as unfree and barbaric. When the movie came out in 2006, the US viewed Iran as part of the 'Axis of Evil' and the greatest threat to American foreign interests in the Middle East. Unsurprisingly, the movie did well at the box office in the US, with the underlying theme of the Greeks (i.e. the West) defeating the Persians (i.e. Iranians).

[25]By becoming more multicultural and multinational, the world has also become less 'nationalistic' in the nineteenth and twentieth century meaning of the word. That is to say, ethnicity and religion play less of a role in defining the modern idea of the nation-state, even though some nations and older generations have struggled to come to terms with this historical shift toward a new world order.

[26]Although some institutions of secondary and higher education still teach Western Civilization instead of World History, most have made the switch to World History in recent years.

end and covering the entire globe, but it does open the discussion to why so much space is devoted to China in most world history texts to-day?[27] As a historiographical question related to the present, students observe the significance of China as a political and economic power in the world and conclude that history is being written not only about the past, but in and about the present. For SOHS students, who enjoy being challenged, these historiographical questions are popular in class. At the same time, these questions teach them to think more critically about their texts and what they are learning in class. Historiographical thinking requires bright and talented students to analyze textual evidence in relation to multiple historical contexts, but more importantly, it requires highly trained, expert history instructors who can spot these historiographical moments in real time and lead students to explore these moments and shifts during class discussions.

If there is a counterpart to a school filled with dedicated and gifted students, it is an equally dedicated and gifted faculty who inspire and challenge students to the highest academic standards while cultivating the emotional and intellectual needs of individual students. At SOHS, history instructors are at the top of their field; they are specialists in their field of study, holding PhDs and awards. Furthermore, they have written professional articles and books on a variety of historical subjects. As highly qualified specialists, they are also devoted to the profession of teaching history, which shows in their enthusiasm for the study of history and in their daily class interaction with students. In emails to their history instructors, students often express their appreciation of their instructors' enthusiasm and professionalism, with words like, 'You are such a great teacher and helped me to succeed. You helped with my paper structure, preparing for quizzes, and you assigned really interesting projects. My love for history is still growing. . . .' Similarly, parents express their gratitude to SOHS history instructors for their professionalism and devotion to their children, for recognizing their child as an individual and teaching to the individual:

> Just a quick note to thank you for how you interact with my son. Your feedback is both very affirming in helpful specific ways, and encouraging towards reaching the next level. That's something so often missing in so many leaders and would-be mentors. I appreciate the impact you are having on my son... Thank you so much for everything this year! [My child] has stretched his perspective and learned a lot in a subject

---

[27]The history faculty has used the 3rd and 4th editions of Robert Tignor, et al. *Worlds Together, Worlds Apart* for World History. This is an excellent and comprehensive textbook. The faculty, when choosing the text, noticed that some other world history textbooks focus largely on the West.

he has formerly not shown any interest. He is showing a little more intrigue with the broader world out there, and history in general. So, thank you!

In a seminar-based setting, history instructors challenge and engage their students on a daily basis in real time; they 'provide rigorous and individualized instruction for talented students precisely through a classroom setting in which students from around the world explore material together with teachers who are experts in their fields.'[28]

2.3 Geographical Diversity in the Online Classroom

When teaching history in a brick-and-mortar setting, instructors are often confined by geography and the socioeconomic conditions of that environment. That is to say, instructors inherit the social and economic experiences of students who live in a particular location or school district. This is more evident in the United States, where education often stems outward from local school districts to the state and federal levels, and where there are noticeable differences between different school districts across the country.[29] Social, economic, and cultural experiences of the student body can affect pedagogical techniques and approaches to how one teaches history in the classroom, depending on where students actually live and go to school. At the local level, race, class, and religion might affect pedagogical techniques in the classroom, as well as course content. A perceived homogeneous student body based on geography or location disappears completely when attending SOHS; in fact, it is geographical diversity that stands out, making SOHS a transregional and transnational learning experience, and defining the school as a truly cosmopolitan place of learning:

> SOHS has from the start featured a strong international representation, paired with considerable geographic distribution across the United States. And so it has been clear from the outset that not only does the online character of the school succeed in concentrating scattered populations of uniquely qualified and passionate students, but it also, particularly in the live, interactive setting, brings directly into contact students who embody the different experiences and perspectives that teachers often struggle to illustrate (or even themselves consider) for their homogeneous students.[30]

---

[28]Scarborough and Ravaglia, *Bricks and Mortar*, 84.

[29]This is clearly the case in public brick-and-mortar schools. Among independent brick-and-mortar schools in the US, the student body might reflect a broader US and international composition, though the great majority of student body will reflect students living in the vicinity of the school (i.e. the same state or a neighboring state to the school).

[30]Scarborough and Ravaglia, *Bricks and Mortar*, 87–8.

This cosmopolitan learning experience provides a rich, fertile ground for historical inquiry and enhances the dynamics of SOHS class discussions.

For history instructors, this online cosmopolitanism is a great advantage. Whether teaching American or global history, diversity among the student body provides a variety of perspectives based on the students' own geographical and socioeconomic experiences. One of the first questions history instructors are likely to ask students on their first day of class—no matter what history class they might be taking—is where they are living: 'What is your nationality? Where have you lived in the United States and the world, and where do you live today? The questions are not designed simply to know the nationality of students and where they might reside, but to inform history instructors about some of their students' life experiences—whether they live within or outside the United States—and how they, as instructors, might frame later class discussions around certain historical questions. For instance, as part of the AP US History course, 'immigration' is a recurring theme during the colonial and post-colonial periods. Often students end up discussing not only the historical events and government policies of immigration, but also the issue of immigration in the present. This is more commonplace in the second semester when students learn about US immigration policy from the Immigration Bill of 1965 to the present age of globalization. During these class discussions, it is not uncommon for students who live in different regions (say, New England or the Middle-Atlantic States) to have different views about US immigration policy than those students living in other regions (say, the border states of the South and Southwest). If students who live in one region dominate the discussion, history instructors have the ability to moderate the discussion by introducing other geographical views and asking students from different parts of the United States to express their own views based on historical evidence, or to express their own historical experiences in different parts of the United States. This enriches the class discussion and can be applied to a plethora of historical subjects and themes, including historical discussions about class, race, and gender.

Equally important at SOHS is the input and life experiences of non-American students. As mentioned earlier, SOHS has the distinct advantage of a multinational student body from different parts of the world (e.g. Canada, Latin America, Europe, Asia, Africa, and Australia). As part of the SOHS community, non-American students not only offer insights into world history courses and how the rest of world views the United States, but how to challenge US students to think about historical events from different perspectives. For example, when teaching the American Revolution, students receive a background in British cultural and intellectual history (i.e. British political ideologies in the seventeenth and eighteenth centuries and the British Constitution) so that they can understand the historical context and language of America's Founding Fathers. In the United States, many students understand the context of the Revolution in the Manichean language of liberty (good) versus tyranny (evil). History instructors often have to deprogram students from this simplistic way of thinking by introducing them to historical and political precedents of the American Revolution—that is to say, they are introduced to British history and political precursors that led to the separation between Britain and the American colonists (e.g. the British Civil Wars, Glorious Revolution, and the emergence of a radical Whig ideology in early seventeenth-century Britain that was eventually transplanted to America in the second half of the eighteenth century). By showing this continuing tradition of a republican ideology, students begin to see the American Revolution in a new (transatlantic) context, as a Civil War between British subjects that tore many friends and families apart. Some might even begin to see it as the First Civil War (or First American Revolution) which eventually led to a Second Civil War (or Second American Revolution), when a new generation of Americans finally addressed the issue of slavery: 'All men are created equal'. With an international online community at SOHS, class discussions include multinational voices and perspectives. The American Revolution, as just one example, allows British and international students to provide American students with alternative visions about their own history and the history of other nations and cultures. This transnationalism has an important role to play in the virtual classroom, especially when providing alternative visions to the class about politics, economics, culture, religion, and foreign policy. Indeed, as part of a cosmopolitan community, SOHS students have the benefit of belonging to a larger community and seeing the world through a transregional and transnational lens. Whether in or outside of class, they encounter a larger and more nuanced world simply by interacting with their fellow classmates.

3   The History Curriculum

With a talented and diverse student body, the history curriculum at SOHS introduces students to the rigorous study of significant historical periods and subjects, ranging from the origins of human civilization to the complexities of the modern world in the twenty-first century. As part of the process of developing historical skills and knowledge, SOHS students are introduced to a sequence of history courses that builds upon their recently acquired skills and knowledge as they progress through the different stages of curriculum. By taking the sequence of courses, they learn how to read and analyze primary and secondary sources, think about historical causation, understand diverse cultures and civilizations in different historical contexts, and write persuasive essays based upon historical analysis and research. In so doing, they acquire historical knowledge and analytical abilities to succeed at the university level and beyond.[31]

3.1   Middle School

In the first sequence of the SOHS history curriculum, students have the option of taking two history courses at the middle school level, both of which require students to have completed Enrollment in Fundamentals of Expository Writing. The first is Introduction to United States History, which provides students with an understanding of the major political events and social-economic changes in the United States between the American Revolution and World War I. Students, during the course of two semesters, learn how to think historically and how to read primary sources (e.g. letters, speeches, images, and artifacts). Through the study of primary documents, students learn how to analyze historical events through the eyes of those who participated in the historical events themselves. They also learn the basics of how to contextualize historical evidence by being introduced to social, economic, and political ideas of a particular time. For example, students might encounter certain words in primary-source readings, like 'franchise', 'suffrage', and 'citizenship'. Through class discussions, they are able to discuss the meaning of these words in relation to a specific primary source, which might include the Thirteenth, Fourteenth, Fifteenth, or Twenty-First Amendments to the US Constitution, the Chinese Exclusion Act of 1882, the Anti-Immigration Bill of 1924, or documents related to the

---

[31]The history curriculum, moreover, uses an interdisciplinary approach, helping students make connections between history and other disciplines in the social sciences and the humanities. At SOHS, there are a variety of courses in the areas of philosophy, art, literature, science, and foreign languages that help students draw these connections while studying in other areas. The courses related to the study of history at the middle school level include: Human Nature and Science, Fundamentals of Expository Writing, Fundamentals of Literary Analysis, and Latin. And at the high school level: History and Philosophy of Science: Great Ideas, Observations, and Experiments, Democracy, Freedom, and the Rule of Law, Critical Reading and Argumentation, Legal Studies: Constitutional Law, Literary Analysis and Argumentation, Textual Analysis and Argumentation, Modes of Writing and Argumentation, AP English Language and Composition, AP English Literature and Composition, AP Statistics, Study of the Mind: Psychology, Neuroscience, and Philosophy, AP Microeconomics, Advanced Topics in Microeconomics, Economics, and a variety of foreign-language courses in Chinese, Spanish, and Latin.

Woman's Suffrage Movement and the internment of Japanese US citizens during World War II. With help from the instructor, students learn about change and continuity, about understanding ideas and events in their proper historical contexts. As one example, history instructors, in the past, have assigned the Naturalization Act of 1790 and asked students what it meant to be a US citizen after the American Revolution? Based on this particular source, students learn that immigrants who came to the United States and became citizens were essentially 'free white persons', while Native Americans and African Americans who had lived in the same region for generations were excluded from becoming US citizens. When combined with other primary sources, like the US Constitution, students learn that the franchise only applied to white, adult males who possessed enough property (wealth), or by inverting the answer, Native Americans, African Americans, poor white men, and all white women were excluded from the franchise or having political rights in the new republic.

As the second course option, middle school students have the opportunity to take the course Empires and World Civilizations to 1800. This course broadens students' understanding of history, focusing on the origins, development, and interactions of complex societies, beginning with ancient Mesopotamia and Egypt and concluding with the formation of global networks in eighteenth-century Europe. In addition to examining the unique features of individual civilizations, students examine the similarities and connections between different civilizations. In so doing, they further develop their historical understanding and analytical skills by reading longer primary and secondary-source materials and developing more complicated analytical frameworks about continuity and change (i.e. scientific, economic, social, and political shifts over time and space). For example, when looking at the global network of ideas, commerce, and migration in early modern Europe, students go back in time to learn about a series of scientific developments in other civilizations, like the compass, astrolabe, and dhow, that eventually made their way to Europe and contributed to a new age of exploration. Equally important is for students to understand the economic and geopolitical shifts occurring in the world around this time, which include the Spanish *reconquista* and the Ottoman Empire's expansion and conquest of the Byzantium Empire, which, in turn, resulted in the Ottomans blocking Europeans from accessing commercial trade routes from the Near to Far East. With no access to overland Asian markets, Europeans developed new technologies from other civilizations (e.g. the caravel) and began to look westward to access markets in the Far East, thus ushering in the European Age of Exploration that changed the social, economic, and political structure of the world. Just as with Introduction to US History, Empires and World Civilizations to 1800 prepares students for further work in the social sciences and the humanities by developing their historical and critical-thinking skills, such as developing larger historical frameworks of continuity and change (like the one above) and learning about historical context. Moreover, it encourages students to develop original creative thinking based on the historical evidence.

3.2   High School

In the second sequence of the SOHS history curriculum, students have the opportunity to develop their historical and critical-thinking skills further by taking the course Revolutions and Rebellions. This course prepares students for advanced work in history through an exploration of the causes and nature of sudden, dramatic changes in modern societies, examining a range of texts and sources, including art, literature, political pamphlets, philosophy, and diaries. Although the study of specific events may change from year to year, this course focuses primarily on the origins, key events, and consequences of the American Revolution, the French Revolution, and the Haitian Revolution. Students build on content and skills acquired in earlier history and humanities courses and learn to analyze how diverse individuals and communities have experienced and influenced major social and political upheavals. While this course hones students' analytical abilities and prepares them for advanced work in history, it also prepares students to take the compulsory AP US History course in the third sequence of the SOHS curriculum.

Once students have completed Revolutions and Rebellions, they have the option of pursuing advanced history studies in either World History or AP United States History. The first, which is not compulsory, introduces students to world history covering the periods from human pre-history to the twenty-first century. Students explore economic, social, and political themes in world history; moreover, they explore religious and philosophical beliefs, as well as developments in science and technology, across a broad range of cultures and civilizations. By analyzing historical accounts, students develop and sharpen their skills in reading primary and secondary sources, answer difficult historical questions, and make connections between the past and present. In a similar way, the AP US History course, which is compulsory in order to graduate from SOHS, develops and sharpens students' historical thinking and skills. It begins with an analysis of Native American cultures in North America and ends with Globalization and the War Against Terror in the twenty-first century. By taking the course, students explore major cultural, intellectual, religious, social, political, and economic themes that have shaped North America and the United States over the centuries, and learn how to analyze historical accounts and understand major developments in their proper historical context.

While taking AP US History at SOHS, students learn how to prepare for the AP exam. Moreover, they learn how to contextualize historical evidence by analyzing social, economic, and political constructs and how these constructs have changed over time. For example, when reading the writings of the Founding Fathers during the American Revolution or Constitutional Period, students learn that most of the Founding Fathers were opposed to a democratic form of government. When reading the writings of public figures during the early republic and the Jacksonian Period of the 1830s, students learn that democracy was becoming more acceptable among the political elite. When reading primary sources, students sometimes struggle with interpreting the meaning of documents because they are prone to associate modern concepts and mores with the past, or the meaning of words in the past with the present. As they develop their historical skills of analysis and the context of words and ideas in the past and present, they sharpen their understanding of other disciplines, like philosophy, art, and literature. For instance, when students encounter the word 'liberal' or 'liberalism' in nineteenth-century writings, they seldom associate its meaning with little to no government involvement in society and an unregulated, free market. Rather, they choose to associate its meaning with the modern idea of government involvement in society and government regulation of the economy. Over time, the meaning of the word has changed significantly; students, reading their primary sources, encounter a shift when Franklin D. Roosevelt initiated the New Deal in the 1930s; they also encounter elements of its earlier meaning in certain movements, like the American 'libertarian' movement of the 1960s, spearheaded by Barry Goldwater.

The World History and AP US History courses, in addition to other SOHS courses, helps to prepare students for the final sequence of the history curriculum. For advanced senior students, they have the option to take a research-seminar course entitled Advanced History Research Seminar. During the seminar, students learn how to do advanced research while studying a major historical topic. Each year the topic changes. In the past, seminar topics have included The Enlightenment, Contemporary History, Empires, and Intellectual History. In addition to learning how to conduct research at the university level, students learn the fundamentals about writing a sophisticated research paper that investigates thoroughly a particular historical issue or problem.

Moreover, they learn the historiography of their topic, engage in historiographical debates, and eventually develop and discuss their own historical interpretations.

During the summer, SOHS history instructors develop and teach non-credit mini-courses as an extension of the history curriculum. These courses, which are part of the SOHS summer program, allow history instructors to create interesting and exciting courses for students who attend the summer program on the Stanford University campus. As non-credit courses, history instructors have the freedom to develop their own historical interests while engaging students in more popular themes of history. They also have the ability to organize field trips for their mini-courses, like the day trips to Google and The Computer History Museum, when students took The History of Silicon Valley course. In addition to this course, some of the other history courses that SOHS has offered during the summer program include Introduction to the Renaissance and the Age of Discovery, The Historiographies of Conquest in Ireland and Peru, The Declaration of Independence and US Constitution, American Abolitionists, Civil Rights and Education, The 1950s, Introduction to the Cultural and Political History of the 1950s, The Beatles, Existentialism, and Ideas of Society. While developing these summer courses, history instructors sometimes team up with SOHS instructors in other disciplines to provide interdisciplinary courses, which they teach collaboratively during the summer program.

4   Conclusion

Since the Middle Ages, the idea of western education has rested largely on two components: the classroom ('lecture hall') and the lecture itself. In recent years, there has been a movement toward active learning and flipped teaching, yet many educators are still reluctant to move in the direction of online education. Much of this skepticism stems from previous online models that are asynchronous and lack real-time contact between individual students and their instructors. As Mark Edmundson and others have complained about online education, as if they are speaking directly about MOOCs as the only model of online education:

> Online education is a one-size-fits-all endeavor. It tends to be a monologue and not a real dialogue. The Internet teacher, even one who responds to students via e-mail, can never have the immediacy of contact that the teacher on the scene can, with his sensitivity to unspoken moods and enthusiasms. This is particularly true of online courses for which the lectures are already filmed and in the can. It doesn't matter who is sitting out there on the Internet watching; the course is what

it is... Learning at its best is a collective enterprise, something we've known since Socrates. [32]

These are valid points if we take them as a response to the fallacy of the so-called MOOCs revolution that would transform education into a low-cost online platform for the masses. With all the media attention given to MOOCs over the last decade, educators have responded to the idea of online education as 'a one-size-fit-all endeavor', as synonymous with the MOOC model. In so doing, they have bypassed one particular model of online education that agrees with the 'immediacy of contact' between teachers and students and learning as a 'collective enterprise' and 'dialogue' in the classroom: the SOHS model.

When Raymond Ravaglia devised the concept of SOHS in 2005, he envisaged, in addition to small seminar-style classes and a highly qualified faculty, that the online learning experience would be synchronous. That is to say, unlike other online educational models, SOHS would have a synchronous platform where instructors would teach their classes live and interact with students in real time. With synchronous, small seminar-style classes and synchronous office hours, SOHS would allow instructors to have a dialogue with their students and provide one-on-one instruction. Moreover, it would allow them to develop their students' creative, critical, and problem-solving thinking skills. By doing this, SOHS would be able to provide an individual, high quality education, and this is what distinguishes SOHS from other models of online education, making it one of the few examples of synchronous learning in the world.[33] One might even think that Edmundson were writing about the synchronous experience of a SOHS seminar class when he writes the following about teaching:

> With every class we teach, we need to learn who the people in front of us are. We need to know where they are intellectually, who they are as people and what we can do to help them grow. Teaching... is a matter of dialogue... Every memorable class is a bit like a jazz composition. There is the basic melody that you work with. It is defined by the syllabus. But there is also a considerable measure of improvisation against that disciplining background.[34]

This model is expensive, since it relies on small seminar sessions and a highly qualified faculty, yet profit is not the driving force behind the school's mission, nor its overall success; its main goal is to provide

[32] M. Edmundson, "The Trouble with Online Education," *New York Times*, July 19, 2012.

[33] This is why Mark Edmundson's critique about online education in "The Trouble with Online Education" (above) does not pertain to SOHS.

[34] Ibid.

students with the best possible education in an online environment. Success, as Scarborough and Ravaglia explain it in *Bricks and Mortar*, 'does not equate to what is financially profitable, nor to what is scalable or represents an incremental gain in instructional efficiency, nor to applications of technology that look good at trade shows. Our duty [at SOHS] is first and foremost to be the best school for our students.'[35]

With an emphasis on synchronous learning, teaching history at SOHS is an engaging and dynamic process between a passionate and talented history faculty and an equally passionate and talented student body. In fact, when it comes to teaching history at SOHS, there are more similarities than differences between teaching online and teaching in a brick-and-mortar environment. As at brick-and-mortar schools, history instructors at SOHS follow a similar curriculum, cover the same material, and engage students in a dialogue about the course content during class discussions. And with recent pedagogical trends toward flipped teaching, brick-and-mortar schools are beginning to take advantage of technological innovation to pursue asynchronous learning outside of the classroom while reserving more time in class for active and interactive learning about the subject. At SOHS, history instructors, like brick-and-mortar schools, utilize their class time for engaging and challenging students in a dialogue about course content and materials, and posing historical questions. Similarly, they utilize out-of-class time for students to learn using asynchronous tools, like recorded lectures, selected primary source materials, links to historical sources and sites, and self-evaluation quizzes on the course material. Together, history instructors are able to play an active role of cultivating students to think critically, chronologically, thematically, and causally.

If there is one major difference or challenge that distinguishes teaching history online at SOHS from your average brick-and-mortar school, it is the faculty's heavy dependence on a talented and passionate student body. Students need to be intellectually curious, mature, and self-motivated to succeed in the online history program at SOHS. If they lack these qualities, they are likely to fall behind or become disengaged from the online seminar classes as the semester progresses. This is especially true regarding the flipped classroom approach to history, where students need to be disciplined and motivated to read the course material, watch the lectures, and do the exercises and assignments outside of class. If students lack the discipline and motivation for the SOHS history program, they are probably better off in a brick-and-mortar

---

[35] Scarborough and Ravaglia, *Bricks and Mortar*, 3. *Cf.* Derek Newton, 'Cheating in Online Classes Is Now Big Business'; Ron Srigley, 'Dear Parents: Everything You Need to Know about Your Son and Daughter's University and Don't'.

school where instructors can continually monitor their body language and engagement level.

Another area where teaching history at SOHS is different from brick-and-mortar education is the geographical diversityof the SOHS student body. The diverse social, economic, and cultural experiences based on multiple online locations and environs provide a transregional and transnational learning experience that enhances class discussions about historical themes and subjects. Whether discussing events in the past or present, SOHS students contribute a variety of perspectives based on their own geographical and socioeconomic experiences that might include different views on immigration, civil rights, federal/states rights, and the environment. At SOHS, students represent transregions of the United States. Moreover, they represent transnations that also enhance class discussions about historical themes and subjects. That is to say, SOHS students are not simply multicultural; they are also multiregional and multinational—they are cosmopolitan in the truest sense of the word.

At SOHS, a dedicated and learned history faculty is committed to promoting academic excellence. Through a broad and comprehensive history curriculum, they introduce SOHS students to a rigorous study of various periods and human civilizations, ranging from the origins of human civilization to the complexities of the modern world in the twenty-first century. While developing these historical skills and knowledge through a culminating curricular process of analyzing primary and secondary sources, thinking about historical causation, comparing and contrasting various historical cultures and civilizations, and writing persuasive essays based on historical analysis and research, history instructors at SOHS teach their students something more than historical skills and knowledge, something more than historical content, dates, and facts; they teach them to think analytically, to use their critical reasoning abilities to understand not only the historical content and topics, but the world in which they live today—to understand themselves and their place in a much larger world. History instructors at SOHS, therefore, do not put the emphasis on *what* students should think in the classroom, but rather on *how* they should think both in and outside the classroom, something SOHS students will develop and cultivate throughout their lives. In so doing, the history faculty and curriculum compliment each other, as well as the Mission Statement of SOHS:

> Through vibrant seminars, the rigorous curriculum challenges students to reason analytically, think creatively, and argue critically... The School's supportive environment fosters independence, strength of character, and a lifelong pursuit of knowledge. . . .

References

Chafkin, M. "Udacity's Sebastian Thrun, Godfather or Free Online Education, Changes Course." *Tech Forecast,* November 14, 2013. Accessed on June 17, 2014.
http://www.fastcompany.com/3021473/udacity-sebastian-thrun-uphill-climb.

Chubb, J. E., and T. M. Moe. "Chubb and Moe: Higher Education's Online Revolution." *Wall Street Journal,* May 30, 2012.

Edmundson, M., "The Trouble with Online Education." *New York Times,* July 19, 2012.

Howard, T. A. *Protestant Theology and the Making of the Modern German University.* Oxford: Oxford University Press, 2006.

Landsberg, M. "More Clicks than Cliques: Love of Learning Propels Students from Around the World at Stanford's Online High School." *Los Angeles Times,* June 17, 2007.

Matusitz, J. *Symbolism in Terrorism: Motivation, Communication, and Behavior.* Lanham: Rowman & Littlefield, 2015.

Newton, D. "Cheating in Online Classes Is Now Big Business," *The Atlantic* November 4, 2015).

Scarborough, J., and R. Ravaglia. *Bricks and Mortar: The Making of a Real Education at the Stanford Online High School.* Stanford: CSLI Publications, 2014.

Schuman, R., "The King of MOOCs Abdicates the Throne: Sebastian Thrun and Udacity's Pivot toward Corporate Training," *Slate,* November 19, 2013. Accessed on June 17, 2014.
http://www.slate.com/articles/life/education/2013/11/
sebastian_thrun_and_udacity_distance_learning_is_unsuccessful_
for_most_students.html.

Sletcher, M. "Historians and Anachronisms: Samuel E. Morison and Seventeenth-Century Harvard College." In *History of Universities, XIX* edited by Mordechai Feingold, 188-220. Oxford: Oxford University Press, 2004.

Sletcher, M. "The Rise of Civic Humanism and Civic Education in Seventeenth-Century Old and New England." PhD diss., University of Cambridge, 2003.

Srigley, R. "Dear Parents: Everything You Need to Know about Your Son and Daughter's University and Don't," *Los Angeles Times Review of Books,* December 9, 2015.

Stober, D. "MOOCs Haven't Lived Up to the Hopes and the Hype, Stanford Participants Say." *Stanford News,* October 15, 2015. Accessed November 25, 2015.
http://news.stanford.edu/news/2015/october/moocs-no-panacea-
101515.html.

Part II

Counseling and Student Life

9

Preface to Counseling and Student Life

In the first book we looked at the various structural aspects of the school and discussed how they worked. In doing so we talked about courses per se, rather than any specific courses as their disciplines would present them, and we discussed a variety of administrative and social services aspects of the school as viewed from the central office, and not from the front lines. As we noted during the introduction, this second book was intended to be an opportunity to examine one at a time the distinct perspectives that were previously merged into a gestalt view of the school. As with high dynamic range photography, sometimes the clearest picture of an object comes not from a single picture, but from a systematic overlay of different aspects of different pictures of the object taken in different ways.

The first section of this book provided an opportunity to hear from each of six academic disciplines. This second section moves out of the classroom into other parts of the school to provide a view of the students and how the school serves them both as individuals and as members of a vibrant community.

It is an embarrassing truth that in the original design of the SOHS we did not give any thought to counseling at all. The focus was largely on the academic subjects—how we would teach them in an online environment, and how we would stitch them together to form a school. We assumed that everything else would just fall into place—after all, we reasoned, these are smart and capable students, what possible need would they have for counseling? That this proved ultimately not to be the case was due in part to the success of SOHS as 'a school' rather than just 'a university-based program'. Because students were investing themselves fully in SOHS we were seeing all of the needs that schools see when they work with students of this age. The students may not have arrived with an expectation that they would be finding a complete school solution rather than just a collection of courses, but that they needed more than just academics quickly presented itself.

The first type of counseling—and here we lump all advising together under the banner of 'counseling'—that we added was college counseling. In the second year of the school, with our students moving toward graduation and beginning to apply to college, it was clear that we needed to play a direct role in the process, in part to help them make good decisions, but equally importantly, to make sure that the colleges understood who our students were and did not just dismiss them out of hand.

During the fourth year of the school the Director of Counseling position was filled by someone who both had extensive experience in independent schools and who had also just completed a doctorate in education with a focus on counseling. What was particularly illuminating about having her join the team was that she brought an expanded cognizance of the broader challenges our students faced and of what we might do to address those needs. We found that the needs our students had were not what some online learning skeptics might have feared. Rather, theirs were very common issues that all adolescents face, and some of which, like perfectionism, are somewhat more acute for highly talented and dedicated students. So the challenge was not that of figuring out how to deal with a school full of problem cases, but rather how to deal with ordinary problems using online tools. And for this reason the experience is illuminating not just for other online schools, but for all schools, as our experience has given us a unique perspective into everyday difficulties and effective strategies for providing support.

Just as it was with counseling, so too was it with taking seriously the supporting activities that our students were engaged in, and the broader community itself. The question of how one builds community in an online school is one that we grappled with from the very inception of SOHS. We knew that unless students felt like this was their school they would not fully invest themselves into it. We also knew that the difference between feeling that your high school experience was 'sitting in your room, working on your computer' and feeling that your high school experience was 'being in lively seminars with your friends, whom you often hung out with after class' was highly dependent on the emergent nature of community. We knew that this was not something that we could create on our own, but rather was something that we could create the necessary preconditions for, after which we would need to see what took root.

Over the first few years in the school, there were a lot of open questions about what the culture of the school would be. Would it be a two-class culture dominated by math-science students on one side and by the verbally gifted on the other? Would it be a school of lone wolves all pursuing solitary projects or would a community emerge?

The summer of 2007, which marked our first residential program, saw thirteen of the thirty students who had been online all year attend, together with seventeen of the entering class of fifty. The ensuing culture clash between the thirteen, who had a sense of this school as being their school, and the seventeen, who did not know what to make of the thirteen, ensured that we would have an active summer. The following year, instituting an e-pal program that paired one or two new students with each returning student provided the returning students with a mechanism for propagating those aspects of their culture that they were most invested in.

Because of the rapid enrollment growth in the early years of the school, each new year would have more new students than there were returning students. This influx, together with a permissive culture of supporting students in starting new clubs and activities, and the fact that the students were increasingly investing themselves into the school and looking to the school to meet more than just their academic needs, led to a fertile ground for community.

By the sixth year of the school it was clear that our garden was in desperate need of some tending. It was not so much that the weeds were choking out the plants, as it was that there was no general sense of landscaping, and as a consequence people would inadvertently walk on things they should not have, hampering their growth and generating resentment. Less poetically put, the scope of the extracurricular activities and student clubs had grown to a scale where someone needed to be put in charge full time. To address this need, the position of Director of Student Activities was created, which the following year expanded to Director of Student Life In the same way that the counseling office began to attend to the overall mental health of the students, the Office of Student Life increasingly made sure that students were part of a community. Whether through organized summer activities, or the graduation weekend, or through working with parent liaisons to encourage meetups in different geographies, the Director of Student Life was increasingly key to ensuring that for the students in the SOHS, their high school experience was 'being in lively seminars with your friends, whom you often hung out with after class, and from time to time saw in the physical world'. This is not to say that all the Director of Student Life did was to manage the 'physical world component'. Rather, it was the recognition that our ability to ensure that the school continued to meet the needs of our students required us to understanding what exactly were the needs of the whole student and to make sure that these needs were being met. This trend would continue further in the eighth year of the school when we introduced a special program for students who were engaged in substantive outside pursuits, providing a mechanism to ensure that such students would remain fully engaged in the life of the school, academic and otherwise, despite the considerable time devoted to their outside pursuits.

Ten years on, it is clear that when one establishes an immersive learning environment, in which students will be spending much of their time, building relationships, and facing real challenges, it is essential to have the depth of structure and support available to do what the best schools have always done—to pay attention to the whole child and to ensure not just the educational development, but the proper social and emotional development as well. This is essential, because if one is successful in building a school, an important part of that success will have been the emergence of a real community and the presence of students who look to the school and the community to meet their social and emotional needs. If the community does not emerge, or if students at the school do not engage in it fully, the students will inevitably find that they are just biding their time until a better school opportunity presents itself—one that does a better job of meeting these broader social and emotional needs. This emergence of a real community is not what just makes SOHS a better school; it is what makes SOHS a school, *simpliciter*.

10

Counseling: Meeting Student Needs Online

TRACY STEELE

1 Introduction

The challenges to educating students' emotional and social development in an online environment are upfront and often seen by some as impossible. For example, how can we offer emotional help to a distressed child living two continents and three time zones away? How can we support students' social lives when they are logging into school alone in their bedrooms? While it may seem perplexing and even paradoxical to imagine supporting students' emotional and social growth online—we have found, surprisingly, that many aspects of such support are in fact both easier and more effective within this virtual educational environment.

As technology continues to disrupt the traditional notions of education, we reimagine how and in what ways we are able to nurture and support the changes that our adolescent students undergo in this dynamic time period. Research has revealed a strong correlation between social and emotional skills and academic achievement. In fact, scholars have found that skills such as resilience may be as important to academic and personal success as IQ or natural talent. Furthermore, students who are able to identify and be aware of their own emotions and the emotions of others are able to take perspective, exercise empathy, and practice compassion to cooperate and be successful in social environments. Therefore, our school concerns itself not only with academic instruction and students' ability to be critical thinkers; we also work to help students develop self-reflection, ways to manage their emotions in productive ways, and strategies for reaching out and asking for help.

Perspectives from the Disciplines.
Jeffrey Scarborough and Raymond Ravaglia.

This chapter explores how SOHS leverages rapid technological advances to support adolescents' personal and social development as they move into emerging adulthood. As the Director of Counseling at SOHS for over five years, I offer specific cases and real examples of working with our students to illustrate how technology can be used to create more personal connection, provide support, and help enable positive change in adolescents. I also discuss the development and implementation of social and emotional learning programs online, as well as the limitations and considerations of meeting student needs in a virtual school.

2   Personal Development

Because many of our new students enter SOHS with a history of academic success and have often times breezed through the academic challenges presented to them in their prior schooling, encountering academic obstacles and challenges can often be a new experience in a student's personal development. Often, new students may be reluctant to ask for help because they hold the erroneous mindset that if they ask for help or admit to having difficulty, then they are no longer 'smart' or 'gifted'.

Take for example, Jacob[1], he had come from his prior school earning straight As—in fact, he had never before had a B on this report card. He decided that he would take a full load of classes at SOHS. They all seemed interesting and he was excited to jump in. In the first few weeks, however, Jacob felt extremely confused. The teacher kept referring to 'lectures' and everyone in the video-based classroom nodded their head and raised their hand to discuss such lectures. But Jacob hadn't discovered the link to the lectures on the learning platform. So he sat there each class, afraid to raise his hand or even chat privately with the teacher, thinking that he simply didn't understand the material—not realizing he was missing an important aspect of the class. As the first few weeks of school passed by, Jacob felt increasingly overwhelmed and he started feeling deep inside that this school was too difficult for him; he was simply not smart enough to be successful.

These beliefs are what Carol Dweck terms a 'fixed' mindset.[2] An individual with such a mindsetcounseling!fixed mindset believes qualities such as intelligence are fixed traits; they do not hold the belief that intelligence is malleable and can develop and increase with learning experiences. In fact, Dweck found that students who have experienced

---

[1]Names and identifying details have been changed to protect the privacy of individuals.

[2]C. Dweck, *Mindset: The New Psychology of Success* (New York: Ballantine Books, 2006).

repeated academic success in the past, similar to most of the students who apply and are admitted into SOHS, are more likely to hold such fixed mindsetscounseling!fixed mindset.

How does working with such students online differ from working with students in other schools with high achieving students? In a traditional school setting, the teacher can more easily support a student and may be able to encourage the student to open up and talk about his or her problem. In an online school, however, it is often easier for a student to be more elusive. Students might, for example, be tempted to feign tech issues rather than admit the real problem. Other ways to avoid contact by the teacher in an online school include not responding promptly to email, logging out quickly after class, or ignoring a private text chat from the teacher asking the student to remain to talk. Avoidance behaviors are not uncommon to see at the SOHS with students who are struggling academically. For such students, engaging in avoidance behaviors is an effort at protecting their self-esteem by attempting to preserve an identity they have developed over the years as the 'smart' student—one who doesn't need to ask for help.

While online schools such as SOHS that rely on technology may inadvertently facilitate avoidant behaviors, it is this same technology that can be utilized to address such behaviors. In fact, online tools and platforms can be leveraged to expedite help and support to a student both nimbly and efficiently, in ways that many brick-and-mortar schools cannot. For example, the use of technology aids in this early identification and notification process of possible student issues. At the start of each month, instructors are requested to update their gradebooks and a report is generated across all classes to identify students who are earning a C− or less in any class. After the first month of classes, Jacob and his family received two grade notifications—a C− in biology and a D in math. Jacob was shocked. He was ashamed. This notification reified his secret belief that he simply did not belong at the SOHS. Of course Jacob's parents couldn't understand what was happening. They saw Jacob studying his math and biology textbooks and he spent hours working on the computer. How could his grades get so low?

Jacob's family reached out to me, Jacob's counselor, for help. Using Skype I was able to meet with both Jacob and his family later that day in order to listen to their concerns. The family participated together virtually—mom from her office in the city and dad and Jacob from their home. We developed a plan of support that included reaching out to his instructors, attending office hours and seeking the help of a SOHS peer tutor.

I also met individually with Jacob to discuss various issues at play including helping him to develop study skills and tools to manage his workload in an independent learning environment. We spent time discussing Jacob's beliefs about intelligence and his identity—who was he if he wasn't the 'smartest boy in the school'? The first sessions with Jacob via Skype were ones in which Jacob's 'camera wasn't working'— often student speak for 'I'm too shy to have you see me'. So, Jacob and I used the instant message feature and typed about how he was feeling and thoughts he had about himself. By the third session, the camera began 'working' and Jacob looked forward to meeting with me for his weekly sessions. He even took time to give me a show of his room and his calendar on the wall, by walking his laptop around the room in a guided visual tour—as part of our discussion on scheduling tools that Jacob could use to improve his study skills.

Not only did technology aid in early identification and communication of problems with a student like Jacob, but we have also found, somewhat surprisingly at first, that students may be more willing to contact and seek help from a counselor in an online school than in a traditional brick-and-mortar school. In an online school, students are able to seek personal help in the comfort of their own familiar bedroom. Students who have a hard time asking or receiving help from others often feel more comfortable instant messaging their counselors online and texting them about their problem.

This was clearly the case when working with Susan, who had been struggling with depression and having thoughts of suicide. She attended our two-week Summer Residential Session on the Stanford University campus and I worked closely with Susan during this time. Yet, it was only after she returned home from the summer program that she felt comfortable enough expressing her suicidal thoughts to me. When I asked her why she waited to until she got home to tell me about her thoughts via text, when we were together in person just a week ago, she said, 'I felt safer texting you these thoughts because I didn't have to see your reaction'. In fact, by texting, Susan may have felt empowered by taking control of the way she revealed thoughts and feelings that may have felt to her, out of control. The opportunity to give students various technological mediums to express themselves are critically important and underscore the importance of suicide help lines, many which give teens the opportunity to text about their problem.

As an online school, we integrate such avenues of communication such as texting that may be particularly effective for teens. Students who may be struggling with a mental illness such as anxiety or depression, the onset of which often occurs during adolescence, may not be able to summon the strength to walk into the 'Counselor's Office' or wait in the office for an appointment as their friends or acquaintances stroll by. Rather, these students at Stanford OHS can begin an online chat and the counselor is able to respond, often in real time. As the student gets more comfortable with interacting and discussing his or her problems, they often agree to meet by video Skype. In this virtual environment the counseling sessions can take on a more personal meaning as the student and counselor can talk in real time over video—with the student never having to leave her bedroom and the security of her own space. In fact, research reveals that individuals, especially those who have dealt with emotional disturbances, social alienation or ridicule, may be more likely to seek help in online counseling sessions.

Meeting student needs in a virtual school is not limited to challenges with academics. As an online secondary school, we work with adolescents whose personal development may be made more difficult by a schedule of daily life that is too overloaded, serious issues with anxiety or communication, problems in the family, loneliness, or depression that the student is not able to manage on his or her own. By providing highly qualified and responsive counselors, SOHS is able to help intervene with emerging issues and assist students in developing an awareness of their own learning needs and an ability to express and receive help more efficiently and effectively than in traditional school settings.

3   Social Development

Similarly, beyond attention to students' personal development, SOHS has been designed to allow for important social connections. Students have themselves adopted technological tools to interact, build, and maintain social relationships with each other. Skype and other instant messaging platforms are the virtual hallways where students' social activity often resides.

Becca: Heya boa, watcha doin

Lisa: super tired cuz of haney's loooong lab report

Becca: me too finished but bout died. Probably flunked

Lisa: right—you always do better than me... oh well. I'm used to it.

Becca: come on, you will be fine... I can't wait till were done with haney's lab reports—they are crazy long.

Students often create Skype groups and name them according to their unique purpose. A group of new eighth grade students who met each other during the Residential Summer Session create the group NKOB (New Kids on the Block), and invited all eighth graders who attended the summer program to join. Or, as often the case, students in a particular class will form a study group to both get and receive academic help and also to interact socially such as the Physics Study group. Students' desire and need for peer connection in adolescence is no different for students attending an online high school—but the medium in which these connections are formed and the ways students interact in these groups may be markedly different. The relationships facilitated by technological communication tools, social media and the ever increasingly personal applications such as Instagram and Snap Chat that are adopted by our students to communicate and engage with each other in novel and dynamic ways.

Not surprisingly, we find that the students themselves make use of the technologies and structures of their environment to engage in age appropriate friendships and connections. For example, often we see middle school students engaged in role playing games with their friends—sometimes across continents. A good example of this would be the budding friendship of Hans, from Copenhagen, Denmark, and Erik from Reno, Nevada. Both eighth grade boys are passionate about playing the video game Civilization V: Gods and Kings. Hans and Nick take classes together at SOHS, and on Friday nights arrange to play the Civilization together in multiplayer mode. Meanwhile, they have Skype chat on and literally tell jokes that make each roll on the floor laughing—enjoying the newly minted emojis that let them express their feelings and silly comments quickly and efficiently. They stay connected to each other while they delve into the intricate game play that spreads out over several hours, with Hans signing off at 1:00am his time while Nick signs off back in the US at 7:00pm, and just in time for dinner. While many parents may worry about their child spending hours in their bedroom because they are not interacting with peers, find that these online games and activities can be in fact very social and inter-active.

As students move into high school, social interaction at SOHS, as in most schools, turns to social media and online communication. With the growing intimacy of peer relationships that adolescents experience comes inevitable social and emotional conflict. Close personal relation-ships for teens are at times fraught with tension and difficulties. Added to this, adolescents are at the same time going through a period of iden-tity development, as they try on new behaviors or roles, to help them to identify those traits that will eventually help make up who they are and later, who they might become. Certainly, part of this experimenta-tion will result in students' hurting the feelings of others as they adopt certain behaviors or may all together ignore or exclude others as they experiment in forming new and different groups of friends.

Of course, this pattern of identity development and conflict in relationships is no different for students who attend school in an online environment. In fact, these behaviors can be seen through the use of the same technological tools that students use to communicate and connect with each other. As Skype groups and other social media platforms serve as students' social landscape and environment, occasionally students become hurt and confused by these very groups. Yet, these actions are not in and of themselves reflective of maladaptive behavior. In fact, adolescents will test new behaviors in their interactions with people they trust and who do not have power over them. For example, they may use an obnoxious verbal comeback or make an off-color remark, but they'll do it with a friend or sibling, not with a parent, teacher or employer. So testing these social limits may actually be a reflection of a strong social bond among the classmates. However, at an online school, these off-handed remarks are often recorded on these technological platforms, so causal hallway conversations can be recorded, searched, and disseminated far more often that a brick and mortar school.

While the traditional notions of bullying and conflict are not absent in an online school, the medium in which they are conducted may be amplified through its written form and its encompassing presence in students' lives. Using hurtful or inconsiderate words, and repeatedly engaging in this behavior toward a particular person, as is the case with cyber-bullying, can have a more permanent sense when seen in the written word and may cause greater problems both for the victim and for the one engaging in hurtful behavior. These records of incidents are now able to be downloaded, swapped, and posted in ways never before imagined in the hallways of traditional schools and playgrounds. Meanwhile, being in an online school may make it more difficult to eliminate interaction in social media or other sites when these virtual sites function as a central place to socialize with friends.

Like all students growing up in today's digital world, everything students type or discuss on the internet, including all the pictures they may send to friends or social media sites become part of their digital footprint. More than most students, SOHS students' main social interaction is online, in print, and available to record, review and to analyze long after a discussion has been had. This makes discussions about digital citizenship a critical component of our work in helping students to develop as a whole child. We are obliged more than most schools to help students understand and realize how what they put out on the internet can stay out there and can come back much later to reflect upon them in ways they may not be considering at the time. Fortunately, perhaps due to the fact that we have the ability to be selective in admissions, students enjoy a safe learning environment and a supportive student body. During our anonymous annual needs assessments conducted by the counseling office, few students report cyber-bullying to be an issue at SOHS.

While SOHS students appreciate our caring and supportive environment, there is no argument that the need for physical intimacy—whether it be a high-five or a warm embrace—is important to the health and social development of youngsters. And, just as with students who feel lonely attending brick-and-mortar schools and who may lack a rich social life, being online can make it easier to be more detached and to have limited in-person connections. For our full-time students, this is most readily apparent when after engaging in a personal conversation online and becoming bonded with a friend, they shut down their computer and find themselves alone in their bedroom—again. They long to spend time with their friends in person.

In order to facilitate these interactions, all students at all ages are invited to 'meet ups' that are hosted by families in which students get together in person at locations that are close to where they live. Further, many students choose to attend the Summer Residential program housed on Stanford campus. Here, students often begin or develop the friendships in person that will last over the course of their time at the SOHS. In addition to attending the mid-year meet ups, students may choose to return each summer to spend time with these friends in person. In fact, surveys from this program reveal that one of the most important aspect to the summer program, especially for our older students, is 'free-time' to simply be with their friends—a coveted luxury that busy schedules and geographical distance make all the more scarce during the regular part of the academic year.

Beyond the meet ups and summer experiences, our SOHS counselors make a point of asking about students' social lives during our meetings with full time students. We flag those students who might be struggling to establish friendships and connections—online or offline. And we work with such students to help them build, develop, and maintain relationships important to students' social growth and development.

4   Supporting Students with Special Needs

Nathan is a passionate, bright and exceedingly optimistic young man who was born with cystic fibrosis and spends much of his time in a hospital bed. Due to various infections that accompany his condition, Nathan often requires days or weeks at the hospital to recover, missing large amounts of school. This had made previous schooling very challenging. However, Nathaniel found an ideal educational environment for him at SOHS. Nathaniel's love of learning and intellectual capabilities matched SOHS's deep curricular offerings. Because SOHS discussion classes were recorded, Nathaniel is able to watch the playbacks of the discussions sections that he misses. In addition, he is diligent about being in close communication with his instructors to create a makeup schedule that is reasonable for him and for the class requirements.

While the SOHS has been an educational boon to Nathan, it has not been easy or without struggle. And, the SOHS does not work for all students with medical conditions. While our technology lowers access barriers for such students, it does not significantly reduce coursework, so if an illness is particularly acute, it can be nearly impossible for a student to catch up on the work and discussion that was missed. Therefore, our approach to working with students who have special needs is individualized and managed on a case by case basis. For students with documented disabilities, our counselors work in collaboration with Stanford University's Office of Accessible Education to provide the appropriate accommodations and support necessary for equal opportunity for success in the classroom. Accommodations might include additional time on tests or a more flexible absence policy if the student experiences chronic health conditions.

SOHS does have a certain number of students identified as 'twice exceptional'. Along with their giftedness in academics, these students may also have a learning disability. These twice exceptional students often need additional support to ensure they have access to rigorous coursework while making accommodations for the challenges they face. For example, a student may be identified in the top first-percentile in intellectual ability while in the bottom thirtieth-percentile for processing speed. This makes test taking extremely difficult as it can take a student double the time to complete a test—resulting in final exams that can take up to six hours to complete.

Moreover, for those students we have who are on the autism spectrum, we find that they may be easily able to do advance computations or recognize complicated patterns in high-level science classes while, at the same time, struggling mightily to identify inference in an author's message. For such students, we might find that they have very diverse course schedules with university-level classes in some disciplines and grade-level or below grade-level courses in others. Many students diagnosed as being on the autism spectrum also report that SOHS provides a much more comfortable learning environment because such students can be easily overwhelmed with too many people, noises and distractions common in large comprehensive high schools. While an online school may work particularly well in addressing these external conditions and issues, often such students require intensive counseling as they prepare for college to find the type of college that can best accommodate their specific academic talents and learning needs.

School-wide workshops offered for students with special needs prove to be particularly helpful to students and families alike. SOHS provides transition workshops for students with disabilities heading into college—providing information, resources, and assistance in helping students advocate for their learning needs. Workshops for students who possess chronic health issues and school-wide workshops on mental health and well-being have been particularly helpful. One of the biggest benefits it provides is letting students know they are not alone and helping students to connect with each other for help and support. Beyond these individualized supports and services, SOHS also focuses on developing and implementing programs and structures in the area of social and emotional learning.

5 Social and Emotional Learning Online

It is getting near to four o'clock pacific standard time and the students begin to pop into the Adobe Connect Classroom. Mark arrives and types a quick hello. Soon, the other students come into the classroom in unison with the text chat starting to take its own shape:

Mark: Hi Everyone :-)

Maize: Hi guys, glad its Friday ;-D

Richard: Hi.

Susan: Sorry, I'm late, but my computer froze on me.

Carla: Hi all! @Susan, glad you made it in. Did you finish the work for DFRL last night?

Susan: No, not yet, but I'm hoping to stay up late tonight to finish and turn it in before the midnight deadline.

The text chat continues to move like a snake down the screen. It's 4:05pm and the guest speaker, Edwin Rutsch, from the Center for Building a Culture of Empathy has arrived in the classroom. As the leader of this group, I turn on my video and microphone.

Hi everyone, glad you could make it to our fifth session of the Social-Emotional Learning Group. Thanks for coming today. As a reminder, last week we discussed the notion of compassion and empathy, and how practicing empathy has been tied to positive outcomes including improved personal relationships and significantly better health. Today, we are going to spend the hour practicing empathic listening through empathy circles.

I introduce Mr. Rutsch and he invites the students to come on to video in the web based conference room. The students pop onto the screen, reminiscent of the Brady Bunch television show, all eight students in their respective box waiting for the next instructions. Edwin leads the group through the practice of listening and reflecting. Once the guidelines have been discussed, Edwin and the students begin to practice. Susan volunteers to go first. Edwin states, 'Okay, Susan, go ahead and just share with me anything you would like to talk about and I will listen and respond.' The small group spends the rest of the hour taking turns and sharing their own experiences, and also practicing listening to others.

The Social and Emotional (SEL) small group counseling workshop described above is one of the many proactive programs and supports that are offered to the students at SOHS. While SEL workshops and courses may be gaining popularity at some progressive schools nationwide—it is the ease in which students can participate in the online environment that lowers the barrier to entry for our students. Students in this SEL group session included males and females with differing levels of knowledge, experience, and skills related to social and emotional competencies. During the sessions, a few of the students opened up and identified as being on the autism spectrum, making social and emotional skills particularly challenging for them, while others disclosed their personal struggles with anxiety and depression. All of the students indicated a desire and willingness to engage in exercises and practices that would help them to develop social and emotional skills that they could use in the classroom, but just as importantly, in their personal lives.

The small group SEL workshop is one such program developed in the midst of a multi-year professional development project at SOHS that seeks to infuse these practices across the academic curriculum. In this development effort, social and emotional learning is not implemented simply as an add-on to the academic coursework. Rather, it is integrated throughout the academic classes and teaching methods. In this approach, we address important aspects of development including reflective thinking, emotional identification and regulation, identity development, empathy, compassion and purpose, and help students to relate these skills and understanding to the social and emotional lives that they inherently bring into the classroom.

While this project is still in its inception, SOHS instructors are leading the way in experimenting with strategies, lessons, and activities that facilitate this integration. We also look to leverage the design of our school, including our homeroom classes, to ensure that we are providing opportunities for students to be exposed to important discussions on topics outside of academics such as the notion of a digital footprint, cyber safety, and physical and mental health and wellness. Homeroom meets once a week through the academic year and provides an opportunity for students to be with age-appropriate peers. It is an opportunity for students to interact socially, to be updated with school announcements and sometimes just to hang out unimpeded by coursework goals and objectives. We use these homerooms to also have our counselors visit classes and once a month, our counseling department provides learning activities in the area of adolescent development.

Moreover, our Social and Emotional Learning (SEL) Committee—a group of instructors and staff interested and dedicated to integrating SEL competencies into our academic classes and within the general school culture—has also experimented in designing specific lessons related to emotional literacy and social and emotional learning to be delivered in homeroom sections. A few of the committee members developed several lessons in the areas of stress, friendship, and college admissions. Survey results of the learning activities with students were promising, particularly the topics and the intimate nature of the discussions. The committee members involved in the experience felt challenged by the lack of time to fully engage in such important yet personal topics. This experimentation, and our findings, will continue to help us create a dialogue through which we hope to see homeroom develop into a more advisory type of program where such topics and closeness might be cultivated. This will most likely require more commitment and training in the area of social and emotional learning for our instructors who lead these homeroom classes. While experts in their academic fields, instructors may welcome and benefit from additional training in supporting the whole child in homeroom sessions.

While it seems redundant to discuss technological tools in an online high school, in fact, it is as relevant here as it might be in a brick and mortar. What is atypical, is not that SOHS employs differing forms of technology, but how it leverages technology in supporting students' personal and social development. For example, we use technological tools to assist students in developing academic support plans, essential components of navigating a rigorous curriculum. As early adopters of technology, Stanford OHS students are often more likely to possess facility and ease with such tools than their peers in a traditional school setting. For example, a counselor can simply send an instant message to a student, 'Did you turn in your lab assignment we discussed last week?' and the message pops up instantly to the student, who at an online school, is most often on the computer during regular school hours. Further, using collaborative tools such as a Google Docs spreadsheet, both counselor and student can work to develop personalized schedules, timelines, and assignment trackers. The counselor and student can pull up the assignment tracker, write notes and discuss time management strategies such as backwards planning and chunking both efficiently and effectively. These documents can be shared in real time with students' families or instructors as a source of support and oversight.

In fact, students who may be shy or reticent about getting help are often more favorably disposed to this type of technological support and can try out these communication strategies in a much lower stakes environment over the computer. Younger students who begin at the SOHS, meanwhile are often not accustomed to a collegiate schedule. Therefore, this support and oversight is very important in helping them to gain and internalize proactive time management skills. As the students gain these skills, the support can be faded, or pulled back to allow the student to assume full responsibility. At an online school, these types of online educational supports and tools work seamlessly and effectively in helping students in their academic work while also assisting them to collaborate effectively among their peers who are dispersed globally. These skills also stay with students as they move into college and work life. SOHS students will most likely be comfortable working in virtual environments with different colleagues in various time zones around the world because they learned to do so at such a young age and have worked directly with the tools that can effectively facilitate this type of collaboration.

Beyond using technological skills for developing individual skills and abilities, we also can use technology to facilitate peer interaction and connection. Students' desire for connection to each other and the need to offer emotional support inspired the development of a student club, BIONIC (Believe it or not, I care). Using the Adobe Connect platform, students come together for club meetings sponsored by one of our counselors. They are trained in skills such as active listening, the limits of confidentiality, and when to seek help. They make themselves available to others for emotional support and help, much like a peer tutor might offer academic assistance. Beyond the direct one-on-one help through our web-based video platform, the group is also exploring ways to connect and support such as a 'kudos' program that sends compliments to students and staff via their email inbox. The use of technology in the area of social and emotional support on a school-wide level is another example of how an online school may in fact provide efficient and supportive spaces for students to learn, connect, grow, and develop as individuals.

6   Limitations and Considerations

While online technologies can enhance student support and help to develop the whole child, it is also important to note the implications and limitations of an online educational environment, particularly when working to meet student needs. For example, among the most important legal and ethical aspects of the school counselor-student relationship are confidentiality and privacy. When counseling a student in an online setting, it is difficult to ensure privacy—a family member may be listening in the other room, or the student might need to attend from a coffee shop or other public venue. Most online video and text chat programs automatically keep records of communications, including full transcripts of text chats. Therefore, SOHS counselors, perhaps more so than their counterparts in traditional school environments, must communicate with students and families about their confidentiality policy and the limitations of such a policy in a virtual world.

Keeping information safe and secure is not the only mandate that online school counselors have in this new digital age; student safety and appropriate channels of support must also be considered. Ensuring the availability of a counselor to respond effectively to students' urgent messages outside of work hours—to be able to accurately assess the situation, respond, and provide appropriate support—is incredibly challenging if not impossible in any school. Providing a school or counseling department web page with after-hours resources that direct students to 24/7 help is an important resource for students in need of urgent assistance, particularly in an online school when a student may be operating in a different time zone from support staff. At SOHS, therefore our school websites include emergency and after-hours resources such as referral sources and suicide hotlines.

Communicating with students online can also present significant issues with regards to the counselors' ability to assist a student in need. As a school counselor, it is important to be able to provide immediate help to a student facing a crisis. It may be much more difficult to do so if the student is not residing in the same city or even the same state as the counselor. Unlike a traditional brick-and-mortar school, the counselor working in an online environment cannot physically supervise a student while parents are on their way or while local safety or referral resources are sought. If a student ends a remote communication session or access is otherwise lost, the counselor may be left without any cues to a student's current well-being. Therefore, our work at SOHS includes counselor training in these scenarios. For example, we may work with local authorities as needed if we feel that a welfare check or other urgent support needs to be provided to a student who is geographically distant. SOHS counselors often refer students to outside support agencies and professionals as well as working directly with students' doctors, therapists and other professionals to help support the student during their time at SOHS.

The fact that our students attend our school from around the globe makes the process of providing referrals a unique challenge. Having memberships in national organizations such as the American School Counseling Association and the American Counseling Association allows us to tap into referral networks across the nation. We also encourage families to contact their local school district for referrals as the counseling offices often have a list of recommended therapists in their community.

For international students, referrals are even more difficult, particularly when cultural differences may include stigmas on seeking mental health assistance. A prime example of this is when a male student from a Middle Eastern country confided in me that he was having urges that are frowned upon in his society and that if he engaged in the activity in question, his father had threatened to commit him to an asylum. He reported having suicidal thoughts and didn't know where to turn. In situations such as these, we have had good success at contacting local agencies, using translators from our instructor pool and at Stanford, as well as contacting private international schools that often work with local agencies and therapists for their expatriate American students living and studying abroad. We are continuing to work to improve our ability to provide efficient and helpful referrals to our students nationwide, including moving forward on the development of a Mental Health Advisory Board that will be comprised of national and international experts whom we can contact for advise on specific student questions while also providing training and consultation to staff.

For a small segment of our population, however, loneliness and disconnect can be a real problem that impedes students from healthy adolescent development and eventually will negatively impact all areas of their life, including academics. As our students value academics and achievement, it may be easier for some to stay at work on their computer rather than make the effort to get out and try to make friends or to become involved in their own communities. Invariably, for some students, they choose Stanford Online High School because it is more comfortable. Students with social anxiety or who have communication problems or challenges find that this school can be a more welcoming and less stressful environment in which they can focus on their academics and be seen for their contributions in this area, rather in their abilities to engage in niceties and appropriate social interactions. While this may be true in certain respects, students are still required to engage in discussions in appropriate and meaningful ways in our classrooms and it often becomes quite obvious if a student doesn't have the social skills such as appropriate turn taking, providing and accepting constructive criticism, or even being able to come on the microphone and camera into the live discussion. The SOHS does require that students do have a certain level of social and emotional awareness to be able to participate fully and effectively in our school environment. And, if students don't have certain abilities in this area, we often find that they are unable to fully benefit from our educational environment. In such cases, the counselor can work with the student and parent to find a school that can better support their needs.

For the majority of our students and families, though, SOHS has been an educational boon. For some, it may be the first time they are truly challenged in an academic environment while for others SOHS allows them to be compete at a high level in a significant pursuit while also engaging in rigorous academic coursework. For all students, SOHS enables them to connect to a diverse group of expert instructors and talented peers from around the globe who are curious, passionate, and committed to pushing today's boundaries in order to continue to improve themselves and make the world a better place.

7 Conclusion

At SOHS we strive not only to develop students' intellectual capabilities but, as just as importantly, to support students' social and emotional development. We provide opportunities for students to connect with other students while also ensuring they have a support system in place. This system includes helping them to develop trusting relationships with adults to whom they can turn when faced with challenging times as they move through the changes inherent in adolescence. SOHS helps students to develop the skills important to navigate the world successfully, including communication, self-reflection and self-regulation. It is this attention to students' social and emotional development that continues to evolve and grow and that sets us apart from most schools, making us unique in the growing world of online education.

As an adolescent school ourselves, we are engaged in a process of constant experimentation and change—with the priority of student emotional health and well-being as our continued focus. We realize that secondary education is not only about academics but about providing students with the social and emotional skills that will enable them to be healthy and productive citizens of the world. While an online educational environment possesses inherent limitations and challenges, it is the unique opportunities not available in traditional school settings that may in fact more efficiently and effectively facilitate the development of the whole child in this new century. While we see clearly the opportunities that this environment provides for a segment of highly motivated students, the next question may be in what ways might these technologies, educational strategies, and school design employed by SOHS benefit all students?

References

Dweck, C. *Mindset: The New Psychology of Success.* New York: Ballantine Books, 2006.

11

Student Life

CLAIRE GOLDSMITH

1 Introduction

'Aren't students at SOHS socially isolated?' This was the question, framed in varying ways, that parents asked me repeatedly over the course of the five years I served in the school's administration, first as Director of Student Life and later in other roles including, ultimately, Director of Admissions and External Relations. Families were often surprised at my answer. After acknowledging that socialization is a key issue for the school, that it's something we rely on parents to help us address, and the school is not the right fit for every student, I would assure them that a thriving, genuine community exists at SOHS. In fact, I would say, the SOHS community is just as strong and vibrant, if not more so, than that of other brick-and-mortar institutions of which I'd been a part.

Ten years of educating academically motivated and intellectually curious students at SOHS have led us to ponder not only what it means to have 'community' at SOHS, but what it means in all schools. Are place—a physical school building—and time—all students meeting together during a defined school day—essential? We know that communities may form in other contexts when people come together, but that these conditions may not be sufficient to form community, and members may not feel the key sense of belonging (a clear example: waiting at the DMV). Conversely, thriving communities can form where we least expect them. When both place and time are stripped away, what is left? If, in our unique meeting of minds we have found real community, what are its essential elements?

Perspectives from the Disciplines.
Jeffrey Scarborough and Raymond Ravaglia.
Copyright © 2016, CSLI Publications.

The first volume of this set discusses the notion of community in schools, arguing that SOHS has indeed created community. It exists both online and in person, through school-sponsored activities and casual interactions, and is made possible precisely because SOHS is not merely a collection of courses but a true school. This chapter seeks to explore the *meaning* of community in the context of SOHS and implications for further study of community in this context.

2 What is Community Anyway?

The success of Stanford Online High School marks an important milestone in the history of schooling—the emergence of a school that looks fundamentally different from most others. It is also the kind of school where observers least expect to find community; skeptical questions about student relationships, isolation, and feeling part of a school come up in most cursory discussions of the school. The academic literature on school community confirms the logic of these questions; educational researchers have always become most concerned with community in schools where it seemed the most unlikely to exist. If the transition to an industrialized school system—and further school reform in the twentieth century—raised questions about the disappearance of community in schools, the existence of online schools raises them in new ways. Because schools like SOHS redefine the meaning of school as existing in a brick-and-mortar context at all, the same questions about how all schools form community must be raised anew.

The first framing of schools as 'communities' emerged only after a perceived threat to community in the late nineteenth and early twentieth centuries. At that time, schools moved from being organizations cemented to local communities, to larger, bureaucratic and professionally-run systems that served changing, often immigrant, populations and sought to prepare a national industrial workforce. Educational theorist and psychologist John Dewey, who in the first half of the twentieth century described schools as communities and emphasized student social groups, did so in the context of a warning against an overly bureaucratic and instrumental school system that churned out an efficient workforce.

Picking up on Dewey's concerns, the last quarter of the twentieth century re-engaged questions of school community as school centralization, student achievement, and social justice became hot-button issues. Researchers over the last fifty years found correlations between strong school communities and student achievement, between strong teacher professional communities and efficacy, and between an 'ethic of care' in schools and increased focus on social justice.[1] Most importantly, this

[1]G. Furman, ed., *School as Community: From Promise to Practice* (Albany:

scholarship leaves us with a thoughtful definition of 'community' in the context of schools, one that is an 'affective experience or psychological state'. That is, if members of the community do not feel a sense of community, one does not exist.[2] This feeling is most commonly associated with a sense of belonging; in other words, feeling 'securely connected with others in the environment' and experiencing 'oneself as worthy of love and respect'.[3] These traits in a communityhave been found to correlate with student success.[4]

Given the definition of school community from Dewey to today—and community's ties to student success—the question becomes how school leaders can foster this sense of belonging. Researchers have posited that the 'primary condition necessary for the development of relationship is frequent and affectively positive interaction'.[5] Moreover, this interaction must occur both in the classroom and outside, and it must be cultivated. Dewey describes this notion clearly, noting that while students are naturally sociable, community requires thought and planning ahead, and educators must create activities 'in which all individuals have an opportunity to contribute something'.[6]

In the context of SOHS, both interaction and the educator's role in creating that interaction foster community. SOHS thrives on the key philosophical underpinning that students must come together at the same time and place for class in live, interactive seminars. Yet they are not necessarily 'together' in the same time and space the rest of the day. SOHS proves that a school need not bring students physically together to interact from 8:00am to 4:00pm to create community. In fact, SOHS challenges the notion of interaction—how much student interaction is really necessary to form community? Is there a minimum requirement of 'synchronousity' for community to form? Similarly, SOHS forces us to investigate how much educators should purposefully direct the formation of community, as it is a school whose adults build community hand-in-hand with students.

The online nature of SOHS is not the only characteristic that would seem to challenge community; it is also the fact that SOHS students hail from across the world and from as many familial, social, educational, religious, ethnic, and socioeconomic contexts as there are students in

---

State University of New York Press), 8.

[2] Ibid., 11–12.

[3] K. Osterman, "Schools as Community for Students," in *School as Community: From Promise to Practice*, ed. Gail Furnman (Albany: State University of New York Press), 167–168.

[4] Ibid., 168–170.

[5] Ibid., 175.

[6] J. Dewey, *Experience and Education* (New York: Touchstone, 1938), 56.

the school. If theorists worried that the transition from community-based schools to large urban ones drawing a diverse population could rupture communities, surely a school like SOHS challenges traditional notions of a cohesive community. Instead, SOHS thrives as a community in part because of the diversity of its students, demonstrating the possibilities for belonging in communities like it and the conditions necessary for that belonging. Of course, selection of a certain student body through admission—a luxury of independent schools—helps to create and solidify this community by ensuring that students understand the mission, values, and expectations of the school they are joining and can contribute positively to it.

SOHS is at the forefront of educational innovation, and it continues to evolve. In recent years, efforts to experiment with blended learning—taking the in-person online and the online in-person—raise yet other questions about community and hold implications for other kinds of schools. This evolution at SOHS and at many schools will continue to challenge our notions of traditional school and community.

3 Belonging: Diversity, and Commonality

While we at SOHS often use our various clubs and activities, meet-ups, and in-person events as a proxy for 'community', these are merely manifestations of community, or ways to foster it—they do not themselves point to an 'affective experience or psychological state'.[7] Instead, the school community is marked by something deeper: a sense of belonging and mattering to others, the presence of trust and safety, and the feeling of connection.[8]

When SOHS moved from being a collection of academic courses to a true school in its early years, its community had to broaden from students identifying with a particular section of high-level math, for example, to a wider school affinity. Devoutly synchronous, SOHS promotes the notion that learning is an inherently social and relational function. The community of the classroom is therefore the most natural. Yet community at SOHS spills out from the classroom to the interstices of the school—the spaces between a class and a club meeting or in-person meet-up. Without a school building or a set time to interact 'at school', our students have created community, and one that is marked by this sense of belonging.

SOHS students speak to the real bonds they've formed with others at the school. 'Although students are separated by space and time', writes

---

[7]Furman, *School as Community: From Promise to Practice*, 11.
[8]Osterman, "Students' Need for Belonging in the School Community", 323.

one student, 'I have developed unique bonds with fellow classmates and friends'. Notes another, 'Despite not being able to see each other every day, the Skype, social media and club communities thrive.'

> On any given morning, I (a 15 year old girl from sunny San Diego, California) will wake up and sign onto Skype to find my friend in East Brunswick, New Jersey, has been up for hours training at the ice skating rink, or I will come home from the store to find my friend has been scuba diving in Oahu, Hawaii.

And from another: 'Truly, SOHS students never let the distance keep them apart, and I believe that the SOHS community is one of the best groups of students I have met.' (The preceding chapter in this volume further describes student social development in an online environment.)

Beyond friendships and ties with other students, students attest to having a group identity as a SOHS student. For them, the community is what facilitates social relationships. Writes one, 'The community at SOHS is so rich and diverse that I have made friends with people all over the world.' In another's words:

> Yet, what makes SOHS special in my view... is the student body! Going to assemblies, entering clubs, or casually debating the ideas expressed in Dostoevsky's *Crime and Punishment*, I am delighted to feel like I am part of a closely connected, vibrant, passionate, and quite simply amazing Pixel community!

This student feels she belongs at SOHS—she is part of something beyond just classes or clubs. The 'student body' is itself a feature of the school, wherein friendships arise. Another SOHS student attests to his feeling of belonging to the school community, calling it a 'surrogate family'.

Students manifest their belonging in the community through their actions as well as their words. Over forty students in the 2015-16 school year led clubs, many of which they had started themselves. Students volunteered to perform at assemblies, lead orientation groups, and serve as Student Ambassadors. The Student Government led Homecoming and coordinated 'eRoses' for Valentine's Day. Students proposed local meet-ups and flocked to them; the SOHS gathering at MIT's fall weekend for high schoolers numbered over 120 including some alumni and current and former employees. From students' claims that they feel at home in their SOHS courses to their willingness to take leadership positions in student clubs to their exuberant group hugs before the cameras at graduation, we know they feel that belonging that Dewey describes.

SOHS found similarly positive indications of school community through a school climate survey conducted in the spring of 2015 by the social-emotional learning non-profit consultancy Six Seconds. This statistically validated, normed assessment of school climate evaluated five elements: motivation, integrity, belonging, accountability, and trust. The results were measured against a database of fifteen thousand responses from students, parents, administrators, and teachers from over one hundred schools in the US, Canada, and Singapore. After accountability, SOHS's highest rating was for belonging, framed as: 'Do people in the school community feel both connection and care? To what extent do they feel part of the community vs. outside?' SOHS's score was 108, compared with an average of 100 across all schools. Indeed, all indicators of school climate were close to or above average.[9] These results reinforce individual student testimonials and actions and point to a widespread and meaningful sense of belonging at the school.

Of course, community is never monolithic, and students at SOHS belong to the school in different ways. Some express their membership in the community by purchasing SOHS gear at the spirit store and wearing it proudly in their home communities. Another student may express this connection to the community by seeking out her SOHS counselor first when facing a challenging issue at home, rather than a support system in her local community or even another school she also attends. Yet another SOHS graduate may tell his college classmates that he was 'homeschooled' but still maintain close ties with his SOHS classmates, valuing the shared experience they had at the school. All of these are ways that students prove the existence of a school community though they may 'belong' differently. Indeed, the School Climate Survey revealed that while on average students felt a strong sense of belonging, individual qualitative results still pointed to socialization as an area needing improvement. Not every student feels part of the thriving community.

Like many of its peer schools, SOHS can acknowledge a strong community but must also pay attention to those students who might not feel a part of it. How pervasive is this feeling of belonging at SOHS? Further study will need to address this question, looking at how it breaks down among certain groups at the school. Do full-time students feel they 'belong' more than those taking a single course?[10] Moreover, do students who attend in-person events, such as meet-ups or who live

---

[9]The results were: Belonging: 108, Accountability: 115.5, Motivation: 96.5, Integrity: 104.8, Trust: 108.7.

[10]While logic would dictate so, there is plenty of evidence of single-course students viewing SOHS as their primary communities while full-time students may in fact 'belong' more closely to an arts community (e.g. ballet) and view SOHS as the school that facilitates that extracurricular engagement.

geographically near other SOHS students feel they 'belong' any more than others? The Stanford OHS community is strikingly diverse, and further investigation should gauge community engagement in the context of the range of characteristics in the study body.

3.1 Diversity of the Student Body

What is notable in this existence of community, in fact, is not just that SOHS is an online school but also, and perhaps more importantly, that its student body is marked by astounding diversity. Students do not gather all day in the same school building; nor do they even hail from the same neighborhoods, play the same sport, attend the same religious institutions, etc. It is both in spite of this diversity and because of it that community at SOHS is so strong. Students often find that they belong where they might least expect it.

The SOHS community is diverse in every sense of the term. Beyond geographic diversity, the most often touted kind of student diversity, Stanford OHS draws from a range of ethnic and socioeconomic backgrounds. It is important to note that these are both aspects of diversity that SOHS has made an effort to increase. In the 2015-16 school year, through a joint effort from leadership in faculty and instruction, the school launched a Committee on Inclusion to focus both on recruitment and support of ethnic minority students in the school through relationships with local schools, mentoring support in the school, and student-led clubs to celebrate ethnic heritage. Simultaneously, the school allocated more financial aid dollars than ever before, bringing the school's 'discount rate' above the national average.

In addition to racial and socioeconomic diversity efforts, the school has begun to recognize clearly the reasons students seek out the school, using this information to drive recruitment campaigns. Over the course of the past few years, the Admissions and Marketing teams studied carefully the demographic groups within the school and identified several for whom targeted messages about the school's value to them would resonate. These included gifted students, homeschoolers, expat/international students, students with significant outside activities, and independent-school families. While each group may be attracted to SOHS for different reasons, the school often touts the fact that all these kinds of students 'fit' at SOHS, especially because all must be highly academically motivated and intellectually curious.

While geographic diversity is just one measure of demographic diversity, it is one that no other school encounters in such an extreme way. The 2015-16 student body included students from forty states and twenty-seven countries. Even boarding and international schools, whose students hail from all over the world, situate their student populations geographically in one place. SOHS students, however, may come together in opposing time zones having entered the virtual classroom from contexts as different as one can imagine.

Moreover, SOHS students may be graduating from the school or taking just one course and have very different perspectives on the role of the school in their lives. One student may have found the school desperate for a solution when his family suddenly moved abroad; another may have contacted the Admissions Office for three years before applying, set on it as her dream school.

3.2 From Many, One

Given this unique student body, the challenge of creating community is significant—students cannot rely on the kinds of similarities that can instigate, if not sustain, friendship groups at brick-and-mortar schools (same neighborhood, extracurricular, or religious community, friendship among parents, and so forth). Perhaps because of the many factors working against community at SOHS, finding commonality becomes an almost urgent need for students. SOHS students belong to the school's community both because of their diversity and because of the resultant thirst for and cultivating of commonalities and shared experiences.

Indeed, SOHS is what theorists have posited as a 'community of difference', one in which 'members negotiate from positions reflecting their disparate norms, beliefs, and values' and 'recognize that. . . there are also some significant commonalities that unite them'.[11] Shields writes:

> *Communities of difference* will not be based on traditions, stereotypes, or unchallenged assumptions about their members; rather, they will emerge through carefully seeking out, and listening to, the cacophony of voices of those who, together, make up each community.[12]

The SOHS community thrives because students take part in this very exercise of defining and holding onto shared experience with purpose.

In the first ten years of the school, the similarity students tried hard to find with one another bonded them together. After all, students are often just as surprised to be sitting in class with someone from

---

[11]Carolyn M. Shields, "Thinking about community from a Student Perspective," in *School as Community: From Promise to Practice*, ed. Gail Furman (Albany: State University of New York Press, 2002), 197.
[12]Ibid.

another continent as they are to find a peer who *also* loves Nietzsche. SOHS students make connections with students who are quite different from themselves based on a similarity that is brought into relief: one student rides rodeo in Texas, another writes poetry on the other side of the country, but they are the two leaders of the Spanish Club, and that becomes enough to tie them together. Two students who lived thousands of miles apart, had had different educational backgrounds before SOHS, and pursued different activities (sports versus music), became fast friends in the age-old way—by investing in getting to know one another and finding they viewed the world in some of the same ways, had some of the same life goals, and just enjoyed one another's company. Even more surprising was the fact that one of the students came to the school primarily for the ability to engage in his sport, never expecting to make friends at school. In a sea of students who looked very different from the peers in his hometown, he found (at least) one close friend who spoke his 'language'.

The search for commonality is universal; we all reach out to find common ground when meeting new people. There is, however, something exuberant about this process at SOHS, when the stakes are so high. After all, the default assumption among students is most likely that they are different. They come from worlds apart—as the administration often makes clear (citing this geographic diversity, the number of languages spoken, or the wide range of outside activities in which students engage). The need to find commonality in this 'community of difference' is thus more urgent.

This student thirst for commonality manifests itself in any large group assembly or event near the start of school. The text chat from an Admit Day event for new students illustrates this desire to build common bonds:

Student 1: lol this is my first year total at sohs, so i have no idea what to expect

Student 2: same here!

Student 3: [student 1], me too

Student 2: we can be totally ignortant [sic] together :p

Student 1: wow! feel less lonely :)

Student 4: me neither! first year too - I'm the new girl again :)) but I'm super excited

Student 5: me too, [Student 1]

The conversation moves toward the various ages of the students, and they break out with enthusiasm upon finding some are the same age. 'yayy twinsies :)' one writes.

In the school's early years, it was commonality enough that students had all chosen to be a part of the school—taking a risk on this quirky place. At prom, they all danced together in one big circle, even though it was clear that for some of them this was their first dance while others were clearly veterans of the high school prom scene. The danced together because they were just happy to all be in the same place at the same time for a change. Years later, prom still has this feel, in part because the culture of the event has been passed on from student to student, in part because the affirmative choice to join this community is enough to bond students together. They know they have all traveled to attend the prom of an online school, they understand both its improbability and its importance, and they embrace that, arm in arm.

Similarity plays a role in meet-ups as well. Fundamentally, in-person meet-ups work best when more than a few students are concentrated geographically in one area. Therefore, just as we celebrate when a student joins our school from a state not currently represented, we celebrate equally when we know we are admitting a new student from an area with only a handful of SOHS students; we anticipate they will have the option of meeting in person.

Throughout the SOHS community, and in so many different ways, students embrace what draws them together, often intensely. A Science Bowl competition, for example, may draw students from across the United States from a range of socioeconomic, ethnic, or political backgrounds. In those couple of days together, however, they are a unified team with a clear common goal. Their interaction is intentional and focused; it is rare that on these student trips the kinds of social dynamics among students that become problematic have time to develop.

In the early years of the school, administrators felt that these must just be incredibly 'nice' students who couldn't be capable of negative social dynamics like bullying when we saw them together. Of course, this can't be the whole story. Rather, the scarcity of the in-person resource increases its value; students are generally on their best behavior in these settings because they know how precious the time is. That the overlap in the same space and time is meaningful but rare leads to a generally positive social dynamic. If interaction is a key to building community, then SOHS proves that it is indeed necessary, but that it need not be constant.

This lower rate of interaction than in a brick-and-mortar context is a feature the school will need to confront as it grows. Will more students from the same context (i.e. more pockets of demographic similarity) make students less likely to seek out similarity and build bonds? As the school organizes more trips abroad or in-person experiences throughout the year, will clusters of students who see one another frequently feel the same need to invest in all-school community building? Or will they form cliques to preserve their distinct social identity? How can the school foster the exuberance students feel for finally finding 'someone like me' as the school grows? Finally, can the school encourage deep, sustained, social relationships among students without in some way marring the 'specialness' of their time together, whether virtual or in-person?

4 Role of the School

4.1 Keeping it Organic

The SOHS community could exist, and students might feel they belonged to it, even without a cohort of well-meaning administrators trying to make sense of it. The school might have taken a 'do no harm' approach and let things be. Yet the pioneering, build-it-as-you-go spirit of SOHS leadership has led to much thought, analysis, and effort to sustain the community. School leaders took up Dewey's charge—and the independent school tradition—that educators build community with intention. This project has persisted for years, handed down along a chain of school leaders, and shifted as the school has grown and worked to solidify its identity.

In the years of intentional community building on the part of SOHS teachers and administrators, a great lesson emerged: for this unique school, community development had to come organically; otherwise, the process by which students found commonality and built relationships became overly mediated. In the end, the approach has settled on one that lets students lead but with a strong measure of adult guidance and support. The school has achieved a balance whereby students initiate relationships or programs that the school fosters, and the school puts structures into place that members of the community imbue with meaning.

This approach manifests itself throughout the school's student life programming. Students may propose new clubs, for example, but they know to do so because of clear messaging from the administration about that option, the guidelines, and the timeframe for doing so. In the 2015-16 school year, a junior decided to start a weekly video show called 'Pixel Talk'. The student sought permission to create the show and use the school's name but did the rest himself, finding interviewees at the level of presidential candidates and major CEOs. No one realized the student intended to find such high-profile guests, and the administration was taken off-guard when the show became a success to the point that outside media organizations considered syndicating it. The administration's response was, of course, to support this direction. The student showed his sense of belonging to the community by creating value within it, and the administration's response underscored trust and safety in both directions.

At the same time, the administration has asked students to step up and provide leadership to fulfill its goals, sparking student involvement in the school community but then allowing students to take the work in their own directions. For example, students serve on committees (such as the one to rewrite the school's mission statement in the 2012-13 school year), participate in admissions and recruitment efforts, and help to plan school-sponsored graduation events. In all of these areas, the school works to support student voice, listen authentically, and act on feedback. Indeed, school administrators regularly engage students to seek feedback, such as on the yearly summer program, making substantive changes based on that feedback. If community rests on meaningful interaction, these types of activities demonstrate that Stanford OHS interaction is not just the presence of two parties in the same virtual space at the same time but an actual exchange of ideas and meaningful collaboration.

It was not always this way. In the early years of SOHS, the community blossomed through student-led initiatives. Students asked for a student government (and wrote by-laws), developed a radio show, and clamored for a barbecue at Graduation Weekend. A Student Activities Coordinator helped to arrange assemblies where students told one another about clubs they could join or assisted the student government in planning for virtual events. The students were deeply invested in the community (they were the pioneers), and the school depended on them to drive the creation of community.

As the administration began to formalize, a Director of Student Life position was created in 2011. The job of the first Director of Student Life took time to define. On the one hand, I was a facilitator not unlike the previous coordinator; on the other, wasn't this the opportunity to build out programming as one would have in a full-fledged student life office? While ultimately, five years later, this role has come into its own, the early year saw conflict between students and the Director of Student Life. SOHS students wondered how an adult could come in and dare set rules for the students leading the radio show. Couldn't club leaders present their clubs however they wanted without conforming to time limits or a number of PowerPoint slides? A more formal, independent school style administration quickly came into conflict with the spirited students who felt they had built the community at SOHS and that it belonged to them.

Over time, it became clear that student life needed both to stay organic and student led *and* feature guidelines and standards to optimize programs, attend to equity, and manage resources (not to mention adhere to broader University rules). Let a driven student start a robotics club out of his garage and call it a SOHS team, but require that he also build an online component of the club open to SOHS students across the world. Give the students resources and claim the club as official, but make it clear that parents must supervise the in-person work. These kinds of negotiations have contributed to a community that fosters students' search for connection and belonging but that also features purpose and structure.

All independent schools balance in this way, guiding student initiative. At SOHS, the need to let students drive student life initiatives is perhaps even more essential to the community's sustainability. In the online context, without the inherent commonalities that exist in other schools, investing in the community takes work for students, so it'd better be work they appreciate and that pays off for them. An inauthentic student life program, applied from the top down, could easily miss the real ways students connect in the school, the commonalities, shared goals, and projects they find on their own. A community of such difference mandates that the commonalities be real.

As the school moves forward, it will need to balance this impetus to keep community student-led with the need to attract students. Increasingly, students applying to SOHS expect student services; after all, they are what differentiate SOHS from many other schools, both online and brick and mortar. For example, the school views it as important to create peer groups for new students (termed 'Pixel Clusters'). These groups go a long way in orienting students to the school, making them feel welcome, and starting those connections that become the building blocks of community. If there were no buy-in from current student leaders, the school would need to decide how to adjust or replace the program to make it meaningful. Similarly, SOHS families increasingly call for travel opportunities (summer 2016 saw trips to Argentina and Rome). Can SOHS, like many other independent schools, hire trip providers and send students along without there being anything unique to SOHS—or anything organic from students? The school will need to confront these questions as it evolves.

4.2   Get the Right Students on the Bus

Knowing what characterizes our community and how we might foster it is one thing, but selecting its members is another. What kinds of students form an interactive, dynamic school community, and how can we select for them? From recruitment through selective admission through orientation, how do we know who will 'belong', and how can we use those processes to increase the chances that students will feel trust, safety, and a connection, that 'surrogate family'? In recent years, innovations in the school's admissions process have sought to address these questions, mainly by taking a holistic approach that looks at criteria well beyond academics.

SOHS has been a selective institution from the beginning. The most important areas in which students are assessed in admissions are academic (through standardized testing, transcripts, recommendation letters, essays, etc.). In order to set students up for success in the online classroom, we also seek students who demonstrate 'independence, self-advocacy, strong time management, and appropriate maturity'. Through yet a third category, called 'Personal Qualities', we seek students 'who will become contributing members of the SOHS community, who will engage with the life of the school and in its extracurricular pursuits'.

At a basic level, our decision to put these criteria front and center on our website makes a statement that we are an online school that actually cares about 'community'. Ever since we have used that language on our website, we have found that more applicants discuss the 'life of the school' in their essays. At the very least, we know that our applicants are aware of this aspect of institution they seek to join.

We assess a student's potential to engage in our community in a few ways. The most 'mechanical' is by asking them to describe their extracurricular pursuits and describe the one that is most important to them. We note whether a student in a brick-and-mortar school is engaged in a school-based activity, such as student government. We similarly note when a student spends over twenty hours per week on an activity, whether it is mainly solitary (piano) or mainly team-based (soccer). These types of engagement tend to indicate students who may seek out 'belonging' at our school and even take the lead on building student community. Even with this information, however, we find we can't tell how much a student will engage in the SOHS community, and if so, in what ways.

Our essay questions in the application take this messaging and assessing a step further, demonstrating that we care about community and asking students to articulate a response to this concept. Over the past couple of years, we have prompted students with short essay questions like:

Please tell us why are you a good fit for SOHS. Then, please explain how SOHS would fit into your plans for next year and beyond.

(In the second part of the question, you may wish to discuss whether you plan to attend SOHS as your primary school or blend it with another school or program and your plans to engage in extracurricular activities at SOHS or outside the school...)

What is it about SOHS that makes you want to be a student here? Topics you may want to address include: rigorous class experience, unique learning environment, instructors, or intellectual community.

Please write your own, brief version of a Student Ambassador Profile, as if you had attended SOHS for one year. You may want to frame your essay as an illustration of your typical day as a SOHS student...

Applicants answer these types of questions well in many ways. One young man who experienced bullying at his past school and thrived socially at SOHS wrote in his application essay, 'I could meet amazing kids who are interested in both school and the outside world. I am looking for a community where my mind will be stimulated...'. Another young man who was a mature and thoughtful middle school leader in his first year, wrote in his admissions essay, 'The best part is taking challenging classes about interesting subjects and meeting awesome kids like the ones I read about on the website.' He later elaborated, 'I like the fact that it has clubs, because then I can meet kids with the same interests as me.' Often, for the many students we serve who have not found peers like them in their current schools, their voices are more plaintive:

Being a homeschooler, I was never able to join an extracurricular club affiliated with a school. I have always wanted to do so, and this will be a wonderful opportunity for me, in which I will certainly join and joyfully participate.

Or, from another young woman:

In my old school, I had good friends, but they did not love learning as much as I did. I began to worry about my looks more than what my brain was absorbing. At SOHS, I hope to be surrounded by learners who will see through my looks and into who I really am. I cannot wait to meet people who love learning as much as I do.

These essays are simple to analyze—the clear social need for SOHS rings out. While these students may go through phases in their tenure at the school—from enthusiastic club leader to 'too cool for school' presence on Skype groups to respected member of the senior class—they typically engage with the community in a meaningful way. In a sense, they are primed to see out relationships with other students and engage with the life of the school.

Yet like most aspects of admissions, which is much more an art than a science, what you see is not always what you get. Plenty of students have neglected to mention a drive toward community in essays but have become integral members of SOHS friendship groups, club leaders, or mentors to younger students at our summer program. One young woman living between two countries outside the US, whose application essay spoke mainly of academics, recently raved about the community, stating she had more in common with her American classmates than with anyone at her old school. Another applicant who mentioned community only perfunctorily in her application won an award for club leadership at the conclusion of her second year at the school. Finally, students with high-level, intensive outside activities—who are drawn to SOHS in order to continue those activities—sometimes neglect to mention the school's community, whether because they are motivated differently or because they see themselves as having a vibrant social life through that activity. One such young man, who was already active in his hometown and in the context of his outside pursuit became an integral part of the SOHS social scene, perhaps despite himself.

While it may not be easy for SOHS admissions to predict accurately whether a student will or will not engage with the community based on an admissions essay, we can usually tell when a student may not be a positive and contributing member of the community. Applications that reveal, through essays, parent responses, or recommendation letters, that a student seeks to avoid 'real school' or peers are flagged, and students who would otherwise be strong candidates are interviewed. Applicants who list no extracurricular activities are scrutinized for reasons why (and often there are good ones). Students who demonstrate they may not engage with the school—or may engage in negative ways—can be denied admission, just as at other independent schools.

The SOHS community is a surprise to many. We know that will be so; no one can quite envision what being a student in our school and forging friendships through it will be like. Moreover, nor would we want to select only students who seem to cry out for the social connection or leadership opportunities SOHS could provide. It is precisely the diversity of intentions with which students join our community that lends richness to the community. All communities need joiners and those who sneer a bit at the sidelines before jumping in, students whose primary social scene revolves around the school and those who bring SOHS students into existing social networks.

At this phase, SOHS does not need to 'socially engineer' an incoming class the way another institution may deliberately select a certain number of athletes or artists and make sure the orchestra has an oboe player or the lacrosse team a goalie. Yet it must stay attuned to selecting students who will be open to joining the community and who can find commonality with at least a few other students. Promoting diversity of all kinds only helps, especially because the commonalities among students—their shared presence at this school no matter the reason or the goal—bring them together.

Moreover, SOHS has the luxury of being able to take students who fit into a range of categories (homeschoolers, expatriates) and who seek out SOHS for as many reasons as there are students in the school. No one worries about whether community will form in this context; the only question is how the community may shift year to year as the student make-up changes. And because SOHS is not a two hundred-year-old institution with a defined sense of what makes a 'pixel' (the school's mascot), its school community and identity can shift, as long as administrators allow it. As a result, the stakes in admission for building community are both low and high. They are low because it is hard to imagine admitting a student who, given she has all the right raw materials, won't contribute in some way to a community that provides so many avenues for participation. Yet they are high in that each student has the capacity to shape the community dramatically given its organic, student-led nature. One student may shape the meaning of the SOHS pixel as much as the school may shape her.

5 Blending Community

The first volume of this set posits that the SOHS community is neither a purely online community nor an in-person one—it is all encompassing, moving with students through their days in and out of the virtual. In recent years, the school has also experimented with more initiatives that are themselves blended—neither just an online course nor an in-person meet-up at a museum. It will be important for SOHS to continue experimenting in these areas if the community is to grow and thrive. In a school whose student life encompasses virtual and in-person activities, the question of whether—and how—those two spheres of community expression interact is key. In these settings, community can mean yet something else, and how it's formed and fostered has implications for many other kinds of learning environments.

Some activities, such as the Student Government, exist in virtual space only; others, such as local meet-ups, are by nature in-person. Yet the lives of students everywhere are increasingly 'blended'. Brick-and-mortar schools 'flip' classrooms to build courses that meet in-person regularly but with important coursework and interaction conducted online. Blending student life at SOHS allows the community to be more inclusive and allows the school to reach students in more aspects of their lives. It also raises important questions for in-person and virtual communities alike.

5.1 In-Person Events

SOHS has found ways to take in-person experiences and blend them, expanding the definition of what the school community can mean. At various points in the school's history, we have often asked how the energy around in-person meetings can be leveraged to benefit the larger, virtual community. The school has never required students at attend any event in person—not even a student's own graduation ceremony— in part so as not to advantage students who may find it easier to travel to Stanford's campus. In that vein, we have made attempts to open experiences on campus available to students who cannot attend physically.

SOHS's Graduation Weekend is an extravaganza of events ranging from an awards ceremony to a senior-instructor dinner to a parent breakfast to a middle school event to the graduation itself. Hundreds of families gather at Stanford, some from the Bay Area and others from the far corners of the globe. In 2012, we decided to engage a broader swath of the community in the graduation itself, motivated in part by the desire to allow graduating seniors who could not attend the chance to be 'present'. Hooking the video feed into a streaming server enabled SOHS families to log onto an internal website and watch the ceremony live or check back to view it later. Despite technical difficulties encountered that year, the rest of the SOHS community has appreciated the chance to connect, and this has become a yearly mainstay.

Of course, making this streaming of a live event meaningful takes thought and practice and raises other interesting questions. Does announcing the names of award-winning students who are not present mean more if there is a chance they may be watching? Could there be a way for virtual attendees to participate in a meaningful way? Would creating those opportunities detract from the in-person event by distracting or changing the flow of the event? Finally, if Stanford OHS Graduation Weekend is meant to be a special, once-per-year weekend (with all the exuberance and positivity surrounding its specialness), should it stay fully in-person or explore virtual possibilities?

Just as we decided to stream graduation in order to make the event more broadly available to the school community, so too have meet-ups experimented with a virtual component. In the fall of 2014, the offices of Admission and Student Life collaborated to create *Start-Up!*, a day-long semi-structured event during the first month of school. Highly publicized within the community and organized more by school administrators than the typical meet-up, *Start-Up!* occurred in several cities across the US. If the goal was to welcome students to the new school year and foster community, we wondered, how could students who lived outside of California or New York, for example, participate? Would we have students carry their friends around on mobile devices? Set up streaming? All options threatened to disrupt or seemed logistically or technically complicated. In the end, we built a question into the scavenger hunt that required students to engage virtually with other SOHS students in some collaborative activity. More than just a nod to the virtual community beyond the meet-up site, this activity gave remote students the opportunity to 'be there', albeit in a different way.

This discussion—whether and how to bring everyone to *Start-Up!*—raised yet further questions. Would giving a remote option for an event send the message that students need not attend in person? If *Start-Up!* sites were necessarily tied to geography (indeed, the New York group attended a local city food festival and took additional advantage of the location), could anyone from anywhere attend remotely? Or just students from that region who happened to have a conflict? If *Start-Up!* sites were connected in some way, perhaps through video conferences connecting locales, what would the benefits be—other than the novelty of the experience? How could events truly tied to geography, such as a visit to a UCLA manuscript room during spring, 2014, benefit the wider community? Or should it simply serve as an impetus for families in other locations to organize their own events tied to their regions? Finally, does the school have an obligation to make school-organized events (graduation, *Start-Up!*) accessible remotely? Fundamentally, the school will continue to experiment in these uncharted waters by providing in-person and virtual experiences and meaningful blends of the two, taking the students' lead as to what really works in the student-led project of building authentic community.

5.2 Blended Learning

Several forays into the blended have been fruitful. The school's most significant engagement in blended activity is with the Malone Schools Online Network (MSON), a consortium of independent schools across the country, all of which, like SOHS, receive scholarship funding from the Malone Family Foundation. SOHS helped to develop MSON in 2012 and remains a member school (one of twenty in the 2016-17 school year). In turn, MSON derives key philosophical principles from SOHS (notably real-time discussion seminars). While MSON exists outside of

SOHS with a professional staff and leadership distributed among member schools, it serves as a homegrown example of a blended community in action.

MSON connects brick-and-mortar classrooms together through real-time, video-conferencing seminars. Students from the member schools attend class from physical classrooms, which are outfitted with a large screen for video conferencing. MSON meets on a college-style schedule, like SOHS, in twice-weekly seminars. The rest of the course is conducted asynchronously. As such, MSON students at most of the schools attend class in the physical setting of their schools, often with classmates or the teacher physically next to them, but join a virtual class with students from other schools.

The innovative aspects of MSON are numerous—as are the benefits to the member schools: courses available to students they would not otherwise be able to take, a classroomof peers from across the country, professional development for brick-and-mortar school teachers, experience for both groups in online learning, and more. The community benefits are clear as well. Students at each school receive local support for their studies (from teachers and peers) and benefit from institutional commitment to the endeavor, yet they attend class with students and a teacher who may be on the other side of the country and therefore situated in a different context. As a result, students are forced to think outside the contexts of their own independent schools, developing a broad awareness that will help them as they move onto college. (Most MSON students are advanced juniors and seniors and therefore close to leaving home.) They understand how a virtual community can feel and the ways in which it can connect with an in-person one.

MSON demonstrates true blended learning that, because of the real-time component, situates students in more than one community at the same time. Students are often surprised to encounter this community. After all, they sign up for MSON to take a particular class whose content they see as interesting or useful. They soon find that the social benefits of the class are meaningful. Yet even program administrators were surprised to see MSON students' desires to go beyond their classes. MSON students have visited one another's campuses during college visits (and seen snow for the first time!), organized MSON class reunions during the school year and later, in cities where they all attend college, jumped on stage to hug MSON classmates who were performing at their schools, and more. Just as at SOHS, students find the classroom community so meaningful that it spills beyond and into the in-person. What is different is that these students have full-time, 'primary' communities at their brick-and-mortar independent schools. Still, the virtual community, formed around commonalities (like finding another student who also loves organic chemistry), is meaningful and strong.

Based on their testimonials and these kinds of urges to seek one another out, MSON students clearly feel they belong to their MSON class communities. Just as at SOHS, educators play a role in fostering this community in the classroom with intention (teachers are chosen in part for their ability to engage students, encourage participation, and build relationships). MSON's format—synchronous, high-definition, and interactive—clearly plays a major role in this community building. Even without the option of clubs and activities and homeroom and assemblies present at SOHS, MSON students have enough contact time with their peers and teachers to feel that sense of belonging. Moreover, as at SOHS, they are a diverse bunch of students thrown together to take Arabic or Organic Chemistry, and that experience bonds them together. They are not required to form community; in fact, notions of MSON community were surprising to all, but they are the right students—they have opted into the program, they are in many cases chosen by their schools both for academics and their maturity and independence. It is no wonder that they connect.

As schools consider blending classes and experimenting with hybrid instruction, they may consider the sense of belonging that students can feel in this kind of interactive online context. Far from being a threat to the in-person communities these students inhabit, it gives them new possibilities for community that enrich academically and expand horizons.

6   Looking Ahead

Community thrives at SOHS, ten years in. Beyond the fact that we have clubs and meet-ups and graduation, the school is characterized by a real sense of student belonging, one built on the kind of interaction and adult intent that Dewey describes. This belonging is forged in an unlikely context—one in which students are as different as can be. Indeed, because they cannot rest on shared past experiences or the more superficial connectors like geography or past membership in a certain defined community, they are in some ways more likely to work to find ties, more exuberant in their discovery of common experiences and goals, and more willing to become part of the shared project of creating a school community. Contrary to the popular stereotypes of an online school, the connectedness to this school in this moment in time may be a deeper and more long-lasting tie than many others adolescents experience.

School administrators all consider how directed student life should be in their institutions. With this group of students, the organic, student-led is crucial. We know that buy-in matters for students. We as educators should create climates of ownership for students, where it is clear that they forge and sustain their communities and adults guide and support. Additionally, the interactive factor that make both SOHS and MSON real communities is a key component in all contexts, and further inquiry should determine just how much is sufficient and whether some communities indeed benefit from interaction when it is limited. Finally, the admissions process clearly plays a role in community formation at every independent school, and SOHS is no exception. All communities of learning should investigate who joins their communities (whether they control it or not) and how that student makeup, especially along the lines of diversity, influences community formation.

As SOHS envisions its community as in-person, virtual, and blended, it navigates new territory, but other schools are not far behind. As more and more schools build blended/hybrid programs, they should be confident that community can exist and that the ways in which they set up programs have implications for community formation. Is there a primacy given to the in-person or the virtual? Where does the most interaction happen, and is it interaction around ideas (i.e. a class) or social (i.e. a class reunion)?[13] Who are the students involved in these programs, and how should those students be selected? Are they given a say in program design? All of these are levers that can influence the community dimension that will develop; they should be considered carefully.

At SOHS, the definition of community will surely evolve—after all, that is the nature of a pioneering and growing school that serves such a range of students. The school may face increasing competition from other online schools, new options for academically talented students, international schools, etc., and the school may continue to define its identify in the face of a wider pool of options. Will students come to SOHS increasingly for similar reasons or from similar context (a certain enrollment status, independent school backgrounds, clusters from the same country)? How would this affect the diversityof students and their need to find commonalities in the absence of more immediately apparent similarities? Moreover, will SOHS's identity as an independent school that fosters student life compel it to provide more adult-

---

[13]The framework of 'academic belonging' versus 'social belonging' provides an interesting framework here—as described in M. Green et al., "Another Path to Belonging: A Case Study of Middle School Students' Perspectives," *The Educational Development Psychology* 33 (2016): 85–96.

led student programming that takes us further away from that organic, vociferous student voice that defined its early years?

If in the history of school change the concept of community in schools has ever presented a fundamental challenge to traditional notions, that time is now. The lessons from SOHS and the questions it raises may help to shape the conversation going forward.

References

Dewey, J. *Experience and Education*. New York: Touchstone, 1938.

Furman, G., ed. *School as Community: From Promise to Practice*. Albany: State University of New York Press, 2002.

Green, M., A. Emery, M. Sanders, and L. H. Anderman, "Another Path to Belonging: A Case Study of Middle School Students' Perspectives." *The Educational and Developmental Psychologist* 33 (2016): 85-96.

Labaree, D. F. *The Making of an American High School: The Credentials Market and the Central High School of Philadelphia, 1838-1939*. New Haven: Yale University Press, 1988.

Osterman, K. F. "Schools as Communities for Students." In *School as Community: From Promise to Practice*, edited by Gail Furman, 167-195. Albany: State University of New York Press, 2002.

Osterman, K. F. "Students' Need for Belonging in the School Community." *Review of Educational Research*; Fall, 2000; 70, 3. ProQuest Research Library, 323-367.

Shields, C. M. "Thinking about community from a Student Perspective." In *School as Community: From Promise to Practice*, edited by Gail Furman, 197-215. Albany: State University of New York Press, 2002.

Tyack, D. and L. Cuban. *Tinkering Toward Utopia: A Century of Public School Reform*. Cambridge: Harvard University Press, 1995.

Index